To Ruth and Charles
with affection and
all good wishes
Routh

December 7, 1997

Rose Ker Foster
A Biography

Rose Ker Foster
A Biography

by
Routh Trowbridge Wilby

Published by The Center for Louisiana Studies
University of Southwestern Louisiana
Lafayette, Louisiana

Library of Congress Catalog Number: 97-67161
ISBN Number: 1-887366-13-X

Published by The Center for Louisiana Studies
P. O. Box 40831
University of Southwestern Louisiana
Lafayette, LA 70504-0831

Contents

FOREWORD

I am both proud and humbled to write about my grandmother, Rose Ker Foster. My memories of her include holiday functions at her Dixie Plantation home where all the family would be together. At mealtimes, the adults would sit at the big table and the children would sit at the small table. It was almost a right of passage to adulthood to graduate to sit at the big table.

Rose Ker Foster typified dignity, grace, and total command of presence. As talkative as the family was, when she was in the room, everyone listened when she spoke. I remember her as always sitting in the same chair, like a queen, enjoying her family.

She was an extremely ethical person with unquestioned morals and she influenced me greatly. I credit her for giving me many of the convictions that I adhere to today.

I am deeply appreciative of Routh Wilby for writing this biography. Routh is a talented writer who has really brought my grandmother to life through her writing.

Hon. Murphy J. "Mike" Foster, Jr.
Governor of Louisiana

ACKNOWLEDGMENTS

Thanks are not enough to give my beloved Mr. Wilby, my husband for 55 years. He has always been my mentor and confidante. During these three years, he has read, suggested improvements, praised and, very often, fed me. Suffice to say we have been happy and no more words are needed.

My first cousin, Warrene Hayne Suthon, was a tremendous help in organizing and reading the three trunks of memorabilia which are the basis for this biography. All through 1993 and 1994 she would come out, or I would bring down to her in New Orleans, grocery bags full of old letters and receipts to read and categorize for me. Never did she fail me. It was not easy. Nineteenth century, Spencerian handwriting is hard to decipher. With faithful promptness she would return them, with explanatory post-it notes on the outside of each one.

My sister, Elizabeth, loaned me her old, family letters and pictures and helped refresh my memory on our early childhood. Her son, Paul Henslee, loaned me the picture of all the family just before they left the mansion in 1899. My cousin, Martha Herbert Walker, her husband, John, were unfailing in their interest, to include pictures and moral support.

Another cousin, Mary Blanchard in Shreveport, granddaughter of Rose's sister Annie, sent me a picture of Rose's mother, Rosaltha Routh Ker, along with papers and letters from the University of North Carolina which detailed our ancestor David Ker's association there.

Sue Ker Hyams from New Orleans loaned me her pictures of the original Ker portraits and gave me a copy of Thomas Jefferson's appointment of David Ker as judge of the Mississippi Territory.

Sister Elizabeth Farley, Associate Director for the Order of the Sacred Heart National Archives in St. Louis, found Rose's registration at St. Michael's Convent in 1872 and sent me the booklet *Society of the Sacred Heart in North America* by Louise Callam, AM, Ph. D. 1937 which described the curriculum at the convent in those days.

Grace Episcopal Church sent me a copy of the record of Rose and Murphy's marriage. Mrs. Young of the St. Francisville Historical Association furnished information on Rose's finishing school at Afton Villa.

Sydney Romero's book *The Political Life and Times of Murphy J. Foster* was tremendously helpful in familiarizing me with Louisiana politics at that time. Then my friend Roger Busbice, Louisiana historian and teacher, checked the gubernatorial chapters to be sure I had the facts straight.

Judy Bolton of the Special Collections Department at L. S. U.'s Hill Memorial Library sent me pictures of Murphy Foster's 1892 and 1896 inaugurations, and the photograph of the yellow fever quarantine camp.

Virginia Dobbs, Public Affairs Director for the U. S. Custom House in New Orleans, sent me pamphlets which familiarized me with that service.

Sally Stassi of the Historic New Orleans Collection Curatorial Department sent me a picture of writer Lyle Saxon as a young boy.

My cousin, Alice Ker Barber of Richmond, Virginia, found a faded picture of the wonderful Alice Wade, who meant so much to Rose and her sisters.

Our Routh cousin, Joess Trimble of Natchez did her best to find a picture of Frank Routh's Kenilworth, but every lead she or I tried was unsuccessful.

Rose's great-granddaughter, and Mike Foster's daughter, Ramelle Foster Townley, found the picture of Murphy J. Foster, Jr., and his pet mountain lion, Bozo.

Marjorie Munson of New Iberia loaned me her copy of the Barrow Family Book and she and Lorraine Bourgeois helped keep me straight on family dates.

Fay Brown of Franklin shared her own papers about the early days in Franklin. Larry Bodin of Franklin gave me a copy of his picture of Dixie as it looked in 1896. Ridgeways in Lafayette took such interest in making finished copies of the old photographs and papers.

My editor, Mary Dell Fletcher, has been wonderful. Not only is she a successful professional in her own right, she has done a capable and caring job of changing and tightening up and making this manuscript better. Personal knowledge of a subject and the research needed to enhance that knowledge can make an author almost too possessive. She has handled me beautifully. We've had a great time working together, we have become very good friends, and I thank her very, very much.

Rose Ker Foster
A Biography

INTRODUCTION

This book had its inception in scribbled notes and scattered papers that I planned to put together for the family. In 1993, as it grew and began to encompass political history of Louisiana, I realized that it might interest an audience far beyond the Foster family. The story is first of all about Rose Foster, but the moment Murphy J. Foster came into her life, she became involved in Louisiana politics, and he, like many of America's finest statesmen, was influenced by the wise and wonderful woman he married. Since his political career has been well documented, this book does not delve into politics except as they touched Rose, but living in a political world, she was inevitably caught up (rarely in an active role) in the affairs of the state—and later, the nation. A retiring and gracious lady, she never sought the limelight but rather lived behind the scenes with her husband, her children, her home foremost in her mind.

Rose and Murphy J. Foster were my grandparents. He was elected governor of Louisiana in 1892 and served until 1900. I wish I could have known my grandfather, but he died a year before I was born; my grandmother lived thirty-five years after his death.

I was very close to my grandmother. My mother, her fifth daughter, married Paul Trowbridge who practiced dentistry in Franklin. When my grandfather's health began to fail, my parents moved to Dixie, the Foster plantation where my mother had grown up. Both my sister, Elizabeth, and I were born and reared there, and neither of us scarcely knew whether our mother was Rose or her daughter Mary. Keenly interested in family history, I often sat at Rose's feet and listened to her tales of the past. She was a wonderful storyteller with a talent for recreating events so vividly that I sometimes thought that her experiences were my own. And I had that feeling again as I gathered up all of my memories and her letters, records, and memorabilia for this book. She must have known that someday someone would dig into and sort out the past as she had lived it, for she was an inveterate saver.

Her early days were revealed to me when I was a little girl. Our confidences were shared, usually every night after supper as I rubbed her feet after we had first soaked them in Epsom salt water. She often spoke of how "Mr. Foster" loved pretty shoes, and how when he went away on trips he usually brought her a new pair. The only problem was that he never realized how wide her feet were. Not wanting to hurt his feelings, she wore the shoes; and she suffered from damaged feet most of her adult life.

As I massaged her feet with Sloane's Liniment, she would lean back in relaxed pleasure and recreate her life for me—growing up during Reconstruction, going to a convent school, getting married, and living in the

Governor's Mansion. She confessed her fear of horses and described her first experience of riding and being thrown off into a thorn bush. She said she had never let her children know she was frightened of horses since they shared their father's love of them. She also had a repertoire of Civil War tales that had been passed on to her, like the encounter between Alice Wade, her guardian, and a Union soldier.

As she grew older and shoes became more practical and foot remedies more modern, my services were less needed. However, the bond between us never lessened, and when I came home, to visit, we always managed at least one good massage and perhaps the repetition of a good story.

In 1986 my husband and I bought Dixie from the other heirs. Living there has revealed much of the past to me—the yellowed letters, plantation records, endless lists and notes and receipts—and allowed me to walk in Rose's footsteps while I was doing this research. Two memorable moments stand out. First I found in an almost-secret drawer of Rose's desk two small faded, scratched and cracked pictures in gold leaf frames, one of Rose, not over three or four years old; the other, of Sarah Ker Towles, her sister, at about seven years. In the same drawer was a faded picture of Ellerslie, where they grew up, taken at approximately the same time. The sorrowful expressions on the little girls' faces seem to reveal their tragedy of losing their parents, being uprooted from their home, and going to live in totally new surroundings with strangers. Memory is kind, however, and most of Rose's stories centered on happy times she had with her new guardians, the Wades, at the beautiful Ellerslie Plantation.

The other unforgettable time came when my two daughters and I drove to St. Francisville to see Ellerslie and then to Ouida, where Rose later lived. We found Ellerslie looking as majestic as ever, but we spent hours trying to find the back road which led to Ouida. Although we finally succeeded, we were very saddened. Today it is used as a storage place for hay. The shutters are closed and the framing is frail. But the family cemetery is still there and our group of three felt the spirits of gallant ghosts. If money were not an impediment, I would take this cottage with all its memories and restore it. I hope that one day the cousins who own it will do that.

A nourishment for this story has come every night when I climb into Rose's big four-poster which was her grandmother Ker's bed. In this bed six of the ten Foster children were born. Remembering, I feel gratitude that Rose was born, and that her children were born, and that I was born.

CHAPTER ONE

As the tired horse pulled the carriage through the Ellerslie gate, Rose drew closer to her Sarah, her seven-year old sister and clutched her hand tightly. Before them stood the biggest house they had ever seen. A wide graveled walk was bordered on either side with cape jasmine hedges. Where the driveway swept in from the gate, it formed a half circle on either side of the broad central walk. The carriage stopped in front of four cedars that, like sentinels, seemed to guard the entrance to the house.

Rose Ker was three. The time was August, 1865, and the journey from Catahoula Lake, Louisiana, to West Feliciana Parish had been a long one. Fatigue and apprehension showed on their small dusty faces. Their two older cousins who had accompanied them understood their feelings. "Look, my darlings," Alice Wade said. "Our family is on the front gallery, waiting to welcome you with open arms."

"Yes," said Elizabeth Ratliff, "why even our old wandering dog, Traveler, is here to greet you all. He must have known children were coming. He loves to be petted."

Their little hands held even tighter, they alighted from the carriage and looked up into the kindly eyes of Olivia Wade, the children's great aunt, who came down the steps with a weakly

Rose Ker Foster pictured about the time of her arrival at Ellerslie.

sweetened glass of lemonade for each. Sugar was very scarce.

As Rose started to drink hers, she stopped and looked up at her elders saying, "Our papa is very sick."

"We know, my darling," Olivia answered, fighting back her own tears. "But your papa and mama both wanted you to come and live with us, and now you are here and we will love you like they loved you."

"Will we ever see our sisters and brother and grandfather and grandmother again?" Sarah asked.

"Of course you will," Cousin Alice answered. "They will visit us when they can, and we will take you back to see them."

"When?" Rose asked.

Sara Ker Towles

"As soon as these miserable Yankees leave us alone," Aunt Olivia answered. Then she added, "I guess this is not quite true. They haven't bothered us much. Thank goodness Ellerslie is too far out of town for them to ransack."

As they entered the house, the little girl's eyes widened once again at the fifteen-foot ceilings and the wide central hallway. "Might as well get used to the house now," Olivia said as she led them through the parlor which was furnished with rosewood furniture upholstered in crimson satin damask. Heavy drapes and lace curtains hung from gold cornices. On the mantel rested a pair of cornucopia-shaped flower holders supported by cupids that held garlands of little pink roses in their chubby hands. A beautiful gilt clock under a glass cover sat in the center of the mantel. They walked across deep-piled carpets through the four other large rooms on the first floor and then up a handsome mahogany staircase which rose from the first to the third floor without a break. As they entered the second floor, they followed their grown-up relatives into a spacious bedroom dominated by two large four-poster beds. Alice said tenderly, "Now my darlings, you two are going to spend your first night in one of these beds, and Cousin Elizabeth and I will share the other. You will have lots of company tonight."

For the first time, smiles appeared on the children's faces. No more separations, for awhile at least. "Can we climb some more steps?" Sarah asked.

"Not until tomorrow. It will be supper time soon, and Aunt Dicey is going to have a big bowl of clabber for you."

With only adults living there, Ellerslie had been a quiet place since the Wade children grew up, but it woke up with the arrival of Rose and Sarah. They played well together and although shy with outsiders, they loved their guardians from the outset. No place in the house or grounds being off-limits to

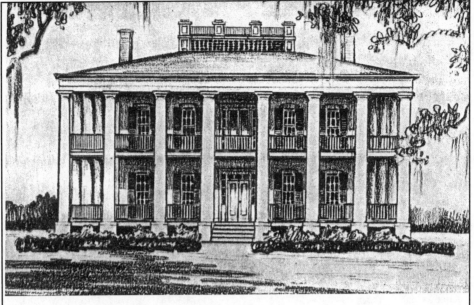

A sketch of Ellerslie, showing an artist's conception of the original cupola.
Drawing by Nan Hagan Wash.

them, they entertained each other with games and frolic, chasing the geese and peacocks, swinging from the live oak trees, giving tea parties for their dolls, and romping with Traveler. And then there was time for their instructions in the niceties of polite society. They were coached in etiquette and learned to sing with their cousins at the piano. They also learned to count and tell time. Always eager to hear stories, they frequently asked for Yankee stories. Aunt Olivia had told them that Ellerslie was so remote, that the Yankees never appropriated it.

She explained, "Ellerslie, as you can see, sits on a high hill, and the Mississippi is right over there." She pointed to the east. "The closest town to us is St. Francisville, founded about 1790 by British and American settlers who received Spanish land grants. When Louisiana became American territory after the Louisiana Purchase in 1803, the Spanish retained St. Francisville and Baton Rouge districts, considering them a part of the West Florida colony rather than a part of the Purchase. The residents of St. Francisville were dissatisfied and staged a small rebellion in which they captured the Spanish fort on September 23, 1810, and declared their independence. Their independence was short-lived, however, because the United States, to the delight of most of us in the area, claimed it was indeed a part of the Purchase and annexed the area.

Sarah's mind was obviously elsewhere, and Rose, yawning, said , "I don't like history. Tell us some Yankee stories; didn't they come here? Didn't you ever see a Yankee?"

Alice Center Wade (1840-1907), Rose's guardian. She was known to Rose's children as "Grandma Wade."

"Oh yes, there was one incident. Two soldiers came to the house one day and pretended they wanted to search the inside for Confederate soldiers. Alice found one of them ransacking her bureau drawers, and when she asked him what he was doing, he sheepishly blurted out that he was looking for Rebel soldiers. 'Well sir,' she replied, 'your Yankee soldiers might fit into my bureau drawers, but our Confederate soldiers never could.' It's a wonder he didn't kill all of us with her talking like that."

"What did he do? Did the soldiers take your silver and pretty things?"

"Oh, no, we had buried the silver and they never found it. We only just dug it up a little while before you came. You all can help me polish it before long."

The girls had begun to fit in and no longer cried for their sisters, brothers, and grandparents.

They looked forward to their visits, however, and were dutiful about writing, even before they learned to "write." Olivia mentioned that it was important for people to learn about their ancestors.

"What's an ancestor?" they exclaimed in unison.

"Kinfolks."

"We know about our kinfolks; they visit us and we send letters."

"I mean farther back—your roots."

"Like trees. We have roots like trees?"

"Yes. Precisely. And when you're old enough to understand, you will learn all about them."

Olivia had always run the plantation while her husband handled his court, and after his death in 1845, the entire burden fell on her since their son was a practicing physician. During Reconstruction, cash was scarce all over the South. In 1866 cotton production was only half of what it had been in 1860. A tax of two and one half cents was placed on every pound of cotton; therefore she struggled with finances. Part of the problem at Ellerslie was the fact that many of their slaves had returned and were being paid. She had always had genuine respect for each of the slaves, and the same warm relationship between Ellerslie and its workers continued to exist. She made it clear to her overseers that they would be dismissed for any abuse or rough handling of the workers. "Old Miss," as she was called, continued to preside over the plantation until she died.

There was always much work to be done and few hands to do it. Rose and Sarah performed many chores around the place that a few years before would have been done by slaves. They rounded up and milked the cows and took care of the milk. Since ice was scarce, the milk was allowed to sour so that the girls could churn the clabber and make butter. In their earliest days at Ellerslie, they were given their own little churns.

Although it was not purposeful on the part of their guardians, the girls had been given little individual identity. They slept in the same bed, did the same chores, and dressed in identical clothing. But as they grew, each began to develop her own distinctive character. Sarah was bold and assertive; Rose shy, and hesitant. She took her older sister's leads and stepped aside to avoid confrontation. Although she possessed an extraordinary kind of beauty—long blonde hair and violet eyes set off by a fair complexion, she seemed totally unconscious of her looks. The girls loved each other very deeply in spite of their differences; in fact, they seemed to complement each other.

Olivia Lane Wade, wife of Judge William Wade, who built Ellerslie. She was Rose Ker Foster's great-aunt.

There was little opportunity for outings, especially in the winter when the roads were muddy and sometimes impassable, but in the company of their cousins Alice and Elizabeth, they attended Grace Episcopal Church in St. Francisville. One day as their carriage approached the town, Olivia mentioned that a Union officer was buried in the churchyard of Grace Episcopal. Excitement filled Rose, who was always eager to hear Civil War stories, clamored to hear the story.

According to the story, St. Francisville was said by Union officers to be "a hotbed of secessionists" during the war. When an agent of the federal government was captured and detained in the town, a Union gunboat retaliated by bombarding St. Francisville and nearby Bayou Sara for several hours, damaging Grace Episcopal Church. On board the gunboat was a scared young officer, Lt. Commander John E. Hart of New York, who apparently had had a premonition about his death. Being from a long line of Freemasons, he had told his commander that if anything happened to him, he wanted a Masonic funeral. Just as the young man had foreseen, he was killed. A truce was declared while the captain of the gunboat asked if anyone on shore was a Mason. When the affirmative reply came back, the captain relayed the young man's request, and it was granted. A longboat from the gunboat came ashore at the Bayou Sara landing carrying the body, which was removed, prepared for burial, and given a Masonic funeral. Then he was buried in the church cemetery. Records do not indicate whether the federal agent was returned, but in any event this is one of the few exchanges of gunfire recorded in the area.

Rose liked the story and added it to her repertoire of Civil War tales. In later years, she repeated it to her children and grandchildren.

In the early years of Louisiana's development, literacy was considered a luxury. During the period of French rule, elementary education depended on the desire of the parents. Advanced schools were administered by the Catholic Church. When Louisiana was ceded to Spain in 1762, the new officials were more receptive to public education, but it did not become a reality until after the United States purchased the Louisiana territory in 1803 when the territorial legislature established an academy in each parish for both elementary and secondary instruction. Real progress came only after 1898, however, when boards were established and given the authority to sell bonds.

Rose and Sarah came to live at Ellerslie shortly after the Civil War ended and lived there during the Reconstruction period before public schools were readily available. Parents were mainly responsible for their children's education. Education was of prime importance in the Wade household, and there being no accessible public schools or available tutors because of the war, the Wades ordered books and taught not only Rose and Sarah but also children of the workers who had remained on the plantation. Both girls had keen minds, but the lovely grounds of Ellerslie called out to them; consequently, they often fidgeted through spelling and arithmetic, especially later when studying Charles Davies' *Elementary Algebra*. Reading offered room for imagination, but Olivia's long readings from the Bible caused stifled yawns, but soon the girls were able to read to her; then stories of the Biblical patriarchs came to life.

Although many Southerners had reservations about books published in the North, the Wade family realized that certain basic books, such as Noah Webster's dictionary and blue-backed speller, McGuffie's readers, and penmanship books, were necessary. The latter stressed the push-pulls and circles which had to be done between the lines of their writing tablets. Hour after hour of this, and then the repeated creation of every letter in the alphabet made them thoroughly familiar with the writing of elementary words.

As they advanced, they often had to copy passages from the Bible whose early King James version was far more difficult than modern versions. They studied the dictionary and learned to use it in reading so that their vocabularies grew. Sir Walter Scott was a favorite, and they sometimes memorized his poetry, not only for its beauty but because their Ker ancestors had come from Scotland and were mentioned in Scott's *Tales of My Grandfather*.

Growing up in an isolated area and in the company of only adults, both girls were shy. They had grown to love the Wades, and their parents were but a dim memory. But the sisters and brothers whom they had left behind remained very much in their hearts since the Wades had arranged for them to visit Ellerslie often. Having been taught about their ancestors, the children often talked about them, especially Great Grandfather Ker, the first to come to America. In her own special way, Alice had made the past come alive.

A Bill From John James Audubon to Judge Ware
for art lessons for Wade's step-daughter, Elizabeth Ratliff.
Miss Ratliff was Rose Foster's guardian.

Instruction for Miss Ratliff	$50.00
March 12 quire of paper	.25
March 23 quills	.37
April 15 quire of paper	.25
April 24 1 yard lace	.18
April 28 Atlas	.62
June 21 Working Cotton	.25
July 23 Slate Pencils	.12
	$52.00
Forward	12.80
	$39.20

The original is in the St. Francisville Museum.

CHAPTER TWO

Dr. David Ker and his wife Mary Beggs, the children's paternal grandparents, came to America from Ireland after he had received a Doctor of Divinity degree from the University of Dublin in preparation for the Presbyterian ministry. He settled in Fayetteville, North Carolina, where he became pastor of Fayetteville Presbyterian Church. To augment his small salary as a minister, he began to teach and ultimately became one of the founders and the president of Chapel Hill School for Boys, which is now the University of North Carolina. According to Kemp Plummer Battle's *History of the University of North Carolina*, Dr. Ker was on hand to greet the first student who enrolled on January 15, 1795. During his several successful years as an administrator and teacher, he began to read and accept Voltaire's philosophy. When he announced himself as a non-believer, he resigned his position as president of the college. He then studied law and subsequently settled with his family in the Mississippi Territory. From there, he continued his friendship through correspondence with a Senator Stone of North Carolina, who had appointed Dr. Ker to his original position at the university. The senator, a close friend of President Thomas Jefferson, recommended Dr. Ker to the president, noting that his philosophy was in harmony with theirs. Therefore, when the opportunity arose, President Jefferson appointed Dr. Ker a judge of the Mississippi Territory as is revealed in the following extract from a letter dated January 25, 1803, from Thomas Jefferson:

> To all who shall see these presents:
> Know ye that, reposing special trust and confidence in the wisdom, uprightness, and learning of Judge Ker of the Mississippi Territory, I have nominated him and by and with the advice and consent of the Senate, do appoint him one of the judges in and over the Mississippi Territory and so authorize and empower him to execute and fulfill the duties of that office according to law and to have and hold the said office with all powers and privileges and emoluments to the same of right appertaining during his good behavior, he to reside within the said territory.
> In testimony whereof I have caused these letters to be made patent and the seal of the United States hereto affixed, etc.

It was considered an important appointment, and Dr. Ker's tolerance and fair play caused him to become a highly respected judge. His sudden death in 1805 was a loss to the area as well as to his family. His wife, Mary, a former teacher, was left to rear and educate their five children. She secured a

David Ker, D. D. (1758-1805), co-founder of the Chapel Hill School for Boys, which became the University of North Carolina. Ker was Rose Ker Foster's great-grandfather.

Mary Beggs Ker (1757-1847), wife of Dr. David Ker.
She is buried at Linden Plantation, Natchez, Mississippi.

John Ker (1789-1850), M. D., the son of David and Mary Beggs Ker. He was Rose Ker Foster's paternal grandfather.

Rosealtha Routh Ker, Rose Foster's mother.

teaching job, not an easy feat in those days, and ultimately achieved her goal of educating all of her children. One son, John Ker (Sarah and Rose's grandfather), after studying medicine in Philadelphia, became a physician in Natchez. He was also a successful planter. His son, John, Sarah and Rose's father, studied law and became a practicing attorney in Natchez and Vidalia, Louisiana, right across the river. He married Rosealtha Routh, and they lived at Roseland Plantation in Natchez until war clouds gathered. Since both their families had farming interests in the Lake Catahoula area, near Vidalia, they moved there, knowing that a Yankee blockade of the Mississippi River was imminent.

The Routh family was of Danish descent who settled in Wales. Jeremiah, the founder of their clan in America, came to this country in 1760, ostensibly because of strained relations with his stepmother. He eventually migrated to the Natchez area with his children Job, Jeremiah, and Mary. Since the Spanish were generous with land grants, he obtained one of the first grants awarded to English settlers under Spanish rule—four thousand acres near the mouth of Cole's Creek.

Job Routh,
Rose's maternal
great-grandfather.

The Routh family prospered from the beginning. After Jeremiah's death, his children carried on. Young Jeremiah moved out on Red River and started farming; Mary married an Englishman, Isaac Johnson, who was appointed *alcalde* (magistrate) of the area by the Spanish governor Carlos de Grandpre. Job, the youngest, obtained a land grant in Natchez, and he and his Swiss wife, Anne Miller, built a home on the site of what is now Dunleith and named it Routhlands. (It was later destroyed by fire, and Job's daughter Mary Routh Dahlgren rebuilt it in 1847 and named it Dunleith.) In addition to his Natchez property, Job obtained a land grant across the Mississippi on Lake St. Joseph in what is now Tensas Parish, Louisiana. Always industrious, Job acquired many slaves and amassed a large fortune on his cotton plantation. His wife bore him eight children, who, as they married, were given portions of the original grant. They, in turn, became planters and erected houses commensurate with their means and social positions. At one time there were fifteen houses in the Lake St. Joseph compound, as well as winter homes in Natchez.

Francis (Frank) Routh, Job's son and Rose and Sarah's grandfather, and his wife Mary Lane built a large Georgian house in Natchez. Named Kenilworth, it was Frank's pride and joy. It was an elegant house with a wide portico supported by Ionic columns and a spacious hall containing twin stairways that curved gracefully from each side. They had two children, and many social events, as well as family weddings, were held there, and the house rang out with laughter and song. Unlike other members of the family Frank had a summer home on Lake Catahoula, where he bought land and developed it into a cotton plantation.

Francis Stebbins Routh,
Rose's maternal grandfather.

Natchez was not fortified during the Civil War, and the town surrendered to Admiral Farragut's fleet in 1863. Although it was occupied by Federal troops till the end of the war, little damage was done to the old buildings and lovely homes with one exception—Frank Routh's beautiful Kenilworth. It was appropriated by a Union commander to become a hospital. When a small pox epidemic broke out, it was turned into a pest house. The disease raged within its walls, and the magnificent grounds became a graveyard where victims were buried in long trenches and unmarked pits. By the time the war ended, the

Rose's father, Capt. John Ker

house was partially destroyed. Frank Routh had spent the war years at his home in Catahoula and after the war seldom went back to Natchez. He never returned to see what was left of his beloved Kenilworth. His wife died in 1868 and he lived on in their Catahoula home with his bitter memories.

His daughter Rosealtha had married John Ker and had borne him six children before he went to war. After word came that Captain Ker had been wounded and captured during the siege of Vicksburg in 1863, their seventh, John, was born. The times were extremely hard for the family: food was scarce, the baby died, and Rosealtha's health was failing. She never fully recovered from the last childbirth, and while her husband languished in a Union prison, she became a total invalid and died shortly after he was released in 1865.

Rosealtha's life at this time contrasted sharply with her antebellum days at Kenilworth. As a child, Rosealtha had visited her mother's sister, Olivia Wade, who with her second husband, Judge William Wade lived at Ellerslie Plantation near St. Francisville, Louisiana. Olivia had first married William Ratliff by whom she had two daughters; one of them, Elizabeth, was like a sister to Rosealtha. After Ratliff's death, Olivia married Judge Wade and had several more children, and among them was another of Rosealtha's favorites—Alice Wade.

Following are letters they exchanged in happier times. At the time of the first letter, Rosealtha was visiting the Wades at Ellerslie while her cousin was visiting the Rouths at Kenilworth. Alice had apparently been on a trip.

Bayou Sara, July 3, 1848

My dear Cousin [Alice Wade],

I wrote last week to "Cousin Frank" [Francina Wade, daughter of Judge and Olivia Wade]. I hope she received my letter in which I mentioned I would address my next to you. It does not make any difference I suppose to her just so she knows that all are well at home. Annie and Belle paid their grandmother a visit last week. They returned to us as well as when they left. I never saw them look better than they are at present. And also Johnny—he is in fine health. I think he's getting very much like my brother, "Willie."

And now for "Aunt" [probably Olivia Wade]—her sleeves are all getting too small. So you may judge what is the state of her health. I have now enumerated all the delicate ones. O, I forgot my humble self. My appetite is still as small as ever. I have only gained 20 pounds since you left. I believe I have. I won't assert it positively.

All the rest are flourishing. Joe, Mary and Bud keep the house in an uproar from morning til night. Mary is kept busy in school the better part of the day, but oh me, she makes up for it when she's let loose. My poor limbs ache when I think of her. Do you not think it's a shame for her to do me so when I never molest anybody in this house. I only sometime play bear for the amusement of Johnny.

We had quite a dance Saturday night. We had the Barrows here— that is, the boys. They stayed all night with our boys. I'm the musician while Cousin Frank's away. It is quite provoking. They will not let me dance any. Miss Haralson does not play, but I think she understands music perfectly.

Well, dear Cousin, I have told you all about home. Now I want to know how you have enjoyed your trip north. Did you stop at Cincinnati? You must tell me all about everything. We are all anxious to hear from you. I hope you have all been well and have had as little trouble with Willie as we have had with Johnny. All join me in a kiss to Papa, Mama, Willie, and Aunt Bettie. Write soon.

Your devoted cousin,
Rosealtha Routh

The following letter gives insight into the relationship between Rosealtha and her cousins and therefore explains why Rosealtha's young daughters were

put into her cousins' care. Addressed to Miss Elizabeth Ratliff, c/o Mrs. Olivia
Wade, Ellerslie Plantation, it was written two or three years after Rosealtha and
John Ker were married.

Roseland, July 9, 1851

Dear Cousin,

To think that I have to decline your kind invitation to pay you a
visit this summer. Is it not too bad? It is, nevertheless, true. We have
determined to stay at home, although everyone around us is leaving.
We have been away from home so much that we feel it our duty to stay
this summer. So you see, dear cousin, we cannot enjoy Aunt's and your
pleasant company nor the nice juicy peaches.

Nothing would please me better than to pay you a visit. Mr. Ker
was saying the other day, "Oh, Rose, would you not like to be at Ellerslie now? It's so cool and pleasant." Whenever he gets very warm he
always wishes to be at your house.

And I know something about the peaches. The summer I stayed
with Aunt when you went north, they were splendid. I wish not to see
finer. I suppose you have been making, or are at the time making,
preserves. You have such nice fruit for preserving,

I can see you and Louise, at the corner of the gallery, with your
furnace, preserving away. (you seated with some interesting book in
your hand, while Louise puts on coal or blows up the fire.) And where
is my dear aunt at the time? Seated on the settee, Bible in hand poring
over its sacred chapters. (If I were to have Aunt's portrait taken, it
should be just as I've described. O, I'd give a great deal to see you all
again. But indeed it's impossible for me to leave home.

Father [Frank Routh, Rose's grandfather] is very anxious for me to
pay him a visit, but I wrote to him I could not. I'm in hopes we will see
each other in the winter. You will pay me a visit, won't you? I'll take
no excuse. I was so provoked that I would not get to see you and
Cousin Francina often in the city. I called twice and you were out, and
then when we did see each other we were in such a whirl we could not
talk.

How does Cousin Francina get on? I hope she's looking as well as
she did in the city. I never saw her look better. She did not look like
the mother of seven children. I heard many persons say she looked
like a girl again. So I suppose she's not going to the Bay for her health.

Caroline Bisland left here for Natchez last Monday. She's going to
be confined. Mrs. Butler will leave in a week or two, but she's not go-

ing for the same purpose! She will stop at Bayou Sara, and pay her mother-in-law a visit of about two weeks. She has a very sprightly baby, but not pretty.

How does my Johnny come on? Kiss him a hundred times for me and all the dear children. Does Cousin take them with her? Do you really know whether it's Cousin John Johnson's wife that's dead? Brud wrote me that "Cousin John's wife was dead," and it may be Cousin John Williams he meant. He wrote me a very unsatisfactory letter. He did not state any particulars.

Poor old Uncle Gilbert's dead. I don't know when I had anything to grieve me so much as his death. I was so much attached to him, notwithstanding he drank so hard. He was so attached to all of our family. I saw him in New Orleans as I was leaving. He was on Father's boat at the time sick. I should like to take Rose if we are able, but I cannot do it. You know she is named for me. I cannot bear the thought of her relations having the children. They are smart children, but very much spoiled. I suppose Father will keep them all.

How did Aunt bring herself to part with Alice? I expect it nearly broke her heart, but I expect Alice is so much grown that she feels able to take care of herself.

I have not told you one word about my darling Willie [her firstborn] for he is a darling, Cousin, and there's no two ways about it. I have him in pants now and they become him very much. He is not a forward child about talking, but all he does say is very sensibly spoken.

I wish you could see him. I expect you and Aunt are rather curious to know if there's not any prospect of another, but be assured there is not. Mr. Ker's quite put out that we have not a houseful at this time, but I told him it's all for the best.

Dear Cousin, you must forgive my long silence, and tell Aunt and Cousin Francina to do the same. We want to see you all very much. Please answer my letter soon and don't give me a scolding. Mr. Ker joins me in love to you all and Willie sends a great many kisses to all.

Believe me, your most affectionate cousin,

Rosealtha Ker

When Rosealtha died the Wade family came to the funeral. After several days of trying to arrive at a solution regarding the future of the children, they decided that the older ones would stay with Rosealtha's father, and the Wades would take the two younger ones, Sarah and Rose. Olivia knew that she was too old to accept the responsibility, but she would make her adult daughters,

Elizabeth and Alice, their guardians. Since Rosealtha had loved those two cousins like sisters, she knew they were the logical ones to accept the responsibility.
Elizabeth and Alice, neither of whom was married, welcomed the opportunity
and from that day forward loved them as if they were their own daughters.

CHAPTER THREE

Although money was scarce, the Wades, with the help of the children's grandfather Routh, were able to arrange for the next step in their education. Rose was eleven and Sarah fourteen when they left the warm security of Ellerslie for a convent school in St. James Parish. Again the feeling of strangeness, loneliness, and dread that had permeated them on coming to live at Ellerslie settled upon Rose. Again she clutched her sister's hand as the Wades, whom they now loved as parents, kissed them goodbye. The date was February 8, 1872.

"But why can't we keep on with our education here? Besides I've already learned nearly everything, and you can teach me the rest, Cousin Alice." Rose said.

"Now, Rose, look at Sarah, how grownup she's being. She's looking forward to school, aren't you, Sarah?"

"But what if the sisters are mean to us?" Rose pleaded.

"They won't be. The Sisters of the Sacred Heart are very kind. You'll see. Look, the horse is pawing; he wants to start now. Get into the carriage now and wave goodbye to us."

Alice and Elizabeth accompanied them to the landing to take a steamboat. At the end of their journey they would be met by escorts from the school. Rose looked back as long as she could see the house. Sarah proudly announced, "I'm excited. I just can't wait. And I know we're going to have lots of fun."

"I'm happy right here," Rose answered.

"Well, you'll have me, Rose. I'm grown up now. I'll take care of you."

St. Michael's, founded in 1825, had established a fine reputation for learning. Known to be the most typically Southern convent run by the Sacred Heart Order in America, it was prosperous and successful from its foundation. There daughters of planters, Catholic and non-Catholic alike, received an education suited to their station in life. The school occupied the original building until 1848 at which time a new building was completed. It was a spacious three-story building, constructed of brick and designed in classic Louisiana tradition. One wing housed the chapel; another, the guest house and parlors. Behind the building stood the kitchen, separated from the main building as a safety measure to lessen the danger of fire. A courtyard covered much of the back area; behind it ran a little lane along which was located a row of slave cabins. Overlooking the Mississippi River, the building afforded a view of a wharf which allowed steamboats to deposit both freight and passengers.

Records indicate that when Rose entered her new school, she was placed in the sixth class (equivalent of present-day seventh grade); her vestry number was 184. Judge Wade paid her tuition and room and board, $141.00 then and later in September of that year, $80.00.

There were about two hundred students in the convent. Rose, always a bit shy, was overwhelmed at the sight of so many girls, so many strange faces; but with Sarah to "run interference" for her, she soon made friends and became a part of the group. Her best friends were the Tarlton sisters, Caroline, Lelia, and Sidonie, from Franklin on Bayou Teche. Although they were younger than Rose, they grew very close; and their friendship continued throughout the school years.

Uniforms, which were worn for special occasions, were made of red twill-like fabric called bombazine trimmed in wide black velvet ribbon with sashes and gloves to add formality. When the weather was chilly, each child donned her black velvet cape; when summer came, colored dresses were replaced by white ones of cotton or embroidered muslin.

Above: St. Michael's Convent, 1825
Below: The new building, St. Michael's Convent, ca. 1872.

When Rose entered in 1872, Reverend Mother Anna Shannon, Vice Vicar of the order of the Sacred Heart in Louisiana, was in residence at St. Michael's. Mother Shannon had been a novice under Mother Duschesne, who was the founder of the Sacred Heart in Louisiana. The Mistress General of the school was Mother Crescence. Mother Noemi Lebesque taught Sixth Class French, and Mother Marie Bertrand had Sixth Class English. The Surveillante General was Mother Mathilde Ratier. The next year changes were made on the staff with

Reverend Mother Susannah Boudreaux replacing Mother Shannon as Vice Vicar and Isabelle du Breuil becoming Mistress of Studies.

The girls, according to requirements, had brought their own bedding, consisting of a mattress (five and a half by two and a half feet), a pillow, two pairs of sheets, two blankets, and a coverlet. Also required were six changes of linen, six towels, a bag for linens, stockings, neck and pocket handkerchiefs, one green sun bonnet, a sufficiency of underdresses, a white muslin veil, a trunk, a work basket, six capes of cambric and one of black velvet, one cloak, a pair of gloves, two pairs of shoes, combs, a silver spoon, a knife and fork, a cup, two plates, a tumbler, a tooth brush.

Rose soon discovered that nuns were not to be feared, as she had heard, *if one obeyed the rules.* But it was hard to be good all the time; it was almost worth punishment to hide the nuns' habits and try to read smuggled-in romances. Planning and carrying out such ventures was a group activity with giggling and whispering and hiding, but when the punishment came, it was an individual experience; and it came with a lecture that made one feel very sinful. Rose suffered both "light punishment," (standing in the corner) and that reserved for "really rascally behavior" (the sting of a peach tree switch).

Sacred Heart's educational program was designed to give the pupils a rounded education which would transform them into "intelligent, active, unselfish women, with minds and hands trained for the sphere in which God had placed them. Cultivation of the memory, formation of the reasoning power and judgment, thorough comprehension of the matter assigned, stress on oral reading to include enunciation, pronunciation, poise, and a pleasant voice were included. Also emphasized were good penmanship, correct spelling, appreciation of world literature so that they might take part intelligently in conversation whether at home or in social gatherings.

Rose's sixth class studies included religion, reading, writing, arithmetic, Latin, French, and needlework. The same subjects were repeated during the fifth class (eighth grade). In the fourth class (ninth grade) emphasis was placed on languages—English, French, and Latin—as well as history. The pupils learned to read and speak French and Latin fluently. In English, they were drilled in all aspects of grammar, especially in correct verb usage. The work was almost entirely oral, with the mistress explaining a new lesson and making practical application of the rules. Then by questioning, she would require the students to exhibit their understanding by defining and explaining. History, including both sacred and ancient, was taught along with geography so that students could integrate the two.

The third class (tenth grade) required a more detailed study of grammar with emphasis on spelling and drills in written work and exercises. Added were poetry, history of literature, and oral reading, the latter usually held in the refectory (dining hall) during dinner and supper on weekends. French history and history of the Catholic Church were a part of the curriculum.

In the second and first classes, the basic courses were repeated on a higher level with added emphasis on compositions, both essays and letters. Arithmetic received small attention in the early courses, but by this time, students had to learn business and household accounting. The latter course insured that the young ladies could be frugal and successful homemakers.

In domestic arts classes, the students were taught to sew, draw, paint, garden, and make artificial flowers. They were also required to take piano, harp, stringed instrument, and vocal instruction.

The academic year usually began in October and ended in September, covering eleven months. Each quarter the school sent a report to parents with notations on their child's health, behavior, and proficiency. Except for letters from parents, all incoming mail had to be addressed to the Mother Superior and was opened. Rose's homesickness was assuaged somewhat by letters from relatives, especially newsy ones such as the one from her grandfather. Frank Routh had lived at Monte Cristo on Catahoula Lake, but the text of the letter indicates that he had recently lost it and was managing the Ker's place for new owners.

Home Place
November 15, 1873

My dear Child,

Your favour of the 9th [of] November came to hand so soon after I had written you that I was in hopes it was an answer to it. I hope, ere this, it has come to hand in which I told you all about myself and a little more.

I have since writing been to Natchez, found all well and have not long returned from the visit. I did not see or hear of the Ker family. I think your Aunt Mary is staying with Henry Metcalf's family some distance from town. The town was extremely dull, but I expect to have a gay time during the week of the fair which commences on the 18th of this month.

Your cousin Eliza Cochran is staying with Matilda Borin. Julia Nutt starts shortly for Washington City to attend to some cotton claims she has on the government. You know, Julia received a claim of fifty thousand dollars this last summer. She says she is certain to get her claim through for a million.

Mrs. Smith died a short time ago and left Irene the only legatee of her immense estate, amounting to two million. She made provision before her death to provide for Mary Louise and Annie Brumley.

I have thought to go to Catahoula as I said in my former letter, but found I was too poor. As to my old servants going with me, gave me little concern for they refused to come to me even where I am. I would like to have had Caroline with me to take care of what little I had, where she could be as comfortable as she is, and as much preaching and psalm singing as she wanted.

I could not be more comfortably situated than if the property belonged to me, having the entire confidence of the gentleman for whom I am agent. When he and Mrs. Ober come to the Place they come as guests and not as owners, and treat me with that kindness and deference that is due between gentlemen. I suppose I could remain as long as I am able to attend to business, but my only object in life is to sit myself in a home that I may take some of the . . . [burden] off your mother's Alice and Elizabeth Ratliff. On bended knee, there is no night they are not remembered in my prayers

I have received one letter from Annie since vacation. I have promised to be present at the examination night. As to the sale of crops the negroes are all broke up here, the worms took our crops early in August and will well make half crops. Last year they would have bought anything, for they had more money than they knew what to do with.

I will try and let you have a little money when I have my settlement for the year. As to Willie [Will Ker, Rose's brother] I am afraid he is not doing much for himself. I am glad to hear he has left Linden, for there he could never acquire money or reputation as a manager. He has all the time and energy to make a good manager.

Now about winding up picking and ginning which keeps me pretty busy. My love to all the family and remember me to your cousin Frank.

Affectionately your grandfather,
Francis Routh

Vacation lasted just four weeks with no holidays except Easter when students were allowed to go home for a few days. There was seldom a holiday for Christmas, but this season brought fun and recreation at the convent—hotly contested games of cache-cache in the mornings, a drama in the afternoon. Afterward came a big Christmas dinner, followed by fireworks set off at the far end of the property.The children, placed at a safe distance, watched in enchantment the brilliant spectacle lighting up the sky.

Rose left St. Michael's when she was about sixteen. Sarah was married shortly afterwards to Dan Towles, a local young man. The Tarlton girls,

younger than Rose, had not completed their course of study, but they kept up
their friendship through letters.

All that remains of
St. Michael's Convent.

Although Rose's education with its
emphasis on the humanities was roughly
equivalent to the present-day baccalaureate
degree in the liberal arts, her education
was not yet complete: she entered Afton
Villa Finishing School, which educated
and prepared young women for life in
polite society. Run by Miss V. Howell, it
was located in Afton Villa house, built in
1798 and one of the oldest and most elegant houses in the St. Francisville area. A
new house was built around the original
structure in the late 1840s. It survived until
destroyed by fire in the 1960s. Elaborate
in all aspects, it contained intricate wood carvings, stained glass windows,
Dresden china doorknobs, and the finest marble and plaster work in the area.
Towers, balconies, and cathedral windows combined to produce a majestic look.
Surrounding it were carefully landscaped formal gardens and terraces. The
place was named for the favorite song of the owner's daughter: "Flow Gently
Sweet Afton." Having escaped the ravages of the Civil War, Afton Villa proved
to be a highly appropriate place to teach Rose and other young ladies how to
take their place in society.

Afton Villa

CHAPTER FOUR

When Olivia Wade died in 1870, her son, Dr. Joseph Wade, became the owner of Ellerslie. Alice Wade with her inheritance bought a smaller plantation named Ouida, located about eight miles from Ellerslie. Although it was not as large and elegant as Ellerslie, Elizabeth elected to divide her time between the two plantations; and Rose and Sarah, who loved their guardians as parents, were delighted to go wherever they went.

Ouida Plantation House as it appeared in 1993.

In the late summer of 1880, Rose received an invitation from the Tarlton girls to go to Franklin for a two-weeks' visit. Lewis Tarlton, their oldest brother, would be in the St. Francisville area in September, and if Rose's guardians would permit, he could accompany Rose on the trip, which would take about three days by steamboat.

Steamboats, freighters of the nineteenth century, made regular trips into the Bayou Teche, delivering general merchandise to the bayou country and bringing out cotton and sugar. The passenger list was usually a long one. The captains of these boats were considered honorable men because they were personally responsible for the cargo and passengers. Therefore, Rose's cousins, Alice and Elizabeth, after much discussion and reassurance from friends, gave permission for her to go. Rose was delighted, and since the visit would be two whole weeks plus almost a week of traveling time, mighty preparations

27

Tarlton House, Franklin, Louisiana, ca. 1881
(Photo courtesy of Dr. and Mrs. R. E. Horton)

started immediately. Which dresses to take, what accessories, how many of what? Excitement filled the entire house, and everyone pitched in to help make selections and to pack. When the trunk and valises were packed, they required a small wagon to carry them to Bayou Sara landing.

Her cousins accompanied her to the boat and very formally placed her in the hands of the captain and her escort Lewis Tarlton.

"Captain, we expect you to watch carefully over Rose at all times." Elizabeth emphasized her last three words.

"Oh, to be sure, Madame. I'll never take my eyes off her. Except when I have to take care of my duties as captain."

"Well, I hope you can do those duties in a hurry. Our Rose is young and vulnerable, and there are so many ruffians around these days just waiting to take advantage of an innocent young girl."

"Madame, I assure you; your Rose will be quite all right."

"Well, be sure she is."

Then turning to young Lewis Tarlton, Elizabeth voiced her expectations of him. "And, you, sir, we trust that you will at all times be a gentleman and conduct yourself properly with our Rose. And see to her well being."

Having listened to the exhortations given by Alice, the young man looked as though the job of escorting this special lady might be a little too much for him, but he smiled and assured Rose's guardians that he was a man of honor.

Rose, eighteen, had grown into a lovely young lady. At five feet six inches, she was considered tall because of her slender build. With blonde hair, slender face, blue eyes set under well-defined eyebrows, and patrician features, she attracted attention wherever she went. She had never lost her innate shyness, but her smile was warm and ready. Her good sense of humor afforded her many laughs.

As she boarded the steamboat, she exclaimed, "This is the most glamorous sight I have ever seen."

The captain said, "I'll give you a tour tomorrow." She wondered if he was trying to fulfill part of his promise to her cousins who had embarrassed her with all their admonitions, but he seemed so willing and gracious that she dismissed the idea.

The next morning he led her atop the decks to the pilothouse, which looked like a comfortable living room with its captain's chairs and padded benches. Rose was impressed with the giant steering wheel and next to it the signal lever to the engine room. The pilot told her it allowed communication between him and the engine room, which took up a third of the lowest deck.

Between the engine room and the pilothouse were the dining room, lounge, and staterooms, where they moved next. The decks were wide—upper decks for passengers and lower decks for cotton bales, mules, or whatever freight needed to be sent. It was not unusual, the captain said, for one steamboat to carry several hundred bales of cotton which covered the entire lower deck. She noticed a crew of rough, salty-looking men working in and around the stacks.

The main cabin reflected the glamour of the packet. Her eyes roamed over white walls, clean crisp curtains, paintings on the wall, thick carpets, and comfortable-looking chairs with the latest periodicals beside them. In the dining rooms were long tables filled with flowers and gourmet food. With the captain's narrative keeping pace with their steps, they moved on through the reception rooms, barber shops, women's cabins, private suites, card game rooms. It was a luxurious floating hotel. The captain further pointed out that the boat had a well-trained staff of maids and stewards to take care of every need and want of the passengers, many of whom were frequent riders and expected excellent cuisine and service.

At night there was dancing with a live band. Lewis Tarlton asked to be her escort, but she was hesitant to accept. Even though she had studied dancing at Afton Villa, she had attended very few social functions such as this. Managing to allay her fears, she accepted and was ready when he called for her at her stateroom. She was dressed in a close-fitting blue gown just the color of her eyes. The young man looked admiringly before taking her arm and leading her to the ballroom where lively music was playing and dancers were swinging all over the floor.

"Do you know the quadrille?" he inquired.

"Yes, I guess so. Anyway, I had it at school."

"We need three more couples. Come on, here are several people not dancing. We can make a set. I'll lead you through it."

The music grew faster and livelier and everyone danced frenetically.
Rose's breath grew shorter and shorter, but she had entered into the mood of
excitement and it kept her going. When the music finally ceased, she asked,
"Don't they know any slow dances? Like a waltz maybe?"

But before she knew it the band struck up a polka. "Not quite as lively as
the quadrille," she panted, "but at least it's a couple's dance, and I won't have to
worry about so many partners."

At the end of the evening, she accepted his invitation to dance the next
night—and the next. And each night there was a full moon and she danced
with the captain and lots of other interesting men. She later told her children
and grandchildren of dancing all night on the boat.

Days were exciting, too. As they steamed up the Mississippi, she could see
the black smoke emitted by the smokestack wafting along on the breeze and

could hear the deep-throated whistle as
they approached a landing, where children and adults alike ran to the river's
edge to marvel at the sight of the big
white packet. Rose, feeling their envy,
thought how very nice her guardians
were in allowing her to make this exciting journey and enter into a world she
had never known before. She wished
everyone could be so fortunate.

Advertisement for the *Teche*, a packet
plying the waters between New Orleans
and Franklin.   From the *New Orleans
New Delta*, February 8, 1882.

The course followed the Mississippi,
into Old River above Baton Rouge, then
down the Atchafalaya, through Grand
Lake, into Bayou Teche, and up the Teche to Franklin. The land had become
flat and the waterways were lined on either side with moss-laden trees and
vines which were inhabited by exotic-looking birds. Their trilling mixed with
the croaking of the frogs to provide cacaphonous sounds. The entire landscape
contrasted sharply with her own hills of St. Francisville.

Franklin was the seat of St. Mary Parish, a land of winding bayous, fertile
soil, and thick foliage, that had been settled by French, Acadians, Spanish, and
Americans. The town itself was founded circa 1808 by Alexander Guinea Lewis. Its main source of income was raising stock, cotton, rice, and sugarcane.
By the time of Rose's visit in 1880, some semblance of the town's pre-war prosperity had returned. Federal troops had been withdrawn in 1877, and white

laborers who had replaced slaves were restoring agriculture production. Many plantation owners sold some of their land in order to pay Reconstruction taxes; therefore sugarcane production had dropped. On the whole, however, the economy was working and the town was expanding.

There were about thirty stores, including a drug store, bakery, and confectionery. Its professionals and tradesmen included three practicing physicians, eight lawyers, a blacksmith; and its businesses, two hotels, four coffee houses, three public halls, a market, a printing office, and a newspaper called *The Planters' Banner* (now *Franklin Banner*). In addition were five churches, a parish office, a fire station, a courthouse, a jail, two shipyards, two sawmills, a door and sash factory, and a corn mill. These establishments provided jobs for quite a few of the citizens. During the time of Rose's visit, Franklin was the main port of the Teche country and had a population of about 1200.

The Tarltons were one of the early families to settle in the town, having come from Maryland in the early 1830s. Rose wondered about the family; she knew and loved Caroline, Emma, and Lelia. And Lewis had been a good friend on the boat, but what about the rest of them? Would they be nice, too? Again, the feeling of strangeness, doubt, and apprehension that she had always experienced in a new situation swept over her as the boat anchored. Then she spied them—all three of her friends standing on the dock, their eyes searching the unloading passengers. Her heart warmed and she rushed forward into their arms. Lewis stood close by, smiling at their teary, laughing reunion.

It was an exciting two weeks for Rose. The Tarltons lived in town and Rose, accustomed to life on an isolated plantation, was an easy guest to entertain. Since all four shared a love of music and literature, they spent much time playing the piano and reading. Then there were carriage rides and walks along the Teche, and berry picking.

The highlight of her visit occurred when an invitation came for a benefit ball to be held at Evans Hall. Mr. and Mrs. Tarlton and Lewis chaperoned the girls, and two carriages were required to travel to the ball. Rose was glad she had danced on the steamboat, for she felt comfortable dancing both the quadrille and the polka. The townspeople gave her a warm welcome and the young men saw that her dance card was promptly filled.

It was a late-arriving gentleman who caught her attention. Their eyes met and soon she noticed him talking to the chaperones and looking in her direction. They explained to him that she was from St. Francisville and had been a classmate of the Tarlton girls at St. Michael's Convent. They added that she loved being in the Teche country, but she was not fond of riding horses and it was fortunate the Tarlton girls preferred musicals and picnics to riding. It did not take the young man long to arrange with a friend, who had the next dance with Rose, to introduce him to her and give up his dance card. As they danced

Rose learned that he was thirty-one-year-old State Senator Murphy James Foster, a lawyer and widower and he had returned home only that day from New Orleans.

The following day Murphy left his calling card at the Tarlton home along with an invitation to Rose to go for a buggy ride. As they rode and talked, they exchanged bits of information. Murphy was the grandson of Levi Foster, an Englishman, who had settled in Franklin prior to 1803 when Louisiana was still under Spanish control. He became a planter and later married Zeide Demaret, whose grandfather, Don Martin Navarro, had accompanied Antonio de Ulloa, the first Spanish governor, from Spain to Louisiana. Levi and Zeide had a son, Thomas Jefferson Foster. Following in the footsteps of his father, he became a sugar planter and one of the largest and most prosperous in the parish. He and his wife, Martha Murphy, whose family was also early settlers, bought Shady Retreat Plantation. Rose was delighted that Murphy's father had been named Thomas Jefferson and told him that her great grandfather had been appointed judge of the Mississippi Territory by President Thomas Jefferson. Rose later said she felt a bond between them at that moment.

Two days later came the invitation from Mr. and Mrs. Thomas Foster of Shady Retreat for Miss Ker and all the Tarltons to come to their plantation for dinner. Rose dressed carefully and nervously for the event, all the time being thankful that she had brought many dresses from which to choose. After choosing a frilly cambric dress, she brushed her blonde hair until it was shining and pinched her lips and cheeks until they hurt. When she was finally satisfied with her appearance; she hoped his parents would approve. "I must remember all that I learned in Miss Howell's finishing school," she remarked to her friends who had gathered around to tease her.

"I've never seen anyone so nervous; you'd think you were going to Buckingham Palace to meet the Queen." Caroline laughingly said, all the time pleased that *the* Murphy J. Foster was attracted to Rose.

The Fosters were a handsome couple; it was not hard to see where their son's dark good looks had come from. Dressed in a white linen suit, he cut a dashing figure with his neatly trimmed beard and brownish eyes. They were escorted into the parlor to wait for the announcement that dinner was served. Conversation was easy and the atmosphere relaxed. The Fosters managed to learn a great deal about Rose without seeming inquisitive. And through the conversation she learned more and more about Murphy. ("Wasn't that the whole purpose of the trip," Caroline remarked, more than asked, when they were dissecting the entire event later. "I mean, they wanted to look you over." Rose answered that she surely hoped they did).

The Fosters were among the early residents of Franklin. Murphy was the oldest son; he had four brothers: Warren, Prescott, Dixie, and Don. A sister

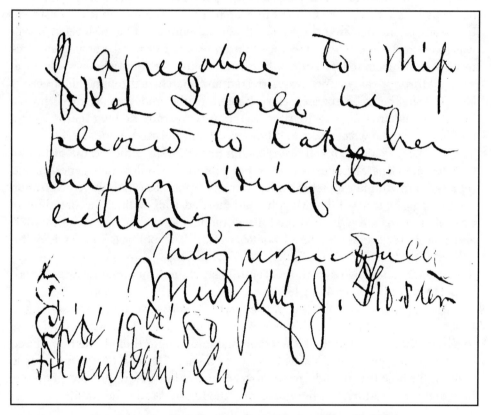

Murphy J. Foster's calling card.

Note from Murphy J. Foster to Rose Ker, September 19, 1880.

Emma had died some years earlier. Murphy had attended private schools for his primary education, his first tutors being the Wilkins just down the road from Shady Retreat. He had attended prep school at White's Creek near Nashville and college at Washington (later named Washington and Lee for its former president, Robert E. Lee). He was graduated from Cumberland University in

Lebanon, Tennessee, and from there went to the University of Louisiana (now Tulane) where he was graduated in 1870 with a law degree. He opened a law office in Franklin, sharing his practice with his cousin Donelson Caffery. They barely eked out a living, because so soon after the Civil War, few had money to pay fees.

Carpetbaggers still controlled the state; graft, corruption, and bribery of public officials ran rampant. In 1873 when he was only twenty-four, Murphy became so concerned for the state's future that he decided to run for representative from St. Mary Parish. He ran on the John McEnery Democratic ticket, and his opponent on Governor William Pitt Kellogg's Republican ticket. After the election, both sides declared victory, and both legislative parties opened their respective sessions in New Orleans in March, 1873. The Republican president, Ulysses S. Grant, declared the Kellog ticket the winner. One of Kellogg's staff was so enthusiastic over their victory that he ordered General Longstreet to arrest those Democratic legislators who were waiting for the McEnery session to open. Murphy was among those arrested and marched through the streets of New Orleans between rows of sharpshooters to the guardhouse; then thrown into the drunkards' cell. When the victorious Governor Kellogg learned what had happened, he was shocked and ordered them released immediately.

This story made such an impression on Rose that she removed the picture of Confederate General Longstreet from her album of Confederate generals and replaced him with her a picture of her father, Captain Ker. As the conversation progressed, she learned that Murphy had married Daisy Hine, the daughter of a Franklin merchant, who had died a few months after their marriage in 1877, and that in 1879 he had entered politics again. The political climate had improved after President Hayes removed federal troops from the state. He ran this time for state senator from the Tenth District, and this time he was victorious. He took his seat early in 1880.

The days flew by with Murphy a part of every day and every thought. When they were in a crowd, his eyes were for her alone. And when they were together, they both felt that they belonged together, though neither dared speak the thought. Then it was time to go home. He took her to the dock to wait for the boat that would carry her so far away, but before he said goodbye, he asked for the address of her guardians, the Misses Wade and Ratliff.

CHAPTER FIVE

Upon her return to Ouida Plantation, Rose's family noticed the change in her. She was ecstatic while talking of her trip. It was a wonderful trip, the boat was wonderful, St. Mary was a wonderful place, the Tarltons had been wonderful to her. And she had met a wonderful man, a state senator from whom they might be hearing. And if they did hear, she hoped very much that they would allow him to come for a visit.

Alice Wade said, "Why Rose, you're breathless. I believe you are love struck! Tell us more about this young man, and if he is as starry eyed as you are, then I'm sure we'll be hearing from him."

And hear from him they did, both through the mail and in person. Alice remarked that he was wearing out both the river and the roads in the Tunica Hills near Ouida. She wondered how a man could practice law and serve in the senate when he seemed to be either writing letters or traveling all the time.

The letters tell of the courtship.

Franklin, La.
October 11, 1980

Dear Miss Ker,

I have always yielded a blind and unquestioned obedience to my impulses and honest affections, and this, Miss Ker, must constitute my apology for this note and new request.

You kindly consented to allow me to visit you at your home with the promise that you "would not fight against my intentions." This promise is very dear to me. It has brought back hope to my life and gathered the shattered debris of youth to a young manhood, proud in a bright future and tender in its regard for you.

And now will it be too much to ask your permission to write to you? Do not blame or censure me for this. I cannot help it. I know that our acquaintance is rather limited, but [for] some hearts there is no calendar and time is a laggard.

I feel that Miss Ker knows that this request is honest and sincere and springs from no other than the most honorable return.

Again, I urge my request.

Very respectfully,

Murphy J. Foster

Franklin, La.
October 19, 1880

Dear Miss Ker -

I received your note this evening and kindly thank you. I do intend to visit you, though you picture "bogs, fens, and deep mires all along the way."

I speak plainly, Miss Rose, because I am dealing in unvarnished truth and reality. I know that I can love deeply and earnestly, and that the one whom I love will hold my destiny in her hands. I will give her a true man's love. My wife shall always be proud of that love and hand in hand I hope we'll climb life's hill together.

This, Miss Ker, is no fancy. I know it to be fact and knowing it to be true, can you blame me for writing as I have? And now, in coming to see you, it will be to tell you that you are omnipotent, that the making or the unmaking of me is with you—that my life is before you, to make or mar. All of its dreams of the future and all of its hopes are given to you.

As I slip forth in the sunlight of a bright future, I feel that indeed, one of God's augurs has been sent to me to lead me to a noble and better end—a new light has been given to me. Will you let me devote that life to the giver's happiness? I do ask you to "express your sentiments." Give me your heart and I promise to guard it as tenderly as my honor and treasure it as a rich gift from on high.

I appreciate the gravity of my request. I feel that I am unworthy of such a blessing, for it would bring more happiness and more joy to my life. Somehow or other, in the hushed stillness of this night, I feel that it may be that you will place your hand in mine and commit your life to my protection. Will you trust me?

I intend to visit you about the middle or latter part of the month, as soon as business engagements will permit. I am somewhat complicated as to the geography of your parish. I will stop at Tunica. Please let Mr. Winn know that I am a "stranger in a strange land." A lone pilgrim traveling to his mecca and easily lost among the hills of West Feliciana.

I thank you kindly for recommending me to your sister. My brother, Don, younger than myself, in formal appearance my superior, whom I can likewise recommend. Please do not take it amiss if I humbly suggest him as my substitute.

You tender your sister and cousin as witnesses of what you actually are. If you consent to be present at the interview I promise to prosecute the examination.

I saw your brother [Will Ker, who was working in Franklin] the other day. He, as usual, is looking well and in fine spirits.

Don wishes to be remembered kindly to you. He says "his bird of paradise" with all her bright plumage has taken wings and flown off to Washington.

I wrote to you the other day. Let my love be an apology for my impatience. And now, Miss Rose, let me ask you again for your love and I pledge you its tender protection forever and ever. Please write.

Murphy J. Foster

Nov. 8th, 1880

Miss Rose—

What credence can you attach to my vows and what assurance can I give to their sincerity. The pledged word of an honorable man. "Society" may have doubted me in many things, but that society, nor its luminous gossips, have ever yet doubted my word when given in the seal of my manhood. And this, Miss Rose, I give.

I do love you—sincerely and devotedly. It is no "infatuation," but the deep, silent, magnetic love of my maturer life. It is as deep as the human heart and as broad as life itself.

Since you left I have realized the potent supremacy of this love. I believe that I am a strong man, but under its influence I have been as helpless as an infant in the grasps of a strong giant. More than this I have been a coward.

While waiting anxiously for your letter I dreaded its reception. When it came I hardly had the courage to open it. I knew that it contained my fate—that it would decide my life, and from its cold pages a mandate would be issued more powerful to me than the decrees of a potentate, and Miss Rose, how can I thank you for your kindness. Let a life of true devotion be a poor reward. I write as I feel.

I believe it was the prisoner of Chillon who, when relieved from the gloom of his dungeon cell, was dazzled by the sunlight of God's bright heavens. Tonight it seems that the great, grand hope which floods my very soul with its beauty and its glory has bereft me all reason and judgment save the one, fond absorbing thought that we may walk together through life in the holy companionship of wedded love.

I hated to tell you good-bye. I saw your brother Sunday and he congratulated me and I told him your happiness is foremost in my life.

I shipped Mrs. T ——— a box of oranges. I hope she gets them before they spoil. This is an unsentimental and unromantic kind of offering, yet it is meant as evidence of my respect.

You will certainly see me next month. Tell your cousins and Minnie [Mary Frances Ker] I confided my case to their special charge and hope when I see them they will be able to tell me you have consented to abide by the judgment as to the date of our marriage. Goodnight.

Affectionately,
Murphy J. Foster

Franklin, La.
November 16, 1880

Miss Rose,

Since you have promised to be my wife, let me tonight talk to you as such. I will not lower the dignity of my great happiness by indulging in sentimental rhapsodies, although I do feel that a great joy and a new life have been given to me. I will simply talk to you as though I were with you.

I shall try to make you a good and true husband. Your happiness shall be my one aim through life, for upon your happiness depends my own. I have sometimes thought that I had the elements of making either a very good or a very bad man. Need I here say that when I know you I felt and knew that it was the pivotal point of my life.

With your love I believe the good will be developed and the bad dwarfed. I know that I love a pure and good woman, Rose, [and] for the first time in years my thoughts go upward to the "Giver of all good gifts."

As I told you, the wise men of the East never looked with keener anxiety for the star of Bethlehem than I have for your coming.

It is no fleeting fancy, but an unchangeable affection, and just as I am proud of you so I hope my wife shall be proud of my love. I need your love. I want it to cheer and brighten my life. I want it to temper my ambition and to elevate my aspirations. I want it as a grand shield in life's hard fight.

I shall leave Franklin the 25th or 26th when I will stop a day or two in New Orleans and thence to West Feliciana. I cannot appoint a day as I do not know the time it will take to go from the city to Tunica Landing. So I thought it might be better for me to stop at Bayou Sara.

I will speak to your brother and ask his consent to our marriage. In regard to your cousin, I am going to ask you to help me. These preliminaries must be gone through, I know. Neither do I wish to evade any of them. But how am I to proceed?

If I tell your cousin I love you, she will no doubt reply that it is perfectly natural that I should. I can't recommend myself, neither can indulge in any eulogies, for this would smack of conceit. I know she loves you and I know it will be hard to give you up, so I am constrained to ask you to come to my assistance. Will you?

It might be more appropriate to postpone this part of my letter till I see you, but as I am in a conversational mood tonight you will excuse my seeming haste. You have promised to be my wife. Is it asking too hastily that you fix the time of our marriage. If not in answer to this letter, at least when I see you.

Miss Rose, I don't believe much in long engagements. Of course every wish of mine shall be subordinate to yours. Yet if you will let me decide, I promise that it will not take place till sometime in February or March. Let me fix the month and you the day!

I saw your picture the other night at Miss Caro's [Caroline Tarlton's]. If you have another, will you please send me one? I want to show it to my mother and my brother, Prescott. I told the latter last night of our engagement. He is a warm-hearted, big-souled, genial boy and I thought he would go wild. He is married himself and for over a year he has been teasing me to "go and do likewise," and all day he has been perfectly delighted. He told me to get your photograph if I could.

Don has been a party to my hopes and fears, and yesterday evening when I received your letter, he remarked that he was glad if not for my sake, at least for himself, that the agony was over. My brothers, as I once told you, are my dearest friends and they are the only ones I intend to tell. But my happiness was so great I had to tell someone.

I sincerely hope that ere this you have recovered from your sickness and are now feeling well. I shall wait impatiently to hear from you and do hope that you can write that you are entirely recovered. If I knew your cousin I would request her to take good care of you and nurse you well, but I know she will do so anyway.

I expect you are weary of deciphering this letter and I will tell you goodnight.

Yours always,
Murphy J. Foster

Franklin, La.
December 10, 1880

Dear Rose,

Should this letter prove uninteresting, disjointed, and desultory, attribute it to physical indisposition other than want of interest or feeling on my part. While sojourning at Mr. Winn's I contracted a severe cold and tonight I am suffering with one of my old headaches.

I left Tunica Wednesday night between 9 and 10, and got to New Orleans about 3 p.m. Thursday. I left the city next morning and arrived here yesterday at two.

Franklin has indeed been in a state of excitement on account of my absence. All have been guessing as to my whereabouts. My brother-in-law, in his return from a trip to the city, told the good people that I had married and was then on a bridal trip to St. Louis.

For four days the matter was discussed. The dear old gossips rolled it as a sweet morsel under their tongues. They laughed and they cried and one older lady actually went to bed in chagrin and disappointment. Like Othello she thought "her occupation gone." Others put their wise heads together to unravel the mystery. I was tracked to the E. J. Gay [steamboat plying between the Teche and New Orleans], and there they lost all trail of me, and were left to surmise and conjecture.

In the midst of the excitement, when the conjectures ran high, John ———— appeared upon the scene. At first he was as mysterious as the Egyptian sphinx, but he could not stand it, and in a burst of passionate grief, he cried aloud that I had married you. And he thought it hard that his young love should thus be doomed to an eternal night. Did you know he was such an admirer?

Yesterday when I arrived back home, it was aggravating, yet amusing to see my friends. From Morgan City to Iberia the report had spread like wildfire. I am not embellishing this story at all. It is impossible to describe the condition of the public mind. Men, women, and children have discussed the matter, and I am questioned and cross questioned on every side as to my absence, whereabouts, etc.

My family, of course, were apprised of my contemplated visit, and now they all know of our engagement. Don and Dixie are delighted with my choice and both send their fondest regards to you. Prescott says he knows he will love his sister Rose. My mother is glad that I am to be married and says she will do all in her power to make our home pleasant and attractive. She knows she will love her daughter, and she will love her with a mother's affection.

I send you by mail Prescott's and Dixie's pictures. The latter is very poor, Dixie being sick at the time it was taken. Of mine, I leave you to judge for yourself. I will have a fresh type put in a locket and bring it with me in January.

And now, dear Rose, I cannot close without telling you how happy I am in the engagement of your love and confidence. Life seems to beckon me on and bid me enter the list of her champions with a new hope, a new courage and a new ambition.

I have always loved you since the first time we met. And now your love comes to me like a sweet echo from the hills of dear old West Feliciana, and I love that dear old parish that much the more.

Remember me to your cousin and sisters and please write to me often, and now, Rose, a sweet goodnight.

Affectionately
Murphy J. Foster

Franklin, La.
December 26, 1880

Miss Rose,

I just read your letter of the 20th.

Do you remember the night you told me you loved me, when you said you were happy, satisfied and contented, and how the sweet confession was baptized with tears? Rose, I want my wife to feel proud of my love. I want her to feel that through life she can lean upon that love with an unfailing confidence and an abiding faith.

And when we go down the hill together and step one after another into the shadows, I want her to feel that even then, she is the same sweet girl who won my heart in the morning of life. I would want you to be happy. Promise me that you will. It is the prayer of my life. I give and endow you with a husband's true love.

I wish you a Merry Christmas. Did you enjoy yourself Splendidly I hope. Did you receive my presents? I received a welcome from Miss Caro, and a necktie and a silk handkerchief, and I thank you for it.

I went to the dance, but language is inadequate to express how hurriedly I regretted attending. It was "Hamlet without Hamlet"—a dance without music, dull, stupid, and funereal. I gave one present outside the family—a toilet set to Miss Caro—she can thank you for this like-wise.

I did want to spend Christmas with you and your pleasant house-hold. Please remember me to them with wishes for a bright Christmas and happy New Year. By the way, we are invited with Mr. Frere next New Year. Without consulting you I took the liberty of inviting him and family to spend next Christmas with us at "Vine Cottage." Will you join me in the invitation?

When I visit you I think I shall stop at Bayou Sara. I like Tunica Bayou very much, but yet I have not much confidence in the place. It is a fine place to stop. But if anyone is in a hurry to go I doubt the safety of relying on that particular spot.

With the most affectionate wishes for a Happy New Year, I am

Affectionately,
Murphy J. Foster

Franklin, La.
January 27, 1881

Dear Rose,

I arrived here last night by the Texas train after quite a pleasant trip. I found Franklin as I expected—full of conjectures and concern as to my absence and whereabouts. But more of this hereafter.

Don, Dixie, Prescott, and Warren were full of interest and made many inquiries about "Sister Rose." After I went home, I had a long talk with Mother. She said she had thought a great deal of me and my marriage during my absence, that she was glad I was to be married and somehow or other, she felt a more than affectionate interest in you. She said for some reason her whole heart had gone out to you. Why, she could not tell, but it was a "something" which told her that, in a great measure, you would fill the void in her heart caused by the death of her only daughter ten years ago.

Our sister, Rose, died when she was just 19—young, beautiful and accomplished. She was the pride of the family and the angel of our household. She was cut down like an early flower in the spring. Through these dreary years a mother's heart has bowed in sorrow and grief under the blow, and now the heart, buried almost to breaking, turns to you. Who knows, but in the providence of all good had the mother of my darling Rose and my only sister taken above by the angels, so that the mother and daughter "below" might lean the one upon each other.

Rose, I have never mentioned the subject to you before, but often in the nighttime I have thought, oh so tenderly, of my orphan wife, so true and trusting. Is it so strange that I should love your Cousin Alice who has been so kind and good to you; or your sister Minnie or your sister Sally? Is it strange that my heart should go out to the kind cousin, though unknown to me, who watched over your young life until it budded into beautiful womanhood.

No, it is not strange, nor is it strange that my mother should feel that she has found her daughter in my young and beautiful Rose. Don't think that I am sad tonight for I am not, unless it be in the sadness of great joy. But I love to think of you in this way. It seems that the feeling comes down from heaven. I know that it draws me nearer to my God.

I want to feel that all through life you will be sheltered from its storms by this same tender and protecting love. I want you to feel that you can always place your hand in mine and say "I trust you even unto death with my happiness alone."

I read your dear letter last night. I know it came from the heart and I feel that now, ever hereafter, your heart is bound to mine by a tie as strong as life itself.

Bring the dear old sofa, darling, just before the fire. Give me my corner next to the door and you will be seated next to me. I have drifted into this strain unconsciously. But love takes some strange breaks and this is one of them. I have never felt in a better or happier mood than I do tonight, and if I continue to write I will dash off on another tangent.

I saw your brother this morning. He is in fine spirits and sends you all his love. He says he will attend our marriage if possible and I know it will be possible.

While going along Canal I saw your little slippers in the show window. I was halfway inclined to buy them but concluded to wait till I could get the pink linen to match them. Since I am to manage the fashion department I think I shall subscribe for Gray's lady book.

Now Rose tell me all about yourself. What did the doctor say about you? Have you had any more of your attacks? I sincerely hope not. I know that you will take care of your health and you will be prudent, won't you?

How is Cousin Alice? I hope she is better. Please remember me kindly to her. Tell Miss Minnie that I will forward her the book on science as soon as I can get it. Say to Mrs. Towles [Sarah] that I think the second edition of Charles O'Malley will be ready about the middle of March.

Write to me often. With a sweet goodnight, I remain

Yours affectionately,
Murphy J. Foster

Franklin, La.
February 1, 1881

Dear Rose,

It is now past twelve o'clock. I've been delving into dry and abstruse law for the past four hours. I am tired and want to have a little talk with you. I have no other paper in the office and you must excuse this.

I wonder what you are doing! If you have kept your promise, and know you have, you are now wooing sleep. Dreaming, I hope, sweet dreams. Let me then see my sweet Rose sleeping among the hills of West Feliciana.

Your dreams may be bright, but mine are equally as bright. I dream, what do I dream, that you and I are in the dear old parlor once more. You, bright, willful and affectionate, as variable as an April day. 1, with a great big foolish heart full of love, don't know what to do or say.

You pique me into saying something hateful and then, with a sweetness all your own, make me heartily ashamed of myself. You tease me into a good humor. We sit down on the sofa to have a real business talk over our marriage. We do not talk much about the marriage, but discuss the difficulties in the way of our meeting the boat. As if we cared, whether we ever met the boat or not! I go into a detailed account of my outfit.

You, well you are busy in disposing of the guests. Don and Warren you have snugly ensconced in the "spare room." That's as far as we get. Something ridiculous suggests itself, and we conclude to discuss other matters. For instance, "Rose, do you love me?" and the tantalizing response "not a bit." I like that answer. It is so original, and at the same time so poetic and replete with such soul stirring sentiment. We must get it copyrighted!

You know the penalty for the answer and here I inflict it, though you don't like it. But I believe you like it, better than you pretended.

Just about this hour, where is the Grecian coil, the artistic crimps and the coquettish curls? All gone. What will Cousin think?

Well, it is difficult to conjecture what she thinks. We won't hazard an opinion on the subject but hope she is too sleepy to notice particulars. Goodnight and bless my own angel.

The people in Franklin are still on the anxious seat about you and myself. You are well known in the parish. The color of your eyes, hair, the number of your shoes, your form, your complexion have all been exhaustively discussed.

It has gotten late and I know you are tired of this production. I have not heard from you yet, but am daily expecting a letter. I am anxious to hear from you.

I am in perfect health. I suffer sometime with my left side. But nothing, more or less, could be expected, when it is remembered that in that locality is a heart full, even to the overflowing, with a grand and glorious love for my special Rose.

Affectionately,
Murphy J. Foster

Franklin, La.
February 9, 1881

Dear Rose,

I was becoming absolutely desperate over your silence. It's two weeks today since I left Bayou Sara. I began to imagine every conceivable misfortune to "dear old West Feliciana," to your family, or to my sweet beloved fiancee, when to day I received your sweet letter of the 3rd. Rose, how can I thank you for all of your goodness?

I was in the midst of a most disagreeable case. I was cross examining a witness and we were certainly not billing and cooing when Dan handed me your letter. When I glanced at the inscription on the letter, the milk of human kindness left me and found its warm way into my questions, and by the end of the trial we were on the best of terms. Ah, Rose, what a potent influence you exercise on me, and it is always for good. I am very busy now and I never leave my office till one.

Now, for our marriage. I am going to leave the details to you. Anything you may do in the premises will be cordially endorsed. I am not particular about the time of day—any hour between "early dawn to dewy eve." But the day is as inexorable as the laws of the Medes and Persians—the 20th. Dan and Warren say that what we do will meet their hearty approval. Tell Miss Towles that on an occasion of this im-

portance and magnitude my brothers must submit to some inconven-
ience.

As for the boats—now, Rose, I have not the slightest confidence or
faith in them. My experience justifies my skepticism. I think that you
and I will languish for some time, either in Bayou Sara, or on the banks
of the River. But with you, even the desolation of Tunica will be
charmed into a paradise. Speaking seriously I leave the entire preliminaries in your hands. . . .

Affectionately,
Murphy J. Foster

Franklin, La.
February 20, 1881

Dear Rose,

Your letter of the 10th is so much like yourself and shows so much
sincerity and appreciation that I will not quarrel with you for asking if I
did not think my visit at Ouida dull and monotonous. Why, Rose, how
could I find it dull when I was with the only being whom I actually
love? If I did find it dull, I shall seek the very same monotony next
month.

I read that portion of your letter referring to your leaving your
home and coming to my mother's. She was very much touched and she
wishes me to say that you already have her love and she will do all in
her power to alleviate the sadness you must feel in leaving your home
and its loved ones.

I went this evening to look at our little home. Miss Allen showed
me all through the house. We had some real good laughs over our pro-
spective house and my anticipation on emplacement of the furniture.
She is a good person and takes great interest in "Rose."

She showed me where to place the armoire, dressing table and
chairs. We had an amusing time affirming an appropriate place for the
mirror. I wanted it in one place and she vowed that Rose wouldn't
submit to any such thing. Adjoining and opening into our room is a
small room. This, she says must be used exclusively as a dressing
room. She knows it will please you.

In the midst of our talk she said, "Murphy, don't you think you will
spoil Rose?" "Spoil her," I answered, "If only I can." She laughed and
said she thought we would be [happy]. We then went into Don's room
and spent time in an imaginary positioning of his furniture.

From the house we proceeded to the garden. The peach trees were in bloom. "This tree," she said, pointing to the one covered with blossoms, "is for Rose and I want her to send me some of the peaches." And how her eyes filled with tears as she thought of leaving her home so dear to her heart. "And Murphy," she said, "I love you and I know I will love your new wife. And now I want to show you the flowers and the violets. Also know that I, in my new home, will be sending up prayers for your happiness."

Oh, Rose, how such disinterested love cheers and brightens one's life. I know that when I take you to your happy home, some of the tenderest chords of your heart will be touched with sadness. A true woman, with an affectionate heart must feel sad, but as compensation I believe I have friends here who will give you a true and affectionate welcome.

There seem to be no less than six weddings on the horizon in Franklin, so we will have company when we launch our little craft on the matrimonial sea.

Rose, I never tire of writing to you but I fear you tire of reading my letters and I will close.

Affectionately,
Murphy

Franklin, La.
March 18, 1881

My dear Rose,

I want to drop you a few lines this morning to let you know of my safe arrival. I arrived here yesterday and was immediately at work till early this morning, or otherwise I would have written last night.

I will not, in this short note, go into the details of my trip. Suffice to say that my experience rivaled the richness of any of my former trips. This morning I am suffering one of my severe headaches. I caught cold and [have] a slight fever. By tomorrow I should be myself again and tomorrow night I will write you long letter.

Tell Mrs. Towles that her flower is in rich plumage, tell Miss Minnie that I have delivered her package, and tell Miss Wade that I will see her about the 20th. This, no doubt, is a piece of startling information.

Dear Rose, overlook this scribble. I write hurriedly for the mail. I feel that I cannot let the day pass without writing. With the fondest love I am yours till death.

Murphy

Franklin, La.
March 21, 1881

Dear Rose,

When I wrote, I promised that I would write again the following evening. Since then I have been decidedly unwell, and concluded that I would not write until I could tell you that I am perfectly well. Please take this letter as evidence of the fact.

When I returned I found Franklin in a more violent state of excitement than ever over our marriage. My protracted absence had excited the suspicions of the people. They knew all about the preliminaries to our nuptials. They knew that my room had been remodeled and refurbished.

Mother had had one, two or three new drapes made and all the family cousins, uncles, and aunts had been invited to give the bride a magnificent reception.

Dixie, Don, Warren and Prescott are perfectly delighted with the idea of my marriage. Even Tommy, our little nephew, wants to know when will "Aunt Rose" come? In less than a month, Rose, you will be my own darling wife. How dear and how precious this thought is to me. What serene joy and calm happiness it brings my soul.

How often when disgusted with the weakness of man, have I thought that I would run up the black flag, neither asking or giving quarters, acknowledging allegiance to no one, and only remembering my colors to the common enemy.

I think of you and what a change! I wear my colors. They are nailed to the masthead. I have a sovereign, a glorious queen enthroned in my heart. And when the oceans rolls and rocks in the thundering conflict of life, how grand to be the subject of such a queen. How glorious to be her champion! And when the storm is over and the conflict ended, under bright skies and over peaceful waters, we will anchor way out in the regions of light—loving and loved—true and trusting. But here I am reminded that I am drifting into beautiful idealities.

It is now about 11 o'clock and your brother, who came up to see me on business, has just left the office. He made a great many inquiries about you all.

He is looking well and no one would ever imagine that he is the victim of disappointed love. Tell Miss Wade that I think he is undergoing the preliminary tortures to another love episode. He has the unmistakable symptoms.

Now, Rose, tell me about yourself. Have you had any more palpitations of the heart, any more chills, any more mumps, any more "confirmed neuralgics," etc.? If so, allow me to suggest as a certain remedy "peppermint." I believe I have witnessed some of its wonderful effects. But seriously, let me know if you are well.

I have censured myself again and again for keeping you up so late at night. Remember me well to Miss Minnie, and Mr. and Mrs. Towles. All in all this is a remarkable letter, but please remember it is from

Your affectionate,
Murphy

Franklin, La.
April 3, 1881

My dear Rose,

How can I thank you for your kind, sweet letter of the 28th, duly received yesterday. No one but one who loves can understand the joy and happiness brought to the soul by such a letter. Your words, written from your young heart, make me happy, and how I shall always try to keep your love, just as it is—so gentle and affectionate.

You thought me sick again. Rose, I was right sick but now I am perfectly well, able to envision Bayou Sara, and if necessary, to walk from Bayou Sara to Ouida. You said I can have reservations on the 17th, but the boats only leave on the 16th and 18th. I will be compelled to leave on the earlier of these days in order to take the precaution against the *Gay* breaking shaft or at least a boiler, and of course we must languish in the city of Bayou Sara which would be delightful.

I am glad that your sisters Minnie and Annie will be with us. My brothers that are coming will yearn for companions. Tell Mrs. Towles it is important to have her at home. I want her along. I want to get a few pointers from her in my trials and tribulations. I want some kindred spirit and when we are waiting for the *Natchez, I* want to feel that, in the festive throng of watchers, there is one good soul which will enter into a full appreciation of the situation.

I do know this—we will have a perfectly heavenly time on the *Natchez.* Oh, Rose, we will have a gay time.

I returned from the city yesterday. All of my arrangements are completed. Court meets tomorrow where I hope to be busy, where I shall be busy until the day of my departure. But I experience great difficulty in coming down to the realities of the practice in court.

All the family send their love. And now again, Rose, let me thank you for your sweet letter. Remember me to the family. With love, I am

Affectionately,
Murphy

After their engagement was announced, a letter came from Lewis Tarlton, the Tarlton girls' older brother who had chaperoned Rose on the steamboat taking her to Franklin to visit the Tarlton sisters.

Franklin, La.
April 8, 1881
Steamer *John Howard*

"Miss Rose,"

Allow me to offer you my congratulations upon the happy event of your marriage, which I learn is to take place on the 20 Inst. Caro tells me that you intended extending Charley and myself an invitation, but owing to certain reasons which she mentioned could not do so. We will consider the intention for the deed, and many thanks.

I suppose we will have the pleasure of meeting you in your new home "in Franklin on the Teche." Although not the "Rose" that bloomed last summer, yet you are always as kindly remembered by us. Accept my best wishes for your future welfare, and hopes that your path through life may truly be one of sunshine and roses. May thee nor thine ever know adversity's frown, or fortune's displeasure; may thy husband successfully weather the contending winds of cross currents of this world, and safely land in the harbor of prosperity and happiness.

May he be, as now, always deserving of you, and you of him, and may reproach and unkindness ever be things unknown to him. Can I wish you anything more? I believe not, save it be, that nothing may happen to mar the pleasure of the anticipated ceremonies, and that your fondest hopes be in every way realized.

Caro [sister Caroline] is coming shortly, but when last heard from, had not decided upon the date. Well, Miss Rose, "Good-bye" and may Heaven's protection always be with you.

Lewis B. Tarlton

Grace Episcopal Church, St. Francisville, Louisiana
Below: Map of the St. Francisville area

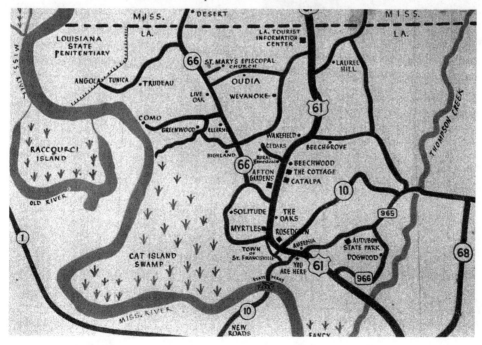

Murphy J. Foster and Rose Ker around the time of their marriage.

Preparations for the marriage finally came to a happy conclusion at Ouida on April 20, 1881. The weather held, and Senator Foster, with his brothers Don and Prescott, reached Bayou Sara without mishap. They stayed at the local inn overnight, and the next day being bright and sunny, they reached Ouida without bogging down on the uncertain roads.

The quiet and simple marriage was solemnized by the Reverend A. Gordon Bakewell of Grace Episcopal Church on April 20, 1881. General W. W. Brandon, Civil War hero and an old family friend, gave Rose away. The witnesses were Rose's brothers-in-law Dan Towles, Don and Prescott Foster, and Thomas W. Butler.

It was a late morning wedding with lunch afterwards for the family and a few old friends. Then Rose and Murphy, accompanied by Alice Wade, Elizabeth Ratliff, and the Towles family, traveled to Bayou Sara landing to wait for the *Natchez,* hoping it would be on time. Surprisingly, it was, and the young Mrs. Foster was hurried aboard before she had time to reflect that she was actually leaving her beloved family; and with travel and money so limited, it might be a long time before she would see them again.

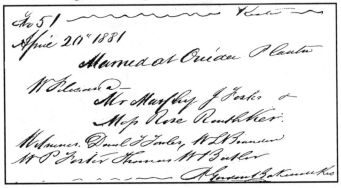

The Foster-Ker entry in the marriage register, Grace Episcopal Church

CHAPTER SIX

Upon their arrival in Franklin, the young couple was given a warm welcome by the Fosters and the Tarltons, both of whom felt real proprietary interest in this happy culmination of events which had begun in their homes eight months before.

Rose's days were full. She loved their small cottage and spent her first days unpacking her trunks and setting up housekeeping. Murphy's parents lived just down the road at Shady Retreat, and were there to help when needed, but they never tried to overwhelm. A steady stream of callers brought gifts and warm wishes, and it was not long before Rose was a happily settled bride.

When Murphy was away, they wrote to each other daily. The Louisiana Legislature had ninety-day regular sessions, usually from May through July. A state senator's salary was $4.00 per day with a travel allowance of $40.00 per session if needed. Special sessions were often held in New Orleans and cost of living was higher there than in Baton Rouge. In a letter from New Orleans dated December 1881, he wrote, "I am changing my boarding house. Senator Morton and I have engaged a room on Bourbon Street—a large and elegantly furnished apartment for $1.00 per day—$.50 cents each. I board at Victor's Restaurant for $1.00 per day, and this makes my living cheap. But when you come down, Rose, we will board at the St. Charles." Accordingly their first Christmas was spent in New Orleans at that venerable landmark of hospitality.

Her Christmas present from her husband was dress material, and they went down to Mr. Brandon, a tailor, to give him her measurements. Rose returned to Franklin leaving Murphy to settle details of the sewing. Apparently the tailor was a bit slow; for in one letter Murphy wrote, "One part of your dress is finished but the skirt will not be ready until sometime later in the week. I think it will make up quite prettily." He had planned to buy her a hat also, but he was not too enthusiastic about what he saw. "The hats are heathenish. They look like dilapidated basins on the heads. Felt is all the style and 'felt' like tearing some of the headgear from the wearer's craniums," he wrote.

By the latter days of 1881, a train ran from New Orleans to Franklin, and when Rose returned home, she made her first trip by rail. She was excited, but Murphy was apprehensive as he expressed in another letter, "How did you spend the time from New Orleans to Franklin? Did Brother Don meet you with the buggy, and how did the conductor treat you, and did you have to call on him for help before you got to Franklin? I hope you were comfortable, dear little wife—I was so uneasy, but could not let you know it. . . ."

In the spring of 1882, Senator Foster had to make a trip to New York on Senate Finance Committee business. His feelings were mixed: he both needed and wanted to make the trip, but Rose was five months pregnant, and he hated

to go so far away. However, his mind was somewhat relieved when her sister
Minnie volunteered to come from Ouida to stay with her.   His letters contain
vivid descriptions of his impressions of the city.

New York
April 29, 1882

My dear Wife,

I arrived here this morning at six o'clock, feeling perfectly well after
my trip. I took a short nap, then breakfast and called on the insurance
people I made a formal engagement to meet them Monday at 11 o'clock.
Can't say what turn matters will take.

My trip here was uneventful. I ate three hearty meals a day, retired at eight and slept until seven next morning. During the day I
read dime novels. . . .

I saw on my way "Monticello," the home of Jefferson, and a few
hours later I was thundering over the valley of the Rapidan, where fifteen years ago the enemies of the North and South met in dreadful
combat. What memories, darling, flashed in my mind as we dashed
over those beautiful plains once red and warm with the blood of our
country's sons. Lee, the great and good—Stewart, the dashing and gallant "Hotspur" of the young Confederacy—Stonewall Jackson, the magnificent soldier, the Christian hero—and the thousands other heroes
who sleep among the hills and valleys of the old Dominion.

Ah, Rose, sometimes I wish that I had worn the "grey." Sometimes
I think the cause too grand for our living to have missed the opportunity. But 'tis past, and with the dead, sleeps the cause of the South.

But let me tack. Otherwise, I'll drift too far out to ever get within
hailing distance. Now, what do I think of New York?

It is a very big place. I've just been promenading on Broadway.
What a sight. What a constant and overflowing stream of human be-
ings. Like the waters of the Mississippi, they seem to flow on forever
and forever, unceasing and unending.

Every imaginable cart may be seen, and at its masthead every
imaginable color—Greek and barbarian, Jew and Gentile, rushing
ahead pell mell like they were driven by some tremendous storm. I
look in wonder and astonishment. Since six o'clock this morning till
now it seems as though the same crowd was onward.

The sidewalks are jammed literally. The street itself one chaotic map of wagons, carriages, cabs, busses, every imaginable vehicle ever seen or thought of. It is like bedlam itself. . . .

I have looked in vain so far for a pretty woman, but have not found one to describe to you. What styles they wear! What dressing, and oh, good Lord, what feet! Their shoes are something to see. And the men—they are worth seeing, too. Tights have come into style again, and these fellows wear their pants as tight as possible, and about six inches too short. I am not exaggerating. . . .

I have not been around much, but have been attending to business so can't say much yet about the places. Will keep looking and how I wish you were up here with me . . . I am

Your affectionate husband,
Murphy

New York City
April 25, 1882

My dear wife,

I've just eaten dinner at the fashionable hour of six. Had a fire made (for it is rather cold this evening), and will spend the rest of the evening with my dear wife in a sociable chat.

I've just witnessed a rather amusing incident at the dinner table. A Mr. "A," one of your bleared and bloated hand holders came into the dining room with his wife and then both took a seat by a Mr. "B." Mr. "A" remarked, "Well, 'B,' I presume that you have been very busy all day." "Very busy," replies "B." "Still," says "A," "the fact is that when I'm with my wife" (and here the little woman gave him rather a delicious look) "she'll not allow me to do anything but talk to her." "Ah," thought I, "what conjugal affection."

In a few moments the lady and the happy husband began a very earnest conversation, and before many minutes they were in downright quarrel. "For heaven's sake," the old fellow hissed, "Maria, remember where you are." "I don't care a cent," she said. Then the old man deliberately turned his back and went to work on the delicate brains before him. In a few moments, however, they were as loving as cooing doves.

Right opposite me sat an old lady with millions, I suppose. She had on magnificent silk, cut a little low for one her age, and her skin was powdered as white as alabaster, and under the treacherous lace she looked artificial. What a hollow mockery this life is. Why, darling, I believe there is more genuine happiness in one of our evenings at home than there is in years of much life.

I went all through Central Park this morning. I had a delightful drive. The air was cool and bracing, the sun clear and bright and the people in thousands were upon the ground. The drive through the park is altogether nine miles. In the heart of the park is also the reservoir which supplies the city with water—nineteen acres in all and thirty feet deep.

These waters are full of swan, fish, geese, etc. The roads as smooth and even as a shell. All through the park were walks, promenades, bowers, swings etc. I went through the menagerie and saw some fine animals. The museum was closed.

These Yankees are wonderful people. Here, almost in the very heart of the empire city, you can get lost in the native growth, for the grounds are covered mostly by native growth. Here the poor and the overworked come, Saturdays and Sundays, to breathe some fresh air and to find rest.

I also saw a very large stone which had been brought from Egypt. It was some sixty feet tall and ten feet at the base, filled with strange and indecipherable Egyptian hieroglyphics. It has cost thousands of dollars to transport it here, where it stood, like some solemn sentinel, pointing the human mind back to the time when another race upon the coast of Africa likewise reveled in wealth, splendor and magnificence— a race where history is only told by the dumb stones and where secrets are locked up in the bosom of the unspeaking and mysterious sphinx.

In the afternoon I took a long walk on Fifth Avenue and saw some of the handsome residences. Some, if not most of the residences, would do for hotels. They are certainly magnificent.

I will stop and finish tomorrow after my interview with the insurance man. The trip is going well.

Your affectionate husband,
Murphy

Soon after he arrived home from New York, the 1882 session of the legislature opened. Apparently it was a long one, and by late June he was very tired, as the next letter explains. Sister Minnie had gone, and Rose's guardian, Alice Wade, had come from Ouida to be with her until the baby's arrival.

Baton Rouge
June 28, 1882

My dear wife,

I am completely worn out this morning. In fact, most of the members of the Senate are pretty well tired out. We are now working from ten o'clock in the morning till eleven P. M. I feel perfectly well but all are tired out. We all WANT TO GO HOME!

I received your sweet letter written last Sunday. I am so happy to learn that you are in good health. Rose, my pet, I could not stay here if you were in the slightest sick.

I had quite a compliment tendered me yesterday. The commencement exercises of the State University begin next week, and I was waited on yesterday by a committee and was asked to address them on the occasion. I was compelled to decline as I felt that I could not do myself or the occasion justice as I am busy day and night [and] have no time to write a speech.

My dear little wife, how I yearn to be with you. This separation, darling, is hard for me to stand. How hard it was to leave you at home. But the anxiety and the worry is considerably relieved by the fact that you are in good hands. May God keep you well and happy.

So the little girl is lively, is she? Do you know I dreamed last night that it was a little boy, and I thought I insisted on calling him "Rose" and we were having a hard time over his name. Finally the little fellow just proclaimed that he would name himself. "Wonderful child," thought I.

I write you a short letter this morning as I have overslept myself and I do not like to keep them waiting at breakfast.

Love to Cousin Alice and with a heart full of love for my wife.

Your affectionate husband,
Murphy

Murphy's stress and fatigue were two-fold: since his senatorial duties were demanding, his hours were long; and since his absence from home at such a crucial time increased his mental strain, he must have been near the edge. Rose, too, was tired. At eight months pregnant, simply dragging her body around was a great effort, and thinking of facing the birth of their first child without Murphy was frightening, indeed. She welcomed his daily letters and wrote many of her own. In one letter she wrote that her sister Minnie, who was staying with her, saved the day when a steamboat had engine trouble and its passengers had to debark. Two of their friends who had to get off came to

Rose's house, and since Rose was in her last days of "confinement," (then it was literally *confinement*) Minnie entertained them.

Minnie attended a few social events, according to Rose's letters. A picnic at Rugby School in Franklin was a spring highlight, and Murphy asked her to accompany him if he was home. Another was the Firemen's Ball. Two of Rose's letters described the town's shock that several unmarried girls planned to go dressed as firemen in red flannel shirts and black skirts: "I am scandalized, Mr. Foster." She wrote, adding "It is going to be so hot at that dance and I am glad I won't be around the aromas which are sure to permeate the whole room. Next thing we know, they will be going to coffee houses and billiard parlors."

On August 4, 1882, their baby girl was born, the first of ten children. When Murphy saw her for the first time, he took her out on their gallery and exclaimed, "Who said I was taking a chance in finding a wife so far away? This little girl will be just as pretty as her mother." They named her Rose Routh, and many callers came to see her. One left this note:

> Stirling
> August 11, 1882

> Dear Mrs. Foster,
>   Please accept these flowers with my love, and congratulate "Miss Foster" on her safe arrival in Franklin. I was glad to hear you are doing so nicely, and I hope very soon to have the pleasure of seeing you both.
>   Frannie desires to be remembered and she wishes to know if the "Rosebud" is on exhibition yet.
> Affectionately your friend,
> M. L. Secornsted

When the legislature was not in session, Murphy returned to his law practice. Their income was limited; but Rose was a frugal housekeeper, and their vegetable garden, chickens, and milk cow provided food they would otherwise have had to buy.

In early 1883 Dixie, the home in which Murphy had been tutored as a boy, was being sold for taxes at a price of $900.00. Murphy had always loved the house, and during their courting and early marriage days, he had pointed it out to Rose. In later years, she remarked, "I felt what Mr. Foster felt when I first looked at Dixie. It seemed so lonely, and yet I could see what we could do with it. Cousin Alice had taught me a lot about old houses and run-down yards. My sister Sarah and I used to help her do repairs at Ouida, and I suppose this is where my interest in carpentry developed. Every time we passed by, the house seemed to almost beckon us. When it came up for sale, Mr. Foster and I knew it was for us."

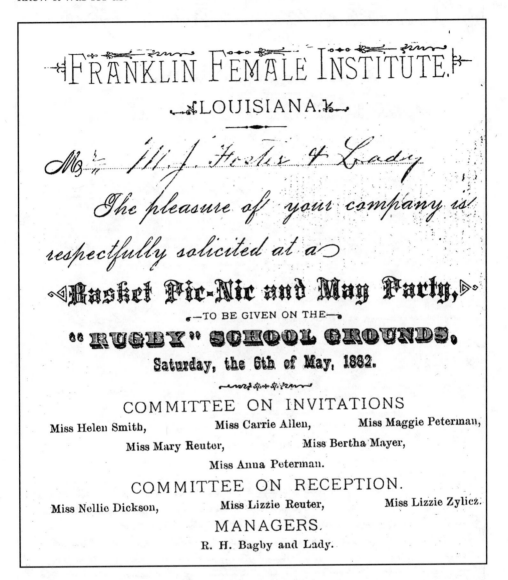

The house was on Bayou Teche approximately a mile from Franklin. It had been built by Euphrasie Carlin in the mid 1830s and owned in the 1840s and 50s by the Wilkins family of Virginia. The Wilkinses improved the house and added more acreages to the plantation. When in 1860 they sold it and returned to Virginia hoping to escape Civil War battles, there were approxi-

5070 Recorded in Book V of Conveyance Page 301, April 7th 1883

CASH SALE.

State of Louisiana,

PARISH OF ST. MARY.

BEFORE ME, *George B. Shepherd* a

Notary Public, duly commissioned and sworn, within and for the Parish of St. Mary, in presence of the witnesses hereinafter named and undersigned.

Personally Came and Appeared *Alvah P. Lappington* a

resident of *the Parish of St Mary* who declared, that for and in consideration of the price and sum of *Nine Hundred Dollars.*

cash in hand paid, receipt whereof is hereby acknowledged and good acquittance and discharge given for the same *he* did and do *es* by these presents, grant, bargain, sell, assign, convey, set over and deliver unto *Murphy J. Foster above resident of the Parish of St Mary,*

here present, accepting and purchasing for *himself his* heirs and assigns,

all and singular, the following described property, to wit: *That entire tract or parcel of land situated in this Parish of St Mary, having a front of Two and one half (2½) arpents more or less on the West side of the bayou Teche; by the depth of Forty (40) arpents for one and one half (1½) arpents of the upper portion of the front of said tract, and the depth to the public road from Centerville to Franklin of the other or lower portion of said front, and containing about One Hundred (100) superficial arpents more or less, together with all the buildings and improvements thereon situated, rights and ways thereunto belonging, bounded above by lands of Lyons Cooke, below in part by lands of Caldic & Sanford, and in part by lands of Mrs. Lucy Ganet and Fluming, in front by the bayou Teche and in the rear by the Siorumps or Sea Marsh.*

10

mately twelve acres on the bayou side of the road and almost seven hundred acres across the road.

Dixie was a bargain they could scarcely afford to let pass, but Rose and her husband did not have $900.00. Since it was strictly a cash sale, the prospect of buying the house looked bleak. However, Murphy's father lent them the money with the stipulation that they pay him back every year from their crop yields; and Murphy's brother Warren, who ran the Alice C Plantation, agreed to manage the crops while Murphy was away. The sale was completed on April 7, 1883, and they started to work on the place immediately.

Having been vacant for so long, the house needed many repairs. Rose could hardly wait to get her hands on it. From April until September, 1883, when they moved into the house, their days were full. Rose worked tirelessly although she was pregnant again. At her husband's insistence, she took some time off in June to visit her cousins at Ouida while Murphy supervised the workers. Then he became ill, suffering from both dyspepsia and a lung problem. Since there were no medical centers near, he went to Virginia for a change of climate and healthful spring waters, which he was advised would help his condition.

The restoration of Dixie was almost complete when Murphy left; and it went on with Rose and her father-in-law supervising and putting finishing touches on the house. Again, the letters flowed.

Allegheny Springs, Va.
August 6, 1883

My dear Wife,

Let us take our seats and have a nice, good chat this Sunday evening. . . . Well, how have you and Pa arranged about the house? The hall floors, I understand, are to be painted as well as the floor of the dining room. This, I presume, will look quite pretty. Now little sweetheart, while you and Pa are getting along so nicely in matters of this kind, you might suggest to him to get some handsome parlor curtains. They would fit so well with the painted floors. I am so glad that the two rooms which you have fixed upstairs look well. Did you have the ceiling of the blue room painted a like color. In the matter of painting the inside—doors, mantels, ceilings, etc.—I would be careful to select good and durable, yet at the same time pretty, paint. . . . By the way I thought it would be well to move that old house in the yard, which we spoke of, using Steve and Walter, with the stable lot and make up a carriage or buggy house. Unless you manage to get something in a buggy house line we will have no place to put our buggies. And yet I dislike to have anything of this kind done in my absence from the fact that Pa will want to have something cheap and worthless constructed.

I throw this out as a suggestion, and if you can secure a carriage house, the more I . . . [think] of it the more I think it highly desirable. Charley might give you some helpful hints on the subject. . . .

I depend upon you and Miss Georgie to contrive some way to have the garden plowed and ready for full planting by my return. Whatever money you may need for this or any other purpose, you can draw on . . . . In fact, little sweetheart, I want to see what is in you in a business line. I have always thought that, if you have the opportunity, you would develop fine business tact, and this summer you shall have a full trial. Don't you think I trust you when I shall leave the whole of the improvement of our future home to your judgment? And I know that you will have done all that could be done, done. . . .

Your devoted husband,
Murphy

Allegheny Springs, Va.
August 12, 1883

My dear wife,

I received two letters and a postal from you today. You will never know how much I enjoyed reading them. I regret that the dogs have been whoring so badly, and have been making such havoc with the poultry yard, yet as every household must have its little troubles, so every barnyard must have its crises. I scarcely know what is the best treatment for the puppies—shooting, drowning, even tying up. I think we [had] better try the last before we resort to the first two. You might put a long leash on them.

Tell me all about the house. How are you getting along and how much has McRae completed? Which is the prettiest room, and when will you commence to hang the pictures?

By the way, you must get Ma to go down with you often. She is very sensitive about these things and you must consult her often and this will be so satisfying to her.

How does the library and reading room look? Get all your book-shelves and have them furnished before McRae leaves. . . .

Your devoted husband,
Murphy

Sweet Chalybeate Springs
Allegheny County, Va.
John Kelley, Proprietor
August 29, 1883

My dear Wife,

Nothing in the world to write about this morning. The same old mountains all around us. The same bright valley spread out before us, and strangers everywhere. We have formed some very pleasant acquaintances in this place. Quite a number of lawyers and as we fraternize on all occasions, we have managed to pass the time very agreeably.

I am counting the days and the very hours. Monday we start and although we will be delayed a few days on the trip, yet we will be homeward bound. How delightful the thought. I feel like a new man—my wife, my baby and our home with all of its love and holy joys. . . .

I shall stop in New Orleans long enough to get some things for home. I shall try to get the carpet and the matting. In fact I don't see why I can't get them both.

Dear wife, how comforting the thought that we will at last be in our own home. Every tree, every plant shall be ours. Even the flowers shall bloom for us. Everything shall be ours. And, as you, Rose, already know I want to see you as its mistress. . . . You shall be its chief ornament and you shall ornament it as you see fit.

A heart full of love, and God bless you.

Affectionately your husband,

Murphy

A letter to Foster from his friend, S. G. Todd, the owner of nearby Arlington Plantation, included this news: "I see Mrs. Foster and baby Rose pass in their buggy every day on their way down to your new home. She tells me the work is going well and I don't know which 'Rose' looks happier. . . ."

After the family moved in, Rose named the plantation "Dixie" in honor of her favorite brother-in-law, Dr. Dixie Foster and the South in general. They hired a housemaid and a yardman, and they also found a farmer to live in the tenant house and work the fields. Sugarcane was the main crop with cotton an important second.

Rose's classes in homemaking at St. Michael's Convent served her well at Dixie. She had learned not only how to take her place in society as a woman of culture, but also how to perform domestic chores such as cooking, sewing, and upholstering. In one of her letters to Murphy, she asked him to get upholstery material so that she could upholster a sofa and chair in the sitting room.

For his part, Murphy began immediately to fill the yard with chickens, geese, turkeys, pigs, two cows and the two horses they already owned. Never again was Dixie to want for devoted owners.

CHAPTER SEVEN

The year 1884 had an auspicious beginning. The second Foster child, Elizabeth Ratliff, was a week old, and Murphy had been elected to a second term in the state Senate. Their first crop on Dixie was a good one, and they were able to start making repayments to Murphy's father.

Their letters to each other usually began each year when the legislature was in session and lasted from April through July or August. During his absence, unmarried daughters of family friends stayed with Rose. Miss Helen and Miss Georgie were devoted friends, and since they were her contemporaries, she enjoyed their companionship. Their names are mentioned frequently in the letters.

> SENATE CHAMBER
> STATE OF LOUISIANA
> May 12, 1884

My dear wife,

I arrived here in fine health and am feeling splendidly this morning. I have run off from the crowd to drop you a line. Everything here is confusion and excitement, a man's very life is worried out of him by the office seekers and one stayed with us last night until twelve o'clock and returned this morning before we were out of bed. This is but a sample.

I have met quite a number of my friends who seem delighted to meet me. All of the reunions are pleasant, though dashed with regrets at the absence of many of our warm friends and congenial companions. Oh, little wife, how I miss you, home, and the bright little babies. God bless their dear little lives, coming right from heaven.

> Affectionately your husband
> Murphy

> Baton Rouge, La.
> May 13, 1884

My dear wife,

I am head over heels in business, excitement and elections. Yesterday I was highly complimented by the best men in the state in selecting me as a candidate for the President Pro Tem of the Senate. I was beaten, but my defeat has but added to my popularity. I would rather have been defeated than elected by the vote which elected my oppo-

nent. This honor was unlooked for and came from strangers and therefore, the more highly appreciated.

Don't, my dear little Rose, take my defeat to heart. I tell you honestly that the men who supported me are the best ones in the state. I
was elected chairman of the Domestic Caucus, which, in itself, was a
high honor and compliment. I will write you as soon as I get the time.
With a heart full of love, and kiss the babies.

Your affectionate husband,
Murphy

Baton Rouge, La.
May 19

My dear wife,

I did not write to you yesterday because I was so busy I could not
possibly get the letter off by the mail. Homer Smith will leave in the
morning and I send this letter by him. He tells me that he will go at
once to see you and give you all the news. How often I think of you
and wish for you.

I am getting along quite well. Tell Miss Georgie that the people
here seem to think a good deal of me, and when I tell them that you all
fuss with me and abuse me, they say that you all must be pretty hard
to please. I then explain that you all abuse me in the same way a mule
kicks—it's only a sign of affection.

Tell her that I am going to have a fine bulldog—a registered English bull, a half-dozen thoroughbred, grown chickens, one or two turkeys, and some fine Peking ducks. All these I will turn over to her.
These are presents from my friends and admirers.

I went to the ball last night. I was on the reception committee, and
soon after receiving the Governor and his party, and making the
rounds I left. You know I usually enjoy meeting the ladies but I didn't
last night. I missed you. A heart full of love.

Your devoted husband,
Murphy

Baton Rouge, La.
May 23, 1884

My dear wife,

In a few moments I go to a committee and will only say how happy
I was made yesterday by the reception of your long, newsy and sweet
letter.

Of course you did right, my darling, in discharging S—. I think it dangerous to have a drunken man around the premises, especially when only you ladies are around. My sweetheart, you acted, as you always do, exactly right.

I regret to learn that old Knight has had such a time. Suthon writes me that this morning, in the storm, he was blown down and his leg was hurt. If this be true then I am afraid his usefulness is destroyed. My dear little wife, you must be brave and true during these difficult times. I will get a leave of absence about the first of next month and spend several days at home.

My love to Miss Georgie, kiss the babies, and a heart full to you from

Your devoted husband
Murphy

Baton Rouge, La.
Sunday, June 9, 1884

My dear wife,

I arrived here yesterday after an uneventful trip. I came from Thibodaux to Burnside Station on the boat, commanded by Bob Allen. He gave me his room and I had quite a pleasant and refreshing sleep. I feel very well tonight.

My friends here all seem delighted to meet me again and have been very cordial and congratulatory in their greetings. Our work will commence in earnest the latter part of the week. There is a good deal of growing bitterness in the fight and expect we will have a lively time.

I have missed you so much today. These Sundays are always so lonesome without you. I have had a right mean touch of headache, but I feel perfectly well now.

I have been particularly uneasy about our dear little Rosebud. I sincerely trust that our little pet is well. By all means have the Doctor. Tell Miss Georgie she will never know how secure I feel when she is with you and the babies and giving you all her love and experience. How have you spent this day? You are busy, I know and I love you so much.

Your affectionate husband,
Murphy

A letter from Rose to Murphy:

Dixie
June 13, 1884

My dear husband,

Received your last letter this morning, and am so glad to know that you are again feeling well. You don't know how I rely on your promise to take care of yourself for my sake. When I think of what my life would be like with you—but I won't go further, for I think you really do know how I want you to be careful.

I see by the papers where you, with others, leave to day to inspect the asylum at Jackson. If you were equal to the journey I would ask that you stop at Ouida to see them there, but don't try it unless you are recovered. I had a letter from Sister Minnie this morning saying she had been busy nursing Brother Dan and young Alice while Cousin Alice was at Cousin Anne Brandon's helping them nurse one of their little girls who was sick with inflammation of the stomach.

Rose is still all right. Has not spent a bad night since you left, and I am so glad I can give you good accounts of her, for I know how uneasy you were, and naturally so. She is as happy and bright as ever.

Miss Georgie is well and we are as busy as two people can well be, getting ready for your return. Oh, I do wish the Senate would hurry and adjourn. I am tired of being at home like a sort of grass widow. How do you like being a kind of "grass widower"?

If the mosquitoes will let me, I am going to write you a long letter tonight, but if you do not hear again tomorrow, just know they decided I should not write to you.

Walter is starting for home so I will have to say "Bye Bye." Goodbye, sweetheart. God bless you and keep you happy during our absence from each other.

Your devoted wife,
Rose

Baton Rouge,
June 16, 1884

My dear wife,

I returned from the asylum yesterday too late to write. I was also unable to go by way of Bayou Sara so had no chance to visit our dear folks at Ouida. My trip was comfortable as far as accommodations , but what a strange and sorrowful world I saw—nearly 500 demented people, all sizes and all ages, and in all conditions of life. There was every conceivable aberration of the mind, from the quietly grinning idiot to the raving maniac.

I will not go into any more detail dear wife, except to say that the sad and helpless impression which these poor people made upon me is ingrained upon my mind forever. I hope we can alleviate some of their problems. There is a crying need to do so.

My stomach has been acting up. This morning I have thrown away my cigar, and when it went sailing over the banisters I thought "if my dear Rose could see you now, she would give you a generous and heartfelt benediction." So you see, sweetheart, that I am doing admirably.

The convention meets today. Everything is politics. I am getting tired!

With a heart full of love,

Your devoted husband,
Murphy

A letter from Rose to Murphy.

Dixie
June 18, 1884

My dear husband,

I wish I had time this evening to write you a long letter, but I commenced work on the "Blue Room" [upstairs front bedroom], and when I tell you I have cleaned all four windows, blinds and facings included, you'll understand that I am a little tired, and as my dress and hair both need arranging before Dixie [Murphy's brother] comes in tonight you will excuse me, I know for not writing at length.

I received your dear, sweet letter of the 6th so full and love and tenderness, and when I reached the end I wanted to tell you once again what you mean to me, and how I want you to come home soon.

Our dear little Bess has been sick, but is all right again. Miss Rosebud is as bright and attractive as ever. Grandma [Murphy's grandmother] leaves tonight for the Jim Murphy's. Mother is looking very well indeed and is just as sweet to me as ever.

That is a dear good husband. Continue to throw the cigars over the banisters, and I'll promise to be anything you wish. Well, almost anything.

Walter is waiting for this so I must say adieu. With so much love

Your devoted wife
Rose

Baton Rouge, La.
Monday, June 22

My dear wife,

I dreamed about you last night. I thought I was home with my wife and babies. Big Rose on one knee and little Rose on the other and little Bessie cooing. But then I woke up and found it was all a dream. What am I to do?

Dear little wife, you will never know how, even amid all this excitement of business and legislation, I miss you all. I will be so happy when the session is at an end. You speak of my health. For some weeks I was troubled with dyspepsia, but I tell you honestly that now I feel better than I have all this year. And I have been free of colds and coughs.

Now, dear Rose, knowing that when I talk about myself you will not consider it vanity, and knowing that my success is dear to your heart I will say that I believe, in this session, I have developed a reputation. My friends tell me that my opinion and judgment is more looked up to than [that of] any other senator or representative in this general assembly.

If you notice my speeches are not much reported, but you will also see that nearly all the time my side wins. I tell you this, darling, because I know it will be gratifying to you, and you are always proud of my success.

Tell Miss Georgia to have everything in readiness for her ducks, turkeys, chickens, etc. I am going to give her plenty of work. Tell her, however, that I intend to rule the roost!!

Your devoted husband,
Murphy

Dixie
June, 1884

My dear husband,

Before I do anything else, I am going to write to you this morning for my last letter was such a brief one and I want this one to atone for it.

To begin with that which I know you are anxious to hear about—our health. We are all very well except Bessie, who is still a little under the weather. Even though her digestive tract is still bad she is the same bright little cricket, and that it is this which makes me keep up my spirits. Everyone tells me that I need not be uneasy, for nine children out of ten are troubled with this same thing when they commence to teethe in the summer. So don't be worried about her, for if she gets worse I shall notify you.

I received your last letter with the fifteen dollars and I fully appreciate your thoughtfulness and goodness which made you send it. Bess has been a considerable drain on the fifteen that you left me earlier this month, for I have been supplying her with both medicine and baby food for nearly three weeks.

Mother and Grandma went to Bayou Sale the other day and drove old King who had the mischief in him. He would not go out of a walk, and when Steve whipped him he kicked way up against the dashboard, getting his foot caught over the axletree.

That feat decided me to what had best be done with his lordship. He is now enjoying this June weather somewhere out in the field, and in his place we have a good, slow old mule who answers every purpose.

Oh, by the way, I asked Father for a barrel of sugar, and it is now in the storeroom. He and Miss Georgie had just returned from Bayou Sale. He loves to go down there so I thought, "This is my very chance." I know he will return in fine humor and I'll strike while the iron is hot. Everything turned out just as I expected. I tackled the old gentleman and met with the gracious reply that I could have a barrel of very pretty brown sugar whenever I could send to the store for it, and I did send today and received it.

Evening—I was called off this morning and have been Bessie's nurse all day which prevented me from finishing my letter. I must say goodnight now. Walter is going home. With a heart full of love from your devoted

Rose

By the summer of 1885, another baby was expected. Rose, planning that her sister Minnie would come from Ouida to be with her during her confinement, was disappointed to learn that she could not come. Her sister Sarah Towles provided her with the family news.

Ouida,
July 22, 1885

My dear Rose,

Have one eye open and the other shut, but will endeavor to write a line or so, as Minnie received your hasty note, and we wanted to let you know how glad we were to hear from you, and to know all of you were well, especially you, for about now we feel truly appraised of your condition. Tell Murphy he must be sure to notify John when your tea party is over.

I know, if it is a boy he will not need to be told. I do hope you will have a little boy this time. Every time I look at my two splendid boys I wish so much you would have one. I know it would be fine, as your two girls are such splendid children.

Min bids me tell you, in answer to your kind invitation, to come by way of Franklin, en route to Jena, that nothing in the world would give her such pleasure than a visit to you on, but she cannot possibly go to see you on account of not having the means. Says she will not be able to return home with Nan if she comes. Nan has set her heart on it, and says she is going to pay her expenses, but Min says she cannot enjoy a visit of that sort.

Yes, Rose, I too would enjoy going to see you and being with you and dear Murphy in your nice home, but this is one of the times where there is a will but no "way." Hard times makes us all succumb to its iron grasp. I had hoped to have paid you a visit this summer, taking with me only baby and nurse, but I find I cannot even do that.

Money is so hard to get. All the cash Mr. Towles got when he left Major James had to go for groceries and making his crop, which is conducted upon the cash system. He has a beautiful crop, and so have I. Haven't a large one, but that is well cultivated. Have a nice large, sweet potato patch and every rain I set out more vines.

How are you getting on with your cropping? Hope you are succeeding. I forgot to mention to you as regards your chickens that you must have your coops with floors in them, or boards laid under the hovels. The best and cheapest coop on each side, two driven down in front (the distance of a door apart), holding the siding door which can be made out of pieces of a plank or the heading of the barrel nailed down by a strip. Be sure and put a brick or something to raise the barrel under the back portion. This inclines it toward the front, and in case it rains very hard there is not danger of the young fowl being drowned.

Whenever the weather is damp and rainy feed high on red pepper (or black if you haven't the red). Gum camphor is splendid for gapes if you commence in time. Give the size of a small pea two or three times a day. Don't wait until the chickens are sitting back on their tails and try to raise them from the dead, but commence on them when they show the first symptoms.

If there is any way of Brother's getting off, couldn't you persuade him to come to see us for a few days. It has been five long years since I have seen him. Sometimes I feel as if he had forgotten us. I think if he knew how much we really want to see him he could come. It is very late so must say goodnight. All send love. The children speak of you and their imaginations are quite familiar with Aunt Rose and Uncle Murph. Be sure to keep us posted about you.

Yours ever,
Sarah

Another daughter, Lucy Price Foster, was born in the summer of 1885. Murphy was home for her birth; however, he had another bout with lung problems and dyspepsia and left shortly afterward for Wisconsin. His doctors had recommended the healthful waters of Waukesha. His and Rose's August 22 letters crossed paths. His told of going through Indian territory in Kansas, changing trains in St. Louis, taking a sleeper to Chicago and on to Waukesha. He said he preferred the waters there to those of Virginia, and this time he hoped for a cure. Rose's letter was brief, with the promise of a fuller one later.

Dixie
Saturday evening, Aug. 22, 1885

Dear Mr. Foster:

Baby is fast asleep. Mother has driven up home, taking Rose with her. Miss Helen is busy upstairs, and Bessie is taking her usual nap, so while "all is quiet along the Potomac" I shall write to you.

Before speaking of anything else, let me mention something that might almost be called a matter of business. Hobson [the tenant on Dixie] told me this morning that the lumber you ordered for the stable had come, and that it had been put out there by his house. Now what I want to know is, being that far away, do you think there is danger of it being stolen before you return? Had I not better see Father and ask him if he can spare a cart and team to haul it into the stable lot itself where you intend to have the building put? I would have had it put

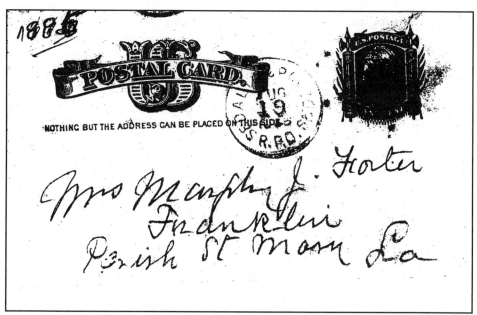

Above and below: Murphy J. Foster's postcard from the Indian Territory

there in the beginning, but knew nothing of it having come until this morning. Write me at once on the subject of this matter.

We are all well. I continue to keep to my room, and shall not go about the house until I enter my third week which will be after this Wednesday. The baby promises to be a splendid one. The last two days and nights she has slept all day and all night, just waking up long enough to nurse and then goes right back to sleep. Her sleep is a natural healthy one, for she has not taken a drop of carminutive for three days.

As I told you in my note last night Miss Helen has had three letters from Miss Georgie and she is decidedly improving. They changed her spring water and the one she is now taking has so much alum in it that her teeth are on edge.

I will write again soon, my dear husband. I miss you so much, but I know the change is doing you good.

Your devoted wife,
Rose

Dixie
Saturday, August 29, 1885

My dear Husband,

Miss Helen just left and, as everything is quiet, I will try to write you at length before I am interrupted.

I hated to see Miss Helen go, for she is so bright and cheerful that her presence helped to keep up my spirits, but she could not stay longer. She had to get back and have a day at home to straighten up everything before resuming her duties at the store. She was up in arms about her passage to New Orleans and would not hear of my getting her a ticket, and she spoke so earnestly about it that I was seriously afraid of offending her, so I did not get it.

Brother drove down this morning to take Miss Helen to the depot and they left here a little early in order to stop at Mother's so she could say goodbye to them up there. She did not want to go back to the city one bit, says she wanted to remain at least a month longer. I was so glad to hear her say so, for, with me confined, I have been afraid she was having a pretty dull time.

Rose will miss Miss Helen very much. Bessie still wants to "see Mama" too much to miss anyone else while I am here. Tonight I commence sleeping with Rose. I will put her in bed with me and I have the baby's crib right by the bed.

Affectionately,
Rose

Sunday evening, August 30th

It looks like I could not manage to write the long letter I wanted to. The baby was quite fretful yesterday and I had to put down the writing materials very often on her account.

Mrs. Caffery and Miss Marie Demanger came to call and then Mother came down to spend the night with the babies and myself. Husband, Mother has been just too sweet and good to me ever since you have been gone. I could not have gotten along without her, and I shall never forget her kindness at this time

Last night I received your letter of the 25th, the one in which you speak of the stable and you say you enclosed a check for $35.00. The check was not in the letter. I suppose you forgot to put it in. I shall get Warren to send Joshua and will try to so boss them to merit your confidence in me to start building the stable.

Mother will take this letter to town, so must close. God bless you and keep you and you don't know how I miss you, but I don't want to see you until they pronounce you cured. A heart full of love from

Your devoted wife,

Rose

Rose and her sisters kept in close touch through letters. Distance and hardship of traveling, along with lack of money, made visits infrequent; however, their letters indicate that the close family bond had never been severed despite their separation as children. Mary Frances Ker (Minnie), Rose's oldest sister and the second child of John and Rosealtha Ker, was never married and lived most of the time with her sister Annie Ogden Ker and her husband Thomas Ringgold in Jena. Her physical condition always fragile, she died in 1888.

Jena
September 2, 1885

My dearest Rose,

I mailed to you a letter from Sally (Sarah Towles, Rose's sister) the day I left Bayou Sara for Jena. I had mailed to you some two weeks or more, but found out only a few days before leaving that my letter was still in the house. Dan [Towles, Sarah's husband], in his hurry had forgotten to mail it. It has been impossible for me to write sooner, since I have been sick with chills and fever which I have not had in fifteen years.

We arrived here Saturday a week ago. On Tuesday morning I was taken with a chill and then came on fever. On Thursday morning at daylight I was taken with one of the hardest chills I have ever had which lasted until breakfast. Then came on the burning fever which did not leave until eight o'clock that night.

Tom says he thinks I had low fever all the next day. He dosed me on quinine and I have not had a return of chills. He has me taking Elixir of Calisaya tonic which I hope will do me some good.

Dear Rose, you are again a mother! We are so glad you and the baby [Lucy Price Foster] are doing well. I am glad you named her as you did. Mrs. Price, I have heard, was such a good woman and it is such a pretty name, but we all had so hoped you would have a boy. I know you were both disappointed.

We found Routh [Frank Routh Ringgold, Annie's oldest son] well, and they are certainly good children. Routh is so much help to his mother. Minnie [Annie's daughter] already thinks I belong to her. Little Belle is a tiny sweet baby, but has a will of her own. I laugh and tell Tom and Annie her spirit is too strong for her constitution.

We left them all well at home. Aunt Alice though seems older. Sal looks better than I have seen her in ten years. I am so glad you are going to pay a visit to Ouida, even if I am not there to enjoy it. Cousin Bett is so anxious to see [your little] Bessie. The old Lady will be with you most of the time.

I must close as Routh is waiting to take my letter to the store. When did you see our dear old Brother? Give him our love and a kiss. With love and kisses for you and yours from Annie and myself.

As ever, your fond sister,
Minnie

By the spring of 1886, the Fosters had much to be thankful for. The crops continued to be good, and the amount of the loan was decreasing. With Rose as overseer the stable was complete. There was room for several horses, a mule, a two-wheeled jumper, and a four-place carriage. Two milk cows had their own stalls separate from the horses. The chickens occupied a larger house, and Murphy's prize turkeys had their own separate yard. His Peking ducks, which preferred meandering along the bayou's edge to having a home, placed

Louisiana State University

—{AND}—

+{——AGRICULTURAL AND MECHANICAL COLLEGE.——}+

D. F. BOYD,
President.

Baton Rouge, La., May 31, 1886.

Hon. M. L. Foster,
    State Senate,
        Baton Rouge, La.,

Dear Sir:

    I have the honor to inform you that you are invited by the Faculty of this Institution, to deliver the Annual address, on Commencement Day — July 5th next; and to request your acceptance.

      Very Respy,

        D. F. Boyd,
        President.

Letter from David French Boyd of Louisiana State University inviting Senator Murphy J. Foster to present the 1886 commencement address.

themselves in dangerous territory, for the alligators discovered their schedule and seemed to know when they would be vulnerable. The yardman, who tried to be alert, killed the alligators when he could, but there were always more waiting for duck dinners.

By May, Rose needed a vacation and a visit to her sisters whom she loved so much. Murphy was away at the legislature, and since she was pregnant again, she felt she should go before she became too awkward to travel. With Rose, Bessie, and Mary accompanying her, she made the journey to Ouida, to visit her cousin and former guardian, Alice Wade, and Sarah, her sister and her family. Elizabeth Ratliff, who still lived at Ellerslie, made a visit to coincide with Rose's. Rose's letter is filled with news of the family.

> Mr. Murphy J. Foster
> Senate Chamber
> Baton Rouge, LA

Ouida Plantation
May 12, 1886

My dear husband,

Mr. Towles [her brother-in-law] sends to town today and it will be the first chance I have had since I sent you that note by Mr. Alexander's driver. I have written to both Mother and Miss Georgie, my letters being dated the 10th and 11th, but will only get them to the office tomorrow.

I am having a very pleasant visit, it is almost like old times to be back home. Cousin Bett [Elizabeth Ratliff, who had chosen to stay at Ellerslie] is here and will remain some time. Everybody pets the children a great deal and they, in consequence, are very happy. I should be perfectly happy if I could only get the mail regularly, for as it is, I haven't received the mail from town since I came, and to be separated from you is hard enough, but not to know whether you are sick or well is almost more than I can stand.

I suppose the session is really underway now, is it not? I hope things will work out during the session. Don't put an end to the lottery until I can take my ticket!

You ought to see Sarah's children. They are simply splendid. Poor little Dan, we were terribly frightened about him yesterday. The nurse brought him in with the announcement that he had cut himself in the eye, and his eye was closed and he had three deep, ugly gashes just above it. We did think his eye was out, but further investigation found that his eye was all right, but he had cut himself on barbed wire. One of the barbs had gone in almost in his temple, and we could not keep him awake, though we did everything in our power to keep him from going to sleep. This drowsiness, immediately following the accident, alarmed us all very much so Mr. Towles sent post haste for a physician.

The doctor said while it was a very ugly wound he did not apprehend any serious result, and he prescribed carbolic salve which is doing, I think, a great deal of good, but is a fearfully ugly place. Poor Sal was almost demented for a while yesterday. Today the little fellow is as spry as ever so we are no longer alarmed about this.

The children get along splendidly together, so you see your fear (in regards to our young ones getting beat) is likely not to be realized. The children are all well and are put to bed early at night. Sal says you are a dear old fellow for sending her that candy. She says there was not a bad tasting piece in the whole lot.

Cousin Alice, in fact the whole family, thanks you for those bananas. Sal made a banana cake the other day when Cousin Mary Ryland and Francina Brandon spent the day.

Cousin Bett's slippers were too small. I knew you were fooled in the number. They are really number four's. At what house did you get them? Cousin Alice says if you fail to come see her while you are so near that she won't speak to you again!

Cousin is in some trouble that I think you can very soon relieve her of by simply telling her what the law is on the subject. Old Mr. Haile, the father of the man from whom Cousin bought Ouida is lying at the point of death and some of his children assert that their father had no right to sell their brother (the former owner of this place) this piece of property and they say they intend to rip the whole thing up as soon as the old man dies.

Now I don't see how they can hurt her, for it is recorded, and Mr. Towles has seen it on the records in Bayou Sara that Mr. Haile bought this property from his father, and when Shattuck and Hoffman took Cousin business they were satisfied with her titles, which I tell her ought to make her secure. But she is uneasy, and she says she can't feel secure until she sees "Murphy." So write me at once what you think about it.

Oh yes, I omitted to tell you that the ground upon which the heirs lay claim to the property is that their father disposed of their mother's property while some of the heirs were minors. I tell Cousin Alice that, if it is taken to law, I know you will do your best for her, and won't you, Husband? Poor Cousin, she is worried no little.

I look forward with great eagerness to tomorrow evening, for then I will get a letter from you. Husband, don't think strangely of my silence for there is little occasion for anyone to go to town, and I don't feel as though I ought to hire a messenger to go just for the mail.

In case of sickness, where you wished to dispatch me, send it to Mrs. Alexander's care, and write on it "imperative," otherwise it would lie in Bayou Sara without my dreaming it was there.

Now, dearest Husband, take good care of yourself and be sure to let me know if you should get sick, which, God forbid, you should be. Rose and Bessie send lots of kisses and they talk about you often. With much love from all here and a heartful from myself.

Your devoted wife,
Rose

A month after Rose's return from Ouida tragedy struck. Little Lucy, age ten months, died suddenly. Murphy being in Baton Rouge, Rose had to go through the ordeal alone—not just her death but the agony of not knowing what had happened—whether Lucy had had a fall without her knowledge, whether in some way she was responsible. She was devastated, inconsolable. Murphy came home as soon as transportation would allow, but it was over. Little Lucy Price had already been buried. He had to return to his duties in the Senate a week later, but his letters attempt to assuage his own grief, as well as offer some consolation to her. The loss was bitter for both of them.

Telegram from Murphy Foster notifying Rose of his return to Franklin following their daughter's death.

DIED.

FOSTER—On Monday, June 21, at 4 o'clock, a. m., Lucy Price Foster, infant daughter of M. J. Foster and Rose R. Ker, aged 10 months, and 12 days.

Affliction and sorrow fell heavily indeed on the home of our Senator, M. J. Foster, Esq., in the death of his youngest daughter. When the father left for Baton Rouge, his family were enjoying the best of health, and to receive a telegram announcing the death of one of his children, and unable to get here even in time to take a last look into the face of the one whom he had built his brightest joys and hopes upon is sorrowful and heart rending indeed.

"Life is sweet to some, and yet
    Its ways are dark and dreary—
  But death is hope and joy and rest.
  A haven for the weary.

                                        M.

Obituary of Lucy Price Foster

                                        Senate Chamber
                                        Baton Rouge, La.
                                        June 30, 1886

My dearest Wife,

    I arrived here last night as expected. My stay in New Orleans was difficult and lonely as you can well imagine. While waiting for transportation to Baton Rouge, I was able to get your drapes and the bookcase we need. Both will come out by the next boat.

    I have been so kindly and sympathetically received by all of my friends. If there be any consolation to us in our loss and bereavement it is certainly the support and sincere condolences of our friends. God knows how deep down in the soul sink these losses. He only knows the sadnesss and utter despair which broods over the heart and almost breaks over the grave of our little dead baby.

Yes, my dear angel wife, when we remember our little one is now with Heaven's angels, our grief is more at our loss than at hers. While we have lost our beloved little bright Lucy she has gained a bright abode lit up with the love of Him who said "Suffer little children to come unto me." While we mourn her and our hearts are broken with grief, we know hers is full of joy and blessings.

Let us, my darling Rose, remember this. I know it is hard, oh so hard to look at it this way, yet it is true. May the kind Father who has taken our child to his own love and abode, pour out the "balm of Gilead" upon the broken hearts of my darling wife and me and Rose and Bessie. Kisses to them a heart full of love and tenderness to my wife.

Affectionately your husband,
Murphy

Their love for each other and for their two little girls made them strong enough to bear the pain, and to look forward to the birth of their next baby.

CHAPTER EIGHT

A new baby, Mary Lucy, joined the family in December 1886. The name "Lucy" was given in memory of the child they had lost the summer before, but she was called Mary. Rose's former guardians, Elizabeth Ratliff and Alice Wade, who lived at Ellerslie and Ouida respectively, worried about this steady arrival of girls. The tone of their letters bordered on condolence, but the plethora of girls did not worry either parent; they welcomed each birth regardless of gender.

The letter below is Elizabeth Ratliff's response to Rose's announcement of the new baby's birth, but it also contains news of a death in the family:

Ellerslie, Jan. 7th, 1887

My darling Rose,

Yours of the 20th reached me a few days since. I was glad to hear that you are safely over your trouble, and both you and the baby were getting along so well. But I was very sorry that you and Mr. Foster were again disappointed in its not being a boy. You must be careful this cold weather, and not take cold, for the past two days the ground here has been covered with snow.

We have had a sad, sad Christmas. The terrible disaster of the [J. M.] *White* [steamboat] has thrown a gloom over Ellerslie that will long be felt. Poor Agnes—her fate was truly a sad one, and what makes it so hard to bear is the reflection that no effort was made by the officers of the boat to render assistance to the passengers.

There were only six ladies and a little girl on board, and if one boat had been brought to their relief, none would have been lost. There appears to have been but one brave man on the boat. He was Captain Wash Floyd, and the poor man, in his brave efforts to save others, lost his own life. He leaves a wife and two children perfectly destitute. The minister and the people of Bayou Sara are trying to get up a subscription for their relief.

Evie says he acted in a most heroic manner. He went to each stateroom, and awoke the ladies, told them to follow him. He soon found they were cut off from the front of the boat. They then fled to the guards, but by that time the flames were bursting up all around them.

There was no escape but to jump into the river, which Evie did, but poor Agnes said "Don't jump Evie, you can't swim." But Evie said she preferred drowning to being burned. What a terrible alternative!

Evie's escape was miraculous. She had on a black silk skirt and, it is supposed, as she jumped the skirt filled with air and kept her up until a skiff from a raft came to her rescue. She was then at least a half mile from the burning boat. She was dreadfully bruised, and extremely nervous and she is heartbroken over the loss of her sister.

Spittoon row aboard the *J. M. White.* The steamboat burned in December 1886 at Blue Shore Landing, near Bayou Sara on the Mississipp River (near St. Francisville).

We were in great suspense over Agnes for five days. We were afraid she had been burned. But thank God, on the fifth day, her body was found near the wreck. She was buried here for the present, but her brother [Dr. McCaleb] and Evie intend removing her next fall to Claiborne and bury her by her mother, as that had always been her desire.

This sad Christmas reminds me of the one when my dear mother was lying so low that every day we thought would be her last, but she remained with us until the last day of December. That was sixteen years ago but will ever be fresh in my memory.

I cannot give you any news of the girls at Ouida. I have not heard a word from them, or seen anyone from there since Christmas. With kisses to the dear children and love to Mr. Foster and Willie. With many kisses to yourself, I am always

Your devoted cousin,
E. Ratliff

In early June of 1887, Sally Foster, the wife of Murphy's brother Don, became so ill that her condition necessitated the presence of a family member. She presumably had a miscarriage (such matters were considered too delicate to discuss), so Rose, leaving her two older children in the custody of their father, Miss Georgie, and the household help went to New Iberia to care for her sister-in-law. Since Mary was only six months old, Rose took her along.

Routh Trowbridge Wilby

New Iberia, La.
June 6, 1887

My dear husband,

I trust this note will find you, Miss Georgie and babies as well as it leaves Baby Mary and myself. I wish I could add Sally too, but she, I am sorry to say is far from well today. I suppose you all have seen Mother, and she has no doubt told you all that there is absolute need for some of Don's family being here to take care of Sally and look after things for a while.

I never in my life met with such a woman as Mrs. Compton, who is supposed to be a help. Sally has now been sick since last Monday. Monday and Tuesday you may say seriously sick, and never once has that woman been inside of her door. No, not even to her door to ask how she feels. Sally says that last Tuesday, when she had a hemorrhage, she called to "Maud" to take care of things, for she could not. Mrs. C. replied that she did not like to housekeep and she never did what she disliked to do. She never went near Sally. Mr. Compton set the table and Don waited on Sally. When Sally told me this, I have now taken charge and do all that Mrs. Compton ought to do. I feel sorry for Mr. Compton. He told Don and Sally yesterday that he felt as though he would go crazy at times, and that if it were not for his children he would have left long ago. I really believe it is on his account that Don and Sally allow them to stay here. I believe the woman is crazy—this is the most charitable construction one can put on her conduct.

Dr. Wolf told Don that after a month he thought Sally would be well enough to go to Franklin, and that he advised her to go because the nature of her sickness inclined to low spirits and the less she was alone the better.

Both Don and Sally beg me to stay. I will do so if Miss Georgie keeps well and can attend to everything for me and you, and if my dear little babies keep well. Bless their dear little hearts. How I would like to see them this morning and their papa too. Tell them Mama thinks of them all the time and would not be satisfied if they were not in such good hands as Miss Georgie's and Papa's.

Do take good care of yourself while I am gone. Drink plenty of hot water and take your pills. You had better persuade Miss Georgie to join you in the pills and tell her I wish she would give Rose and Bessie a dose of quinine now and then. I feel uneasy about that typhoid on the place.

If you get any letters please don't forget to send them up. How are you and Miss Georgie thriving on our dairy products? And Morris and Johnny—how do they look? Morris started on the 19th and Johnny started work on the windows May 24th, so you will have an idea when you pay them.

Don, too, has gone back to hot water. He says he is sorry now he ever stopped taking it. Tell my dear little babies that Mamma is going to bring them slates, pencils and chalk when she comes home, and we will start the ABC's.

Sally and Don's children are frail, especially little Louise. I am homesick and I miss you all so much. Mary is just as sweet and friendly as she can be. Everyone speaks of what a jolly little thing she is.

Love to Miss Georgie, kisses for the babies and so much love for your dear self.

Your devoted wife,
Rose

Again, Murphy's and Rose's letters apparently crossed in the mail.

Foster & Mentz
Attorneys at Law
Franklin, Louisiana
June 6, 1887

My dear wife,

This Monday morning I will enjoy writing you. Everything is going along fine. Yesterday morning I brought the girls up to Sunday School and waited at Ma's till school was over when I took them home. They were good and sweet all day. Every now and then one or the other would ask "When is Mamma coming home?" When I told them I was going to write you Rose said, "Tell Mamma I am a good girl" and Bessie wants to let you know that the kitten is well, and the mamma cat is staying at home.

I had a good horseback ride early this morning and called on the Morris Robicheaux's. We had such a pleasant time. What nice people they are. He and I are hoping our dairy will improve. Milk production has slowed.

Court opens this morning. I shall not go home to dinner today but will dine somewhere with my friends. I am so glad you are with Sally.

Court will keep me busy and fully employed. Although the weather is getting intolerably hot, it will be a very busy session.

I must close my letter as the office is filling up with loafers and clients.

Your devoted husband
Murphy

P. S. I must tell you that all the animals are behaving well, except the hogs. You remember our old lady with the little pigs. Well, she got on a first class jamboree yesterday. She ate two or three chickens. After this, she looked with fond affection upon her little unoffending young and she selected the fattest, prettiest and she deliberately ate it up. Whereupon Willis, swore like a trooper and talked to himself and everybody else the whole day long.

Rose herself was full of news when she wrote the next letter to Murphy, who was trying a case in New Orleans. She reminded him to add to his shopping list two bobinet bars, adding that she could not get them from Warren's store for less than $4.00 each, and also the quality of the material was too coarse. Bobinet was a type of net that was attached either to the tester of a four-poster bed or a top frame of an iron bed. It dropped down the sides and tucked in under the matters so that sleepers had air but also protection from flying or crawling insects. There being no screens on the windows, these bars were lifesavers from mosquitoes at night. Until her final illness, Rose slept under her bar every night. Rose also requested that Murphy get her some strong upholstery goods, complete with tacks and tape, so she could cover the lounge and a chair in their sitting room

Then came the farm news:

Everything about the yard is coming along very nicely. I took off a hen yesterday with fourteen little ducks. We have now about seventy-five little chickens and I have thirteen hens now setting. . . . A hawk caught one of the chickens yesterday and I shall be on the lookout for him and hope to have him killed. . . . The babies have colds but thanks to cod liver oil their colds do not amount to anything much. Miss Georgie is well and I can't keep her out of her garden. I don't want her to wear herself out. . . .

In early 1888, a fifth daughter, Willia Ker Foster, made her entrance into the family. Every congratulatory letter was qualified with the familiar words "and yet another girl—she is number five, isn't she?" Murphy and Rose merely smiled, thankful for another beautiful little girl who had arrived in good health.

Rose's sister Sarah and her husband, Dan Towles, lived at Ouida and managed the plantation. Money was scarce and jobs hard to find, so during slack times with the crops, Dan had to take work anywhere he could find a job. Sarah's letter to Murphy epitomizes the strain, fatigue, and weariness of the post-war South where gentlewomen, who had been reared in the plantation tradition, were reduced to doing the work of field hands. At the time of Sarah's letter, Dan was working at Angola between farming seasons.

Ouida
February 22, 1888

My dear Murphy,

You must excuse my not answering you sooner, but really I haven't had the time in the day and, as usual, too sleepy at night, for weary Nature demands her rights and I haven't force or will enough to defeat her claim.

We were glad to get the news of the new babe's safe arrival, but unlike you terribly disappointed at its gender. I will hope for a boy every time so I cannot join you in this great hour of your rejoicing, altho the little darling will have just as warm place in her Aunt Sarah's heart. Say to Rose that just as soon as I get all my work in the fields under good headway and I can collect my wits I will write her a nice, long letter.

Cousin Alice hasn't a hand on her place this year and she is not the only one in this fix. Nearly every plantation here is bare of hands. It looks as if the labor has vanished.

I have plenty of corn and beans and by selling what corn and peas I did not need I have the cash to hire day labor. You see, the few negro families around here haven't the team to keep all their plow hands busy at this season, and in that way I can get hands to break up my land, and after that I can hire whole families on Saturdays. They must have a little cash to spend at the store.

Mr. Towles is at Angola, working for $50.00 a month and this will furnish us with supplies and cash to work my crop. I have much to contend with, and sometimes I think the billows of care will engulf my frail back if it was not for the sake of her [Alice Wade] who has been father, mother and everything to me and mine. I would sink, but this thought steers me over the rough waters.

Tell Rose that I am glad she named the baby for Brother, that is what I would have done if I had been asked. Tell Rose and Bessie I thank them so much for wanting to name their baby for me, and am so glad they love and remember me that well.

Murphy, are you coming to see us again? I know we live in an out of the way place, and the home is a simple one, but the hearts that beat within are warm and sincere, and you will find a hearty welcome.

It is late and I must go to bed. The effects of my black coffee have died out, so here's a good night to you. Cousin Alice and the little folks are now fast asleep, but the last thing they said was to be sure and give their love to Uncle Murphy. With love to Rose and children, you must write when you find time to.

Your affectionate sister,
Sally [Sarah]

Burdened with problems of the economic depression, inefficiency of the postal service, Sarah's husband Dan had written to Rose knowing of her concern about Ouida and her family. Rose responds with a suggestion.

Dixie
February 25, 1888

Dear Brother Dan,

I suppose, by this time, you have come to the conclusion that you will not get an answer to your letter, but, when I tell you that little Miss Willia Foster was only six days old when your letter reached me, and that she had been badly spoiled from the start, you, who know something of bad babies, will make every excuse for my silence.

I don't understand why it is that Sarah did not get my letter. I am afraid the trouble is at the [post] office for Sister Annie makes the same complaint against me, and I wrote to her just before I was sick and Mr. Foster wrote when the baby was only two or three days old telling her of its event, and she has not heard a word from either of us it seems, for day before yesterday a dispatch [came] from Dr. St. John in her name to Mr. Foster asking after my health.

I wrote her a long letter today, which it is to be hoped she will receive. Since the Baby's birth Mr. Foster has written Sarah twice and I have written to her once and have not heard anything from her since, and that has been two weeks ago. Do you know whether or not she has received these letters?

In your letter you asked me about the box that brother asked me to send to Sarah. I sent that box the very last part of August or the first part of September. I don't know exactly which, but I know it was either one or the other month.

I thought it had been received ages ago. What in the world could have become of it? I am quite sure it left here and I suspect Mr. Irwin's crew could tell you something about it.

I was so sorry to hear that your crop was a failure! Brother Dan, don't you think it would be best for Cousin Alice to lease her place to someone and to move near some town in a snug little house and live off that rent? Then Sarah and herself could raise poultry for market, sell butter and milk and they could, for a small amount, send the children to school, and best of all, they would not be way out in a lonely piece of country alone as they are, and which, I think is dangerous for them to do.

I tell you it is dreadful for people to live so far from all means of communication. We have already seen that living where Cousin Alice and Sister Annie do, that those that you love can be dead and buried before you know of their being sick.

This is a very serious thing—one that I just can't get over and I am crazy to see Jena [her sister Annie's place] and Ouida left behind by those I love. Do, please, agree with me and talk up a change in affairs. I tell you, no woman has a business with a plantation.

I sincerely hope you will do well this year. I would get my pay out of the Major [at Angola] too when it becomes due if I were you. Write to me whenever you have the time. I will always be glad to hear from you.

With love from myself (Mr. F. is not at home) and kisses from the little people, I am

Affectionately your sister,
Rose

Ouida
May 7, 1888

My dear Rose,

As Towles is going to Angola tonight, will write you and Sister Annie a few lines. On Saturday night received a letter from Nan written on the 11th telling us of Tom's illness. We just chanced to get the letter by a negro from the other place, who I asked to inquire for our mail in Bayou Sara, Pinckneyville being our regular post office. I had sent every week, expecting her in person every day as she said she had just returned from a visit to you and would start for Ouida soon. As she didn't come we thought the children had taken the measles or mumps and felt anxious and uneasy.

Poor dear Nan has had her cup brim full of trouble. I suppose Tom is well or convalescing by now. If the worst could have happened we certainly would have heard by now. I scarcely look for Nan at all now. I had so hoped she would come. It has been such a long, long time since I saw her.

You speak of going to spend August at the Springs with Nan. I am so glad for you, but do you ever intend to come to Ouida again?   As you did not come last year I thought you might this year.

Mr. Towles has, by his desire, given up on his job at Angola, and is going on the Railroad. They are such poor pay in cash. They force him to take upon his work for Major James if he cannot do any better, but if he can get a place anywhere else he will take it. Says he will not stay at Angola if Major James gave him two hundred a month. Says there are ten dozen bosses, even the convicts. They give him all the responsibility and no authority.

I wish you would find out from Brother what he did with that diamond pin of Cousin Alice's and mine and Mr. Towles watch sent to him to pawn to raise money to pay S and H the interest. Please see about it for I would not have that pin lost for the world.

You ask about Carrie. I haven't seen her for nearly two years. Heard she has a fine boy and that her mother and self have made friends. Mr. Towles is waiting so goodbye. Love to you and Murph, and kisses for the children, I am

Your loving sister,
Sarah

In the 1888 session of the legislature, Murphy was elected president *pro tempore* of the Senate. Wanting to share his pleasure with his six-year-old Rose, as well as with his wife, he wrote her the first letter she had ever received:

Baton Rouge, La.
May 16, 1888

My darling daughter, Papa sends his dear little girl a newspaper's picture of himself. It makes Pa look like he is mad, but he is not. Papa sends his good little daughter and his sweet little Bess a heart full of love and a hundred kisses to you. Kiss Mama for me.

Your loving papa

The newspaper picture Foster sent to his daughter.

Rose's sister Minnie died suddenly in late 1888 while staying with Annie in Jena. The family was devastated. This was the first break among the five siblings (Willie, Minnie, Annie, Sarah, and Rose). Since Minnie was the oldest daughter and unmarried and had at times stayed with all of them, they naturally felt closer to her. Rose's grief was intensified perhaps by not being able to see her or attend her funeral, which was held in Jena. The distraught relatives had to share their grief by mail. Elizabeth Ratliff sends her condolences to Rose:

Ellerslie
November 1, 1888

My darling Rose,

It is with sad heart I write to express my sincere sorrow and sympathy for you in your great bereavement. Our dear Minnie was taken from us so unexpectedly I don't know when I was more shocked than I was at hearing of her death. I have seen no one who could give me the particulars of her death. I heard she had died of pneumonia; that has always been so fatal to your family.

Your Cousin Alice and Dan Towles went up immediately on hearing of her illness, but arrived too late to see her. She was buried the day before they arrived. I also heard that your brother arrived in time to see her for which we should be thankful. I know it was a great consolation to both of them.

Dan has returned but Alice is still with Annie. As soon as I possibly can I will go up to see poor Sally [Sarah]. I should have gone before this but at this season of the year you know how it is on a plantation. The hands are so busy you can't get them to leave their work.

Remember me affectionately to Mr. Foster. With much love and many kisses for you and dear little ones, I am as ever

Your devoted cousin,
E[lizabeth] Ratliff

In the following year, Rose and the three youngest girls—Bessie, five; Mary, almost three; and Willia, two—visited Annie and her family in Jena while young Rose stayed with her father at Dixie. Rose and Murphy exchanged letters frequently.

Franklin
August 24, 1889

My dear wife,

Your sweet and affectionate letter reached here yesterday and it
brought a great deal of happiness and satisfaction to me. I was a little
disappointed at the prospects before you and children and it was hard
to leave you, but I felt what was lacking in comfort etc would be made
up in the pleasant companionship of Annie. I know how fondly you
looked forward to a sojourn with her and it was a pleasure to me to con-
tribute in this small way to your happiness. Rose, my sweet wife, you
do not know how much comfort it is to me to feel that I can give you
more happiness and to bring more sunshine to your life.

I feel politics here is red hot. I am on the go most of the time. I will
certainly be glad when the election is over—too much excitement and
too much intensity of feeling.

Everything around the yard is getting along well—chickens, turkeys, horses, cows, etc. Rose wrote you a letter yesterday, but when I
asked for it this morning she could not find it. She was much distressed
about it, but says she will write another.

Ma sends love and Rose, kisses, and with love.
Murphy

Franklin
August 30, 1889

My dear wife,

I have just come into the office behind a big demonstration on its
way to Glencoe. Just to say, that as the election comes off Tuesday and
everything will be in a state of confusion and excitement, I will not be
able to write again before Wednesday. I have been going night and
day and am literally broken down and broken up. In a few minutes I
will start on a ride of over thirty miles. All well at home.

Today is two weeks since you left and I have only received one letter from you. While I know you have written yet you don't know how
lonesome it is without you and your letters.

Little Rose asks about "Mama" and wants to know why you don't
answer her letter. The little darling took so much trouble and was so
proud when she finished it that you ought to write.

somehow or other, dear wife, it seems that my heart would have been lighter and my spirits higher if I was carrying next to my heart some sweet message of love from my absent wife.

    With much love to Annie, and with a heart full of love for you and our dear little girls,

Your affectionate husband,
Murphy

Apparently there were some healthful springs near Jena, and Rose and Annie, along with the children had been spending some time there to perk up both them and the children.   Murphy's lack of mail, about which he complained, probably stemmed from this and other activities that kept them busy.

Jena, Louisiana
August 30, 1889

My dear Husband,

    I received two letters from you yesterday and I assure you they were welcome. I am beginning to miss you terribly, notwithstanding I am having a real nice time, and I am still in favor of remaining until the 15th, for the children are improving fast—old Bess has bright color and her eyes are clear and bright.

    Sister Annie speaks of the loneliness of this place, but she has had company ever since I have been here. Mr. Miller drove all the children in from the Springs the day we came here and has been here ever since, making himself generally useful and pleasant. He is a real nice gentleman, so perfectly deferential to ladies.   Brother Tom and Sister are great friends of his.   We have had several nice drives since he came, thanks to his team.

    Mr. J. H. R_____ is now here. He returned from New Orleans the other day. He wanted me to drive with him yesterday evening but I declined. Last night we were rather crowded for a Mr. L_____, a connection of ours, was here also. He also wanted me to go driving, and had he been an elderly gentleman I should have done so, but as he was both young and handsome I declined his invitation also. He did not like it a bit—said he had been "Cousin Volney" with all my sisters and had known me when I was a little thing and he did not think I would have refused him.

Jake R_____ was decidedly miffed at my refusing, but I did right, did I not? There would not have been any actual harm in driving with them, but the times are so fast that I don't think anyone, and particularly a young married woman, can be too particular.

I never saw anything like the fruit up here. The other evening Brother Tom, Sister Annie, the four youngest children, Mr. Miller and myself went in his double seated conveyance and called by a neighbor of Sister Annie's who had insisted upon her sending for some fruit. He had filled a cotton sack with the finest sort of peaches and we can get apples and peaches in abundance.

Tell Rose that the bugs did not get away with me at the Springs for the simple reason that I left when I did. Otherwise, I think the children and myself, like Berthard's covering would have been carried off. I can see the old gentleman now as he stumbled along with quilts, pillows etc. tucked under his arms.

Husband, do remember what I asked you in regard to being particular and not get into trouble during the high run of politics in St. Mary. Remember to be particular for my sake.

Louise [perhaps the children's nurse] has just told me to tell you that I am getting fat. I suppose you are glad to hear it as there was room for improvement.

Give Mother ever so much love for me. I shall write to her again soon. I hope she won't have any trouble with the housekeeping. Tell my dear little girl that she must be sure to write me often. Louise and the children talk about her often.

Please get me Caro [Caroline] Tarlton's address. Also Sally Allen's and give them to me in your next letter. Please don't forget. I wish I could see you now, but I know it is too far to expect to see you. With fondest love,

Devotedly
Your wife

His answer to her lack of time for writing seems to be a stiff upbraiding from a jealous husband.

Franklin, Louisiana
September 2, 1889

My dear wife,

I got home this morning at four o'clock, and just as I got in the room, your letter was found on the table at the head of the bed. I was weary, worn and tired out, so I saved the opening until I could get in bed.

Rose, I must epitomize your letter. You wrote hurriedly. You first stated you had only begun to miss me. Then that Bessie was well and not a word about precious and bad little Mary nor a line telling of sweet and tender little Willia.

You then tell me that a young and handsome stranger, a Mr. L_____, and that Mr. R_____, a married man, a rejected lover and a notorious and disgusting libertine, had each asked you to take a buggy ride with him in the unfrequented and almost untravelled piney woods, and that you had declined each invitation and you ask me what I think of it.

My opinion is that the insult was so deep and pointed and the proposition, in its very nature, so compromising, that every instinct of a wife and mother should have been shocked and horrified.

I don't understand. A young married man and a stranger proposes a buggy ride to a young married lady—the mere thought suggests a cowhiding of the lout at the hand of the husband. A miserable and unscrupulous wretch without character, who will contaminate, even by association, the good and fair name of a woman—a married man proposes to you a buggy ride! Such insults from such a source could not be wiped out with the blood of the wretch.

You tell me that there would be nothing actually wrong in accepting such an offer. Why, Rose, you must have written this letter to fill up the pages of an hurriedly written letter. Do you young married ladies go buggy riding even in town and in the country with strange young gentlemen and fast married men? And these GENTLEMEN, after offering you, in my opinion, the grossest and keenest insult, actually condescended to become miffed at you.

Why, Rose, what are you thinking of when you write lightly on this subject? Do you suppose that either of these creatures could have even suggested such a ride had your husband been with you. Do they suppose that your visit to Annie's as a hunt on your part for buggy rides? Was not Annie's house sufficient for you?

I write, dear wife, in no spirit of anger or of reproach to you, but I did not think you would ever have been subjected to such an insult and indignity.

I consider R_____ and L_____ dangerous men for any lady to associate with for the reason that they have no appreciation of women's character and they are both full of vanity and conceit.

Rose, I have written much too much, and I will close by saying if you could make your arrangements so as to come to Alexandria on the 15th it would be more convenient for me to meet you. Court opens this week and I could leave here on Sunday and we could then get back Monday morning and I would not lose a day.

I am glad you have had such a nice time otherwise, and I am glad you did not go with those scoundrels. I have missed you so much. Love to Annie and love and kisses for you and the girls.

Affectionately your husband,
Murphy

Politics did seem to heat up during Rose's visit to her sister when a near-tragedy occurred on the Franklin courthouse steps. However, it took Murphy's mind off the thought of Rose almost accepting a buggy ride.

Franklin
Sept. 3, 1889

My dear wife,

It is now four o'clock. I write you in the midst of great excitement and to correct our newspaper reports which might reach you, and for the further reason that in all times my love and my heart turn to my darling wife.

A terrible tragedy took place in Franklin poll this morning. Joe Jacobs ran up against George Palfrey, and as Jacobs was going down the courthouse steps, he attempted to draw his pistol. I immediately sprang in front of George. Jacobs continued to draw. When he about got his pistol out, I drew mine. The fellow was then in the act of shooting me, as I could not get my pistol cocked, when a friend standing by shot Jacobs down. It was all done in less than a minute.

We all think the wound may be fatal. The man fell like a beef. The bullet entered his side. I believe that unless my friend had not been standing by I would have been killed. At least this is the opinion of the crowd. It seems that the man had a spite against me too.

I was almost moved to tears at the universal affection shown toward me. Today the man who did the shooting is almost idolized for saving my life. I write in great haste, dear wife, for fear that some distorted report may reach you.

Jacobs thinks that I shot him, but twenty men saw the shooting and the party that did it does not pretend to conceal it from his friends.

With love to you and kisses for the little girls.
Affectionately your husband,
Murphy

Two days later, another letter to Rose came from her husband.

Franklin
Sept. 6

My dear Rose,

Your sweet letter of the third received, and while I am glad to learn that you are having a nice time I am sorry that the little ones have colds, but I trust they will soon be better.

I enclose herewith my interview with the New Orleans papers on the shooting here. Everything is now quiet and I am glad to say Jacobs is getting much better. There is a deep undercurrent of feeling, but I think it can be easily controlled, and I would like to write you at length on the whole situation, but even now there are four or five men in the office.

It was first reported that I had been shot, and I never saw such a wild feeling as was abroad. I believe if Jacobs had wounded me more blood would have been shed.

I will meet you in Alexandria on the 16th. That is a Sunday night. I will leave here on the morning of the fifteenth and will see you about 10 o'clock.

With love to Annie and the children, and a heart full for you,
Your affectionate husband,
Murphy

They were glad to see each other!

CHAPTER NINE

In the spring of 1890, Rose, who had never had a serious illness, was stricken with grippe, an influenza-like virus. Since she was five months pregnant with their fifth child, the illness hit her very hard and lasted for several weeks. Elizabeth Ratliff's letter shows her concern.

Ellerslie
May 12, 1890

My darling Rose,

Your letter of May 4th reached here two days ago. It's always a pleasure to hear from you and yours. I had begun to think strange of your long silence, and am very sorry to hear that it was caused by illness, and of all diseases the grippe.

It certainly is a fearful disease. I am well acquainted with it. The doctor [Dr. Wade] was seriously ill for six weeks with it, and complained, as you do, of excessive weakness. He was taken sick the first of February, and it is only in the last three weeks that he has been able to attend to his business. His illness was caused by his exposure in traveling to Carolina for hands.

We lost this year about twelve or fourteen hands, and having heard by going to Carolina he could replace them, he concluded to do so. He brought out twenty for himself and eight for Mary Ryland.

The doctor is very much pleased with the hands. They are good workers and, between you and myself, I think it's a good thing to let our negroes see that we are not dependent on them and they can be replaced whenever they choose to leave.

I had not heard about your illness. I have not been to Ouida for several months. I was over and spent ten days with Mary Ryland. We had planned to go to church last Sunday, and go from there to Ouida, but it rained and put an end to all our plans.

I was delighted to hear that your little folks were getting on so finely in their studies. Tell Bessie I feel quite proud of my namesake. You are truly fortunate in having a good school so near. How does Annie stand her separation from Routh? It must be hard to have him so far from her. [He was staying at Dixie that year in order to go to school at Franklin.]

I trust, my dear child, that you will get safely through confinement. I shall feel anxious until you are safely over it. I hope this time it will be a boy.

Carry Reeves Barrow has two children, a boy and a girl. I was amused at what you wrote me of your little Mary. She must be a mischievous little toad. I do so much wish to see you and all the children. It appears an age since I last had the pleasure of seeing you.

I am glad to hear that you were not much troubled with the high water. The water is still very high in our swamp.

I must close. With kind regards to Mr. Foster, with kisses to the darling children and lots of love for your dear self, I am as ever

Your devoted cousin,
Elizabeth Ratliff

When the acute stage of the infection was over, Rose was left with extreme weakness. Since she was five months pregnant, her recovery was slow. She later commented, "A first serious illness is one you never forget, and my dark days that long ago spring are etched in my mind." But the recuperation process was finally over and the rest of the year was a banner year for both. Murphy led the Louisiana Lottery recharter fight, which was coming to a head in the legislative halls of Baton Rouge, and Rose gave birth to their first son.

The fight for rechartering the lottery is well known in the state's history. It proved to be the greatest fight in Murphy's career. From its inception in 1868, Murphy had felt it was morally wrong. Aware of the stranglehold it had upon people who could ill afford it and disgusted at the influence it had over the legislature, he knew the state could never move forward with constructive legislation as long as lottery money was buying the votes of some of his fellow legislators. He discovered that in the fourteen sessions of the legislature between 1872 and 1884, a total of one hundred fourteen days at a cost of $1,500 a day had been devoted to lottery interests at a cost of $200,000 to the taxpayers.   It paid dividends to its stockholders and donated $40,000 to the Charity Hospital in New Orleans. It was a heavy financial burden on the state.

The lottery, first chartered in Louisiana in 1868 for a period of twenty-five years, was nearing the end of its allotted time. During the year of 1889, the stockholders began preparations to secure the recharter before the expiration date of January 1, 1894. John A. Morris, president of the lottery company, issued a statement to the people of Louisiana declaring that his company would pay the state $500,000 a year for the next twenty-five years with one third of that amount going to the public school system of the state, one third to charitable institutions, and one third to construction, maintenance and repair of levees. Governor Nicholls opposed the recharter, for he, like Murphy, knew the lottery would continue to control the destiny of the state by influencing the election of both state and federal officials.

Sides were drawn, and because Murphy's record of integrity was unimpeachable, he was chosen to lead the fight for the anti-lottery forces. Then another lottery company appeared on the scene, causing Mr. Morris and his company to raise the ante to $1,250,000 per year. Murphy counter-attacked by accusing both companies of trying to influence legislators. He, therefore, introduced a resolution providing for the appointment of a committee of five to investigate charges that both companies were trying to influence legislators. The pro-lottery forces offered a substitute resolution which would have carefully selected pro-lottery legislators to do the investigating. Murphy presented letters and other evidence as proof of his charges; then he forced the issue: ". . . in the name of Louisiana, in the name of her virtue, in the name of her patriotism, we challenge you to an open contest upon the floor of this chamber."

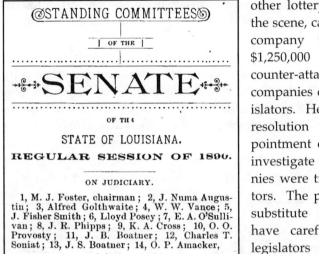

@STANDING COMMITTEES@

| OF THE |

SENATE

OF THE

STATE OF LOUISIANA.
REGULAR SESSION OF 1890.

ON JUDICIARY.

1, M. J. Foster, chairman ; 2, J. Numa Augustin ; 3, Alfred Golthwaite ; 4, W. W. Vance ; 5, J. Fisher Smith ; 6, Lloyd Posey ; 7, E. A. O'Sullivan ; 8, J. R. Phipps ; 9, K. A. Cross ; 10, O. O. Provosty ; 11, J. B. Boatner ; 12, Charles T. Soniat ; 13, J. S. Boatner ; 14, O. P. Amacker,

Murphy J. Foster served as chairman of the Senate Judiciary and Rules Committees during the 1890 legislative session.

With Murphy leading the way, the anti-lottery forces maintained that the state's revenues were enough to meet the expenses of government without lottery money. But the other side mustered the votes to pass a bill calling for the lottery recharter to be brought before the people. Then the anti-lottery group tried to defeat the bill by proposing amendments. One amendment called for dividing the lottery's revenue with the state on a fifty-fifty basis. Another would require the lottery to repay all parish and municipal taxes. There were others, but they were all defeated. After much oratory and many accusations, the pro-lottery faction was able to pass a bill calling for a referendum.

Murphy and his anti-lottery forces responded by calling a convention to organize their forces, and the 1892 gubernatorial contest entered its first phase. Since Murphy had played a key role in the organization, he was chosen to address the delegates. He stressed the point that the state's honor was at stake, that the lottery company was mistaken in believing that it could be bought. His words "for my country and her honor, for my state and her good name, for her dead and her living, I vote no" became the standard rhetoric of anti-lottery oratory.

The intensity of the fight grew when the anti-lottery forces enlisted the support of their U. S. Senator Edward Douglass White. Mindful of the adverse effects of the gambling interest on the state, he called upon the support of his colleagues in Congress to pass a law making it illegal for the lottery to use the mails. Stymied, the pro-lottery forces were furious, and the newspapers responded by accusing Congress of taking away freedom of the press.

Meanwhile back at Dixie, Rose was keeping up with state news through the newspaper. Having seen firsthand gambling's demoralizing effects on the poor people of the area, who often bought tickets instead of food, she felt both joy and pride in her husband's work, despite knowing that defeating the lottery would take him away from home at a time she needed him most. But the activities at home went on—caring for the children, overseeing the farm, and the thousand other duties of a mother. The children wrote often to their father.

Receipt for tuition payment for Rose, Bessie, and Routh Ringgold,
a nephew visiting from Jena, Louisiana.

Dixie, May 11, 1890

My dear papa,

We went to the picnic Saturday and we had a fine time. I am going to study hard. We played ring around the rosey. May has a little colt and it is almost white. I wish I could see you. How are you getting along? Mama is going to get us a doll. She is going to get Routh a knife. Willia is as jolly as ever. Willia can run. Willia is all the time calling Mama. I want to see you.

From your little daughter Rose

Routh, the busy young cousin, wrote his uncle, too.

Dixie, May 12, 1890

Dear Uncle,

I hope you keep well. Aunt Rose and the children are all well. I went to the Picnic and had a good time with some of the boys. I had lots of good pie and cake.

Willia is as quiet and spry as Mary who is very spry. May had a little colt and it is almost white. Miss Fletcher says that the water is going down in the bayou. Your colts are looking fine. I am trying to learn very hard. School will close for me in the last of June. I am glad.

Your nephew,
F. Routh Ringgold

Dixie
May 14, 1890

Dear Husband,

I did not get this letter off in today's mail because I could not send Johnnie from here in time, as that long looked for Flat Boat with corn made its appearance and Johnnie had to help John store away that feed. The Flat Boat tied up here at the Rice Mill, and the old gentleman who sells the corn told me that you had engaged 15 barrels from him and he asked if you still wanted it. As John told me that 15 barrels would not last you until corn came in again, and as you were saved freight and hauling by buying this, I took 25 barrels.

I hope I did right. Please let me know in your next letter if what I did meets with your approval. There was such a rush for this corn that Warren, who came down immediately, could not get 25 barrels for himself—in fact, he did not get a single barrel of it.

I send you in today's mail letters from Rose, Bessie, and Routh. The latter, much to my surprise, handed me his at the same time Rose and Bessie handed me theirs. The children are studying well. They have to learn their lessons before breakfast, as the mosquitoes are unbearable at night. I make it a point to hear their lessons, and help them all I can in this way.

Mary is as bright and as great a "case" as ever. Willia is as gentle and sweet as usual. Rose and Bessie still cough a great deal, but all seem well. Louis has gotten over his sore throat, and Miss Georgie keeps well. Mother was down yesterday and remained until this morning. Says she will be down again in a day or two to stay some time.

The horses all look well. Colts are looking splendidly . May and her fine looking offspring are both doing well.

Joshua will complete the cattle shed this evening. He says he made it 30x18 as it did not take any more material than he at first calculated it would. I have settled with him for it.

And now that I have told you all the home news (of news from town I have had none), tell me about yourself. I received your letter of Saturday yesterday morning. I am glad to hear you are feeling better. I sincerely hope that change of work, though it is still mental labor, will be of some benefit to your health.

I wonder that the *Times Democrat* of yesterday has the face to try to so misrepresent Governor Nicholls as it did when it printed his message in the same paper. The Lottery Company is certainly making a desperate effort to hold its own, and I am afraid it will win the day. From all I can hear, almost all of the Senators are bought over.

Still, single handed and alone, I know you would do your duty to fight with self respect and that honor and integrity that a true man holds dear—all the wealth in Christendom should not buy it. I am so proud of you, dear husband.

Your affectionate wife,
Rose

Franklin, La. May 20, 1890

My dear Papa,

I have got whooping cough. Rus got sick and died. Bighead's colt is not very spry. May's colt is as spry as ever. We are all sorry when Mr. Jones told us that Rus was dead.

How are you getting along? I wish I could see you.

From your little daughter

Rose

Franklin, La.
May 29, 1890

Dear Papa,

I am going to try to wear my bonnet. How are you? Routh is very bad. He loves the bayou. Mama wants to see you. I wish I could see you. I am going to study hard. Barbee is sick. I have a bad cold. Mama thinks that I have whoopingcough. Mary is all the time getting hurt. I was all the time at school when Rus died.

From your little daughter Bessie

A few days later Rose received two letters from Murphy giving her the first real insight into the political struggles going on in Baton Rouge.

Baton Rouge, La.
May 18, 1890

My dear Wife:

I have snatched a few brief moments from my busy life here this Sunday evening to write a few lines to my dear Rose. We are fighting day and night. I am on the "go" all the time and I thank God that I believe the fight will be with us. Should I succeed in defeating this lottery I am willing to return to the shades of private life.

Your letter was received with a great deal of satisfaction and I am so glad to learn that everything is getting along smoothly. You did exactly right about the corn. I will send you a check in a few days to cover your expenses etc.

I spend a great deal of my time with the governor. The more I see of him the more I like him. I had dinner with him in his bachelor apartment and I must say his company was far better than the food.

How I wish, dear Rose, I could be with you this evening and how, in all of this strife and trouble I wish that I was with you all. If we win the fight, I am coming right straight home for a while.

Write often. Your letters mean so much. Love to Miss Georgie and kisses to the girls and yourself.

Your devoted husband,

Murphy

Tell the little girls Papa will write them and thank them for all their letters.

Senate Chamber
Baton Rouge, La. May
May 23, 1890

My dear Wife,

I have just made a speech on the lottery question. I did not expect to make it, but we were provoked into debate, and I don't think I have ever received more praise and hearty congratulations. Old and young came up to shake my hand and thank me, some with tears in their eyes.

I did not finish the speech, but will conclude this coming Thursday. I write to tell my beloved Rose for I know she will be proud and glad to hear it.

With love and kisses
Your affectionate husband,
Murphy

Included was a note to his daughters:

ESTABLISHED, A. D., 1852.

HOME INSURANCE CO.
OF NEW ORLEANS.

No. 78 Camp Street.

New Orleans, _____ **MAY** _____ *1890.*

M Alice C. Wade

Shattuck & Hoffman

The Insurance effected by you as per

FIRE *Policy No.* 29613 _____ $500

On Fire

Oneida Pct

W. Fel. Par. La

will expire on the 31st *day of* **MAY**

at 12 o'clock at noon.

Respectfully,

JOHN G. BYRD,

Secretary.

Rate : _____

PLEASE RENEW.

ask Murphy J. Foster

at Franklin La

as to renewal

Murphy J. Foster found time in his busy schedule to help with insurance problems.

My dear little daughters,

Papa, when he read your dear sweet letters, felt just like coming home and taking his darling little girls to his heart. I was so glad to learn that you are feeling better. I was worried. I know that you study hard, except when you're sick, and you will be at the head of your classes. You don't know how proud Papa is of his little girls.

So old May found a colt. I thought when I left home that she was hunting all around the stable for a little colt, because she looked like she felt sad when she saw all the other horses with their little colts.

You must write often. With lots of love for Mama and Mary and Willia and yourself from

Your devoted papa

In June the girls sent more letters.

Franklin, La.
June 21, 1890

My dear Papa,

You asked me what should you bring me. So then bring me a sash. I'll learn a piece of poetry for you. When will you be home? Will you dispatch when you are coming home? Aunt Annie is coming down here. Routh has Lelia for his sweetheart and Martha and Emma and Daisy. He wants to get married and he doesn't even know how to spell. I can write better than this but my finger is still sore. Mary sends you lots of kisses. Willia is very funny. The flowers are very pretty. The clovers are coming up fast. Mama is going to get me a canary and Routh is going to make a cage.

From your loving daughter Rose

Dixie
June 22, 1890

Dear Papa,

How are you getting along? We miss you so much. I will learn you a piece of poetry if you will bring me a sash. We catch crayfish on the bayou bank. You ought to see Grandma eat them. Mama is very well. Grandma is very well. Routh goes crawfishing every day. We are having such a hard rain. We are having such a nice time. Aunt Annie is coming down here to get Routh and then they are going from here to Ouida. I send you lots of kisses and a piece of my hair.

Your loving daughter Bessie

The chaotic session wore on that summer, and Rose must have told him she felt neglected, for in his next letter he asks her not to misconstrue his preoccupation with his work for neglect.

Senate Chamber
Baton Rouge, La.
June 30, 1890

My dear Rose,

For heaven's sake don't think I am neglecting you. I would give worlds to see you and to have your presence over here in this great fight going on. I am busy day and night. One day last week I became utterly exhausted mentally and in the midst of a conference I was compelled to ask my friends to let me lie down till my dizziness passed.

You cannot realize the intensity of the excitement and the vast amount of work, conferences and commotion which are necessary.

Every night I am up till one, two, or three o'clock and I say it in no conceit, but every man depends upon my advice. You can get some idea of my intentions when I tell you there are some forty men, each with different ideas and each wanting to consult. I am writing this as still another debate goes on. The governor has been sick and I have had to preside over the Senate. When in the chair I am bound to listen, or try to listen, to the debates and arguments.

How this fight will end I do not know. It all depends upon cousin Willis Prescott the lottery men claim absolutely. I don't know what will be his vote. The fight has now gone into the depths of diplomacy and we are all treading over dangerous ground. How this thing will end God only knows. I still trust that right will triumph.

With a heart full of love for you and the girls. I think of you and hope you are well as possible.

Your affectionate husband,
Murphy

On July 5th a last happy letter arrived from the Senate Chamber.

My dear wife,

The session is about over, thank heaven!

I will leave here Friday morning and possibly get home Friday, if not Saturday at the latest. How happy I will be, and I don't think I shall have to leave home again soon.

God bless and take care of you, dear Rose.

Your affectionate husband, Murphy

Murphy returned home in time for the birth of his son: William Prescott Foster, who arrived two weeks later. Joy reigned at Dixie. He was named after each of their brothers—William Ker and Prescott Foster—and he was born into a bevy of deliriously happy little girls and proud parents and excited cousins. Rose announced that, unlike the girls who always called her "Mama," this son, and any that followed, would learn early to address her as "Mother."

Her husband agreed. All in all, it was a happy summer.

CHAPTER TEN

With the end of the strenuous session, Rose and her husband were able to enjoy time at Dixie together. Their new son was a healthy baby and they, as well as the little girls, delighted in him. A steady stream of callers came to Dixie, friends who expressed their pleasure over the Foster girls finally having a brother and Rose and Murphy a son. The children welcomed their father home, and as they had promised in their letters to him, Rose and Bessie recited poetry in his honor and showed off their reading and writing skills while little Mary and Willia colored pictures for him. He took them for carriage rides and gave Rose and Bessie riding lessons. To provide equal amusement for Mary and Willia, he led them around the yard on his horse or put them in the saddle in front of him. Although Rose was concerned about the little girls, she tried not to caution him too much.

Soon after Prescott's birth, Alice Wade came to Dixie. Welcomed with open arms by all, Alice shared her time with each of them. She loved to talk politics with Foster and family with Rose. The little girls reveled in her bedtime stories, many of which concerned Rose's childhood and hard times. She brought each a little butter churn, and they had a "butter-churning" or "gather-the-eggs" or "feed-the-chickens" party every day. It was delightful to all of them to have their mother's guardian whom she loved like a mother, share their lives for a brief time. When the time came for her to return to Ouida, tears rolled down the children's cheeks and Rose and Foster wore long faces. As her carriage pulled out of the gate, young Rose turned to her mother and said, "Oh Mama, no wonder you love her so. We do too."

Foster took pride in all the new colts, the geese and turkeys and pigs, and Black Annie, the fine new cow, who gave the most and best milk they had ever tasted. With the vegetable garden producing well, the household was almost self-sufficient. The improvements at Dixie that Rose had overseen in Murphy's absence proved very satisfactory to him.

The quiet weeks passed too quickly, and before Rose could become used to having Murphy at home, the Anti-Lottery League called a convention in Baton Rouge, and he was off again. Nine hundred delegates representing fifty-three parishes registered. Foster was elected one of the vice-presidents, and plans were made to defeat the amendment in the 1892 general election. Murphy's popularity grew, but his political stance was even more popular, and by October, 1890, it was evident that the 1892 election would be more about lottery re-charter than candidates.

All through the winter and spring of 1892, Murphy made speeches around the state lining up different organizations to join the Anti-Lottery League. One of the most important was the Farmers' Alliance, led by T. Scott Adams. They were anti-lottery, but since farming was primary on their agenda, their support was somewhat half-hearted. Even when Murphy returned to Franklin, he was caught up in politics with callers both at his law office and at home. Rose was a gracious hostess and the children learned early how to be at ease with adults.

One memorable experience occurred at home and made its rounds over the state. In the habit of taking a short nap after the noon meal, Murphy one day fell asleep on the sofa in the living room instead of retiring to his bedroom. Three-year old Willia had always loved his thick hair and flowing beard, and often when he had a headache, she rubbed his head. On that occasion she removed the ribbons from her doll and tied up her father's hair in little bunches, and having achieved the desired effect went on with her play. Shortly afterward, three gentlemen callers arrived, and when Murphy greeted them at the door, there was dead silence. Then they burst out laughing, and one said, "Well, Senator, this is one more colorful side of you we have not seen before." It was then Murphy caught a glimpse of himself in a mirror with Willia's pink, blue, and white ribbons woven into his hair. His friends never let him forget that day, and little Willia became known as her father's hairdresser.

While Murphy was touring the state with his powerful anti-lottery message, conflicts were building up within his own Democratic party. Some members were pro-lottery; therefore they were divided on who would represent the party in the 1892 election.

Rose was aware of the turmoil, but she was involved in her own domestic affairs and felt the best way she could help Murphy and his cause was to take care of the home and children and be there for Murphy when he did get a chance to come home. Although she loved him dearly and wanted him with her, she was willing to sacrifice because she knew the state needed a man of integrity. Her burden of caring for six children and a big plantation was great, even with a cook, a housemaid, a butler, and a yardman to help her. Finances were no small matter. The wages of the staff members averaged fifty cents a day or $15.00 per week. The cook usually stayed on the place while the others stayed nearby. All took their meals at Dixie, as did some of their offspring who played with the Foster children. With Murphy averaging about $40.00 per week, she stretched the remaining $25.00 to feed and clothe her own family. Since the Dixie crops yielded fair income, they had reduced their debt to her father-in-law and planned to pay off the loan in a few years.

The legislative session of 1891 opened in a fevered state since decisions were close at hand. Candidates had to be carefully chosen by each party in order to insure that its political philosophy and agenda be put forth aggressively. Some who were not opposed to the lottery on moral grounds questioned the financial soundness, believing the state could not afford loss of the lottery money. Many complex questions entered into the decision making. Murphy worked day and night to unite the different anti-lottery groups under the Democratic party umbrella. Both the Anti-Lottery League and the Farmers' Alliance had favorite candidates whom they favored to lead the anti-lottery fight in the 1892 election. After many meetings and heated discussions, they finally agreed upon a slate of candidates. The Farmers' Alliance was given the offices of governor, treasurer, and superintendent of education; the Anti-Lottery League was given the offices of lieutenant-governor, auditor, attorney general and secretary of state. T. Scott Adams was to be Farmers' Alliance candidate for governor.

Murphy was pleased that the two groups had reached a compromise, but his efforts as peacemaker took its toll. Fatigue and stress combined to bring him down with chills and fever heralding a return bout of malaria. He did not tell Rose of his illness, but she found out and wrote the following letter.

Dixie
June 22, 1891

My dear husband,

I have just heard through Father, who had seen Mr. Hine, that you have had a fainting spell. What caused it, Mr. Foster? What is the trouble? How are you now? God grant that you are well. I shall see Mr. Hine today and find out the particulars of your attack.

I hope you can go with Mother and the children right off today to Cooper's Wells for I feel certain you will improve right away. It is good that they were on their way to Cooper's Wells and you must go with them. And one more request—please stop the use of tobacco also for I am sure this will keep you run down. Do all that you can on this trip to improve your health—your state needs you like we do—and when you get home I promise to do all I can to keep you well and happy.

I have the "blues" this morning. The news of your sickness was such a shock to me. I feel if anything happened to you I would never get over it. The thought of you being seriously ill makes me realize how very dear you are to me and I wish I could be with you. Thank goodness Mother is with you for I know her good nursing and affectionate care will help you to improve quickly.

The children here are better. Willia is better and so is Prescott. Tell Rose we miss her and I am glad she is going to Cooper's Wells with you and her grandmother. Tell her Bess says not to wear out her good dresses for she intends to go on a trip too.

Samson is lame but with the help of antiseptic John says he is getting better every day. The colts are fine. I am planting six pretty cedars and three nice size pine trees this morning. Miss Molly Harris brought them to me after her trip to Lafayette. As this planting should be done before the sun gets too hot I shall say goodbye. Tell Rose to behave herself. She promised me she would not give her grandma and yourself any trouble. Stay until you really feel like your old self again.

I am enclosing a lovely letter from Cousin Alice. You have been such a help to her, dear Husband. It is terrible to think that young Routh is gone. Just a year ago he was writing and telling you what a good time he was having with us at Dixie. Pneumonia is a terrible thing.

With love,
Your devoted wife,
Rose

This is the letter from Alice that Rose enclosed:

Ouida, June 16, 1891

Dear Rose,

You don't know how glad I was when I opened my mail to find a letter from you. Do you know this is the second one we have received since you all left Ouida? That is too long, my child, to keep me in suspense, your children are all too dear to me for me to lose sight of you for too long.

I am sorry to hear my sweet, good natured boy has been sick. He is a little darling. Sarah says he is the sweetest baby she ever saw. Rose, can you realize that my old, long child Sarah and her little ones have gone from Ouida? It was a sad morning when I took the little ones [five of them] that I had cared for so long, one by one in my arms and gave them their parting kiss. Alice cried for two or three days. She is devoted to her mother and an affectionate little thing with the children, my parting with John was the sad part. Sarah writes me that he can't speak of me or home without his eyes filling with tears.

Katie feels a great deal and follows her like a shadow. She says she thinks the child misses me and is homesick. She says Dan and Roberta are perfectly satisfied. I feel sorry for Sarah. I never saw a greater struggle between love of home and duty.

Mine was a peculiar position. I could not say go, it is your duty, for fear she would think I was pushing her out. And if I said stay, it would look as if I was selfish. I could not advise her. I left it entirely with her. I suppose it natural she should wish to be with her husband, he is certainly devoted to her, and a kind, patient father with his children.

The mail that brought your letter had one also from my poor little Annie. Rose, I can't tell you how my heart has ached for that child. Tom has rented a nice house in Pineville and moved her and the children from Jena. She seems pleased with her new home, and the change will be good for her mind. She dwells continually upon her sorrow. Routh's death was a sad thing. Poor little fellow, he was an unselfish, obliging child.

Your cousin Frank is with me, has been for two weeks. Ann Brandon has had the old house at Como pulled down and they are having a large, two story house put up. They have seven carpenters hard at work, expect to finish it in two months. Francina is at home helping Ann. Sadie, with her little anxious self, is at Mary's. Her Yankee beau is up from the city on a visit to her, he has been very ill with abscess of the liver and his physician orders him north for the summer. God forgive me, but I could almost say I trust he will never get back.

You asked me to tell you all about myself. Well, to start with, I have not a hand in my yard. I do all my own cooking. I can make pretty light bread. Sally Lunn, biscuits, flannel cakes, rice cakes and batter cakes. I am doing everything in my power to pay Murphy something on that debt. His kindness I shall never forget and I know he thinks I have no gratitude because when I feel the most I can't express it.

How are all your dear little children? Is Willia as handsome as she was when I was in Franklin? That head of hers was beautiful. I hope Rose and Bessie are good children and help you. Do they go to school? I make Alice and Sarah get their lessons every day and say them to me at night. The day's work is over and I can give them my attention.

How is your health and when you get sick come home and I will pet you up and send you home all O. K. God bless you, my dear child, and help you to do your duty under all circumstances, be true to yourself, and remember all I said to you. Alice and little Sarah join me in love to you all.

Your devoted old cousin, Alice

Dixie
June 26, 1891

Dear Husband,

John went for the mail and I am hoping to hear that your fevers are easing and that the waters at Cooper's Wells expel the malaria from your system.

I heard to day that Mrs. Mentz [the wife of Murphy's law partner] is quite ill. I had hoped to visit her today but it has rained so hard I could not get to town in the carriage. I sent word to Mr. Mentz that I would be happy to take care of Alvin for them while Mrs. Mentz is sick, and that I did not offer to nurse her myself because I could not leave our own children. But I told him one more would not make any difference here.

Prescott has missed his 21st day without a chill and fever and he seems so well. Mary and Bessie are fine but Willia is uncomfortable. I think she is cutting her last jaw teeth.

John says everything is going on well at the stable. The 16 sacks of oats and bran were put off here by the "Round Boat" several days ago.

I must catch the mail so I will close. My love to you, and to Rose and Mother.

Affectionately yours,
Rose

Later that summer, the family went to Cote Blanche Island for the air and saltwater bathing.

Rose stayed on with the children and friends, Miss Molly Harris and Miss Caro Lyman, after Murphy returned to work. The change did her good, and she returned to Dixie feeling rested and ready for what she knew was going to be a busy political year.

When the Democratic Central Committee met at the St. Charles Hotel on October 14, 1891, a tally showed the pro-lottery members with thirty-nine votes and the anti-lottery members with thirty-eight votes. Anti-lottery members wanted the lottery issue to be decided on when the delegates were selected for the State Democratic Convention rather than at the General Election, but the pro-lottery forces were firmly against that proposal. They battled to a draw, each side suspicious of the other. With no compromise in sight, the State Central Committee adjourned until December 14, after calling a meeting of the Democratic State Nominating Convention for December 16, 1891, in Baton Rouge.

In the meantime, more of the anti-lottery Democrats were unhappy with Mr. Adams. Conceding that he was a fine man, they declared they needed a more forceful leader since everyone knew they were the underdogs and had less money than the pro-lottery people. The situation came to a head in November when former governor Samuel McEnery, who had held office from 1881-1888, decided to throw his hat in the ring. He had never declared openly that he was pro-lottery, but it was known the Lottery Company was supporting him. The group threw a tremendous bash for McEnery in New Orleans on October 27 to announce his candidacy. Fifteen hundred people attended.

As a counter-measure, the anti-lottery group held their rally in New Orleans a week later. To their disappointment, only three hundred came. This was a bad opening for Adams, and after some questions and suggestions he agreed to withdraw if the Farmer's Alliance asked him to. The fight for delegates was emotional and charges and counter-charges flew. By the time the actual meeting was held, the two factions of the Democratic party had split, and the two sides held separate meetings—the McEnery followers in Pike's Hall on Third Street and the anti-lottery delegates in the Old Capitol in the hall of the House of Representatives.

More opposition to Adams was developing among the anti-lottery forces. Although recognizing that he was an honorable man, the leaders of the group asked him to withdraw his name for the good of the party. He finally agreed to do so if "they will give me another place on the ticket." The groundswell of support turned to Murphy, and on December 16, he was nominated for Governor, along with Charles Parlange for lieutenant governor and T. Scott Adams for secretary of state. To direct their campaign, they formed a state committee, composed of one member from each parish, one from each representative district of New Orleans, and twenty-five members from the state-at-large.

Soon after Murphy hit the campaign trail in January 1892, his father died. His death was a real loss for the family, for he had never failed to support them in whatever they did. Having some health problems shortly before his death, he told Rose, as well as his son, that if anything happened to him, he did not want any crepe hanging or interruption of the campaign. He knew time was crucial for Murphy, and felt that the state was in dire need of his leadership. Murphy obeyed, and the day after the funeral, he left for a rally in Monroe. He gave a simple but powerful speech which contained the following points: there were many good Democrats among the lottery supporters; he would not engage in mud-slinging; the lottery was commanding complete attention of the state; the only issue in the campaign was lottery or no lottery, lottery-paid retainers were fanning out in the country seeking constituents' signatures so that they could influence legislators to vote for passage; the Charity Hospital, the Institute for   the   Deaf   and   Dumb,   and   the   levee   system   were   all

The 1892 Democratic Party ticket (left to right): Thomas S. Adams,
Charles Parlange, and Murphy J. Foster

debt free; the anti-lottery ticket was not made up of deserters from the Democratic party, but rather deserters from the lottery party.

Vigorous schedules and much travel gave Murphy an early lead, causing
the opposition to worry. An open letter written by lottery President Morris declared he was getting the message that maybe Louisiana did not really want a
lottery; therefore he would not operate a lottery if the amendment should pass.
Then McEnery proposed that both Democratic tickets should withdraw and an
entire new slate of standard-bearers be nominated. Both central committees
agreed to consider the proposal. On February 16, 1892, Murphy submitted his
resignation saying he neither sought nor wanted the nomination and he now
returned it to the committee to reach a decision. The anti-lottery committee refused the McEnery proposal since they doubted Morris's pledge to abandon the

lottery. Another factor was that as soon as the word got out that Murphy had submitted his resignation, parish conventions were called and the delegates went on record saying they wanted no change in the Foster, Parlange, and Adams ticket. All of this support led to a final compromise, resulting in a primary election in which all Democratic white voters would select their ticket on March 22. The candidates receiving the most votes would represent the party in the General Election.

Back at Dixie, Rose read the accounts of the Morris letter and McEnery's proposal. She did not like what was going on, and she told Murphy so.

DEMOCRATIC TICKET.

STATE OFFICERS

For Governor,
MURPHY J. FOSTER.
Of St. Mary.

For Lieutenant Governor,
CHARLES PARLANGE,
Of Pointe Coupee.

For Secretary of State,
THOMAS SCOTT ADAMS,
Of East Feliciana.

For Auditor
W. W. HEARD,
Of Union

For Treasurer,
JOHN PICKETT,
Of Bossier,

For Attorney General,
M. J. CUNNINGHAM,
Of Natchitoches.

For Superintendent of Education,
A. D. LAFARGUE,
Of Avoyelles.

The 1892 Democratic Party ticket

Dixie
February 14,
1892
My dear husband,
Through the papers and hearing the "boys" talk I have learned of your being in New Orleans and for what purpose you are there. I wish I could make you understand how much I feel for you in this trying ordeal when it is so difficult to know just what is best to do.

I think it an outrage that some of our own side should turn faint hearted and advise a compromise when victory was sure to be ours. I think it an outrage that they should propose a change of ticket when they had begged and pleaded for you to run. Worse than this, I think they propose to do you a greater wrong still when they would insist upon your trying to maintain your place at the cost to others on your ticket, some of the very men who labored to put you at the head of the Party.

I don't know when I have felt so indignant as when some of your friends should propose for you a course that would put you in an office seeking light. If your party sinks, it is your place to go down with it, but I cannot see why there should be any compromise. I cannot think of anything worse for you than to go on a combination ticket composed of such men as Crandall, for instance. I don't think for an instant you will consent to any such course. I only express myself thus because I have no one to talk to and it is a relief to let off some of my indignation in words.

But, Husband, what I started to write, I have not really told you, how in this moment of anxiety and doubt, when it is so hard to tell you just what course to pursue, that if it is any comfort to you to know, you are constantly in my thoughts and I wish there was some way in which I could help you.

May your side come out victorious, my old Louisiana come safely into her own, in spite of the breakers ahead. This the prayer of

Your loving wife
Rose

P. S. I enclose you a letter from an old teacher of mine Mrs. V. Z. Howell, the Principal now of the "FFCI" of Jackson, La. Should the program be unaltered and you should go to Jackson from New Orleans, I would be so glad if you would see Mrs. Howell and explain that I could not leave home just now. I shall write and thank her myself for her kind invitation, but I would be glad if you would see her.

The children are all well. Frances is back and I am glad to have help in the house again. She seems better than she has and all is running smoothly. Mother has stayed with us some and she is remarkable. We all miss Father terribly.

Your Rose

St. Mary Speaks.

MORGAN CITY, LA., Feb. 16.—At a meeting of the Foster Democratic Club at this place this evening the following resolutions were unanimously adopted:

Whereas, we have ascertained through the State press that there is a movement leading to an adjustment of the differences now existing in the ranks of the Democratic party; therefore, be it

Resolved, That we are opposed to any compromise that does not include the return of Foster as governor and Adams as a orotary of state; that we oppose the introducing of any new ticket in the field; that we recognize the Hon. Murphy J. Foster as a true Democrat who has rescued our State from monopolistic slavery, who has trampled the hydra doaded lottery monster to the earth, who is the exemplification of honest statesmanship and as such is fully qualified to lead his party to success and is entitled to the office for which he has been nominated by the Democracy of the people of Louisiana; that we pledge our firm and unswerving devotion to the Democratic party and to its tenets and to its gallant standard-bearer, Murphy J. Foster, whom we hope, please God, to see governor of this fair state.

Meeting of the Foster Democratic Club. 1892.

After the compromise, the campaign became more bitter and more frantic. Rallies and mass meetings in different parts of the state were an almost daily occurrence. Rose and the children saw little of Murphy, and the separation was very difficult for all of them. Three days before the primary election she wrote him.

Dixie
Saturday evening,
March 19

My dear husband,

I have been worried because I have not been able to write to you, but I have not known where to write to you, for while the mass meetings were published to take place at certain places at certain dates, it did not say which of these meeting you would address. The *Delta Times* would say that your party would leave such a place "this evening" to address a meeting, "tomorrow" at some other place which would not give me time to get a letter to you in time.

When you stayed over at Homer, had I gotten my *Delta's* when I sent for them I could have written to you at Shreveport, but I did not get my *Delta's* of Saturday and Sunday for Mr. Mentz and Mrs. Shepherd were not in the office. I am being this explicit because I want you to know I have not neglected you intentionally.

I am just in receipt of your letter telling me that you will be in New Orleans until after the election. This is a great disappointment to me for I have half-way expected you this week, and had so hoped to see you today or tomorrow.

However, I do think it a wise move to stay in New Orleans until after the election, for even though all here seem certain of you winning here, it is well for you to keep up the enthusiasm in New Orleans by having you there.

While I have worried over our strained last goodbye, I have missed you terribly and I know this is hard on both of us. I am better now. In fact I have been having a very gay time for such a quiet person as you know I am.

Miss Jennie and Miss Lizzie Rogers, both of whom I like so much, have been visiting us the last two weeks. We have been driving around a great deal as the weather has been delightful—a little too cool, but bright, beautiful days we have had ever since they arrived.

I was a little forlorn after I drove them to the station, but I brought Mother down and we have so enjoyed our visits together. Dixie, Don Caffery, Percy Saint, Jim Smith, Lawrence Tarlton, and Prescott have all been down to see the girls. Quite a number of ladies called and we were invited to Caro Brady's for dinner. That part of the Teche along Irish Bend is beautiful and we went down and had a delightful day of it. We so often wished for you.

Children and all are well, except for the chickens. They have nearly all died in spite of every remedy, and I have worked on them faithfully.

Your crayon came and it is the most perfect likeness I ever saw of anyone. For whom are the smaller ones? It is late and I must get this in the office before it closes. The children are always talking about you and keep asking why you don't come home.

With much love, dear Husband, and hoping that you will be rewarded by victory for all these long, arduous trips.

Devotedly yours,
Rose

When election day came, both sides predicted victory. Because of the slow procedure of vote counting, in addition to getting the returns from all the parishes, not much was known until March 26th when the *Times-Democrat* predicted a McEnery victory by over 2,000 votes. But it was March 30 before the committee of seven, composed of three McEnery supporters, three Foster supporters, and a man from out of state, counted the votes and officially determined that Foster had more votes than McEnery. McEnery supporters did not agree with the count, and they ran their man in the general election which followed two weeks later.

On April 19, the Foster ticket received a commanding vote over all the other candidates, and the lottery amendment was decisively defeated by a vote of 157,422 to 4,225. The people had spoken, and Louisiana had a new governor. And the Fosters could become a family again.

CHAPTER ELEVEN

Rose joined her husband in New Orleans after the votes were in. Their separation having been long and difficult, it was a special time for them. Although the vote count had not arrived from the remote parts of the state, the signs pointed toward a Foster victory, and they became more confident with each passing day.

In order to join her husband, Rose had made careful arrangements to leave Dixie. The five children, as well as household affairs, were placed in the care of Miss Georgie, Murphy's mother, and members of the staff. With her family and Dixie in good hands, she could relax and enjoy being with her husband. Before leaving, she told the children that since the crops were not very tall, they could see the train as it passed through the Dixie fields and that she would wave a white handkerchief. Each of them was given a handkerchief for a response. Enchanted with the idea, the children waved her off, and enjoyed it so much that they continued the practice as long as trains remained the chief mode of transportation.

After Rose had been in New Orleans several days, the final vote count was announced, and Murphy was declared to be the next governor of Louisiana. She received a letter from ten-year-old Rose, who seemed much more interested in the affairs at Dixie than in her father's upcoming inauguration.

Dixie, La.
April 27, 1892

Dear Mama,

I am going to drop you a few lines. Yesterday we made lemonade. You ought to see Prescott jump from the first step. Mary says she is going with us to see Papa take the othe [oath]. She says she is going to wear slippers.

I hope you and Papa are having a pleasant time. I saw you wave from the train. Prescott, when he heard the train coming, said, "Bye Bye Mama." He waved too. He stood on a chair. Mary and Willia send you lots of kisses. I am going to bed now as I have nothing new to say.

From your affectionate daughter,
Rose

The inauguration was planned for May 16. While she was in New Orleans, Rose went with Kate McCall, a friend, to shop for fabric for the dresses needed for the inauguration—a day dress for the swearing-in ceremony and a gown for

Rose Foster in her inaugural gown, 1892

the inaugural ball. She located the fabric for the day dress easily, but the latter was not so simple. The wide variety of choices overwhelmed her as she later

told her family: "New Orleans always had so many balls that I was almost defeated by the bolts and samples from which I had to make my selection. Finally we found just what I needed. It was a white silk faille material, as they
called it, and the seamstress trimmed it with pearl prassmentarie and white
chiffon which was a new French trimming. It was beautiful."

Before she returned to Dixie, Rose was able to have two fittings on the
dresses. Miss McCall checked out the final touches before they were sent out to
Rose.

Back at Dixie, plans were made to take the four little girls with them to Baton Rouge for the inaugural ceremonies, but little Prescott was to be left at Dixie
with the staff. Murphy's mother, his brother Don, and Don's wife Sally would
go with them from Franklin.

One of Rose's first acts upon returning to Dixie was to write a letter to Mrs.
Nicholls, wife of the outgoing governor, whom they had long admired. A Confederate veteran who had lost an arm in battle, Governor Nicholls had been
elected in 1876, but the carpetbaggers had tried to prevent him from taking
office. He was finally able to take office and was reelected in 1888 with a strong
anti-lottery vote. He had been one of Murphy's strong supporters. Rose received a reply to her letter almost immediately.

Thibodaux, La.
May 12, 1892

My Dear Mrs. Foster,

Your very pleasant letter was forwarded to me here from New Orleans, and I write at once to thank you for it, and for your kind expressions regarding my husband.

I hope your little daughter has entirely recovered and that you are
no longer anxious on her account.

I hope you will take all your children to see their father inaugu-
rated. I have always regretted that I took only my three older children
15 years ago in the first inauguration of their father. It is something for
them to remember and even if they are too young to remember, they
can still say they were there, which will be a happiness in after year.

This will be an exceptional inauguration also, and one that the
women of Louisiana should exceptionally value and point out to their
children and their children's children as the triumph of right over
wrong, of honesty over the love of money and of pure government over
corruption. You are a thrice blessed woman that you are the wife of the
man who led this crusade against evil.

I am proud that my dear husband's only hand was the first raised against the Louisiana lottery when he refused the bribe of one hundred thousand dollars for the levees.

It is with regret that I have to say that I will not be at the inauguration of your honored husband. My daughter, Mrs. Bradford, whose health has been poor for several months (in fact with a miscarriage) so that I fear to leave her for any length of time. My other daughter will represent me and will enjoy being with you.

Mr. Nicholls writes me that you and Governor Foster's mother will arrive on Saturday. My daughters will go up on that day and I hope will meet you on the train. They will be the guests of Mrs. Garig, so you must feel at home from the first at the Governor's house which I think you will like.

Governor Foster can tell you that two years ago I bought the furniture and arranged that house for you, and it is unspeakable happiness to me that you will be mistress there. A piano is still lacking. I did not buy it as I wanted it to be new for you, and it will be a pleasure for you to get it.

I shall come to Baton Rouge when Carrie is well and I can assure you it will give me pleasure to meet you and see your improvements. With sincere and kind wishes for your future, I am

Truly yours,
Caroline B. Nicholls

On May 11, Murphy, who had stayed in Baton Rouge, wired Rose that he had made reservations for her, the girls, and his brother Don and his wife to come the day before the Inauguration Day; and that his mother, Rose, and the girls would stay with Governor Nicholls at the Mansion while the others went to the hotel. Rose was eager to get a good look at her new home.

The day before the inauguration, the Fosters left Franklin for Baton Rouge. Although Rose had already planned to take the four girls, Mrs. Nicholls' suggestion made her feel more comfortable about it. The children were elated, filled with wonder and anticipation comparable only to Christmas Eve. Rose and Bessie maintained a degree of dignity to distinguish themselves from the four and five year olds. Mary was a jumping jack, popping up and down the stairs, dressing and undressing, and in general creating chaos. Four-year-old Willia, fearing being left behind because of an eye infection, remained quiet and calm. The entourage boarded the train amid much excitement in Franklin (the little town would soon be on the map), and soon the train was approaching the fields of Dixie. All handkerchiefs appeared at the window to wave to baby Prescott, who was stationed on the front steps with his nurse and Miss Georgie.

Murphy met the train in Baton Rouge and took them first to the hotel; then Rose and the girls to the Mansion. Although the family was excited, they had not expected the degree of enthusiasm with which they were met in the city. Up to this point the idea of anything more than a personal victory for Murphy had not penetrated their consciousnesses; when they saw the city bedecked with streamers and flags and heard the people cheering, they realized that the victory belonged to the people—that Murphy J. Foster belonged to the state and to history.

The governor's mansion, Baton Rouge. ca. 1892.

When the carriage pulled up before the Mansion, Governor Nicholls and his daughters were waiting to greet them. The children held their parents' hands tightly as they walked up to the house. Rose and Bessie were the epitome of little-girl sophistication, and Willia whispered to her mother, "Mama, my eye feels better already." Mary had remained very quiet until she was inside the house and spied the tall graceful winding stairway leading to the upstairs. She immediately dropped her mother's hand and went running towards the stairs crying, "Mama, Papa, can I please slide down the banisters, please, please. . . ."

"Not today, little daughter," her father answered. "We can't have you tear your good clothes up when you've come all this way to see Papa take his oath."

Rose, standing by, was experiencing a sense of *déjà vu*. She was seeing herself and Sarah alight from the carriage, holding hands tightly and staring in awe at the magnificent Ellerslie that was to be their new home. Governor Nicholls and his daughters were transformed into the kindly Wades who welcomed them, and the beautiful winding stairs became the Ellerslie stairs on which they had loved to romp.

Feeling a bit disoriented, Rose heard Governor Nicholls saying, "Before my family leaves, we will have the banisters polished once again just for Mary." Coming back to the present, Rose apologized for Mary's noisy entrance, and the governor replied, "Madam, I can see that our old mansion is going to enjoy these spirits of the young."

Inaugural Day dawned sunny and bright. Rose dressed carefully in her newly made "day dress" of creme-colored embroidered lawn with a high neckline and double puffed sleeves. Her husband was delighted with her dress, her accessories, and her whole demeanor. He appreciated his lovely wife, but since she was not used to being in the limelight, he felt that his compliments would make her less shy and apprehensive over the limelight into which she was about to step. Perhaps his praise, as well as her finishing-school training made her comfortable because she showed a perfect blending of modesty and decorum.

Louisiana's state capitol building, ca. 1892

Later that morning, carriages brought the other Franklin guests to the Mansion. Governor Nicholls and his daughters hosted an early lunch for the gubernatorial party before they departed for the State Capitol grounds where the ceremony was to be held. A platform in the corner of the Capitol grounds had been built and elaborately decorated. Seats for the governmental officials had been arranged, and in addition chairs had been placed around the platform for the public, who began to arrive early. At 12:30 the excursion train arrived from

New Orleans with three coaches of visitors. The trip had been uncertain, for part of the track between Baton Rouge and New Orleans was under water because of a crevasse near the Bonnet Carré break. A tremendous cheer went up from the crowd at the station when four hundred seventy-five members of the Anti-Lottery Party stepped down from the train, led by Colonel Wycliffe. For them it was the culmination of many months of hard work. They marched to the Mansion where one of their leaders, Judge Monroe, presented Rose and the Misses Nicholls with flowers. After Senator Edward White, who was at the Mansion, responded on behalf of the ladies, the group marched back to the old Capitol grounds.

The carriage with Murphy and Governor Nicholls led the gubernatorial entourage followed by Rose and the children, the Nicholls family, and the Foster family. North Boulevard was lined with spectators, and they cheered the families as loudly as they cheered the governors. The Corps of Cadets of Louisiana State University, led by the Continental Guards Band of New Orleans and the Washington Artillery Band, escorted the governor and the governor-elect to the platform.

The platform's centerpiece held portraits of Governors Foster and Nicholls which were both outlined with flower arrangements, and when the governors took their seats of honor, more deafening cheers went up. The little girls began to put their hands over their ears, but their mother shook her head and their hands went down. The program opened with a prayer by Dr. Owens. Then Supreme Court Justice Fenner administered the oath of office to Murphy, after which a cannon boomed a salute to the new governor.

In his speech, Murphy paid sincere tribute to Governor Nicholls, thanked their successful struggle, and declared that the war between a free and independent state and a powerful gambling corporation had been won, and now the evil could pass into history:

> My policy will be to limit the appropriations to the annual revenues which are derived from the constitutional limits of taxation. The doors of my office will be open to the humblest and the highest of citizens of this state . . . Two of my first objectives are to encourage immigration and second to foster the public school system. If we are to develop this fertile soil, we need more people—other states are far ahead of us—and to attract new settlers, we must have schools for their children. A third effort will be directed toward our levee system. This state receives an annual accumulation of water from many states, and I hope to work with senators and representatives to establish national control of our levee system. [*Baton Rouge Advocate*, May 17, 1892].

Then he beamed a warm smile toward Rose and his daughters and paid tribute to the women of the state who worked so long and so hard against the lottery forces.

Murphy Foster's 1892 inauguration

At the end of his speech, Judge Monroe presented him with a floral ship of state from the Women's Anti-Lottery League of New Orleans. Then after more cheers, the ceremony ended. The two governors went into the Executive Offices with Lt. Governor Parlange and accepted the congratulations from supporters and admirers.

Rose, with the girls and her family, returned to the Mansion where a *Daily Picayune* reporter was waiting for her. The interview was rather short. The reporter requested, "Mrs. Foster, please tell me the story of your life," and Rose answered, "I was born in the country, educated in a convent, married at nineteen, and I have been in the nursery ever since." After thanking the Nicholls for their hospitality, the Fosters returned to their hotel to rest before the ball that evening. Martha Foster said she had enough festivities and would stay with Mary and Willia while the two older girls went to the ball with their parents and aunt and uncle.

Rose felt very elegant in her ball dress and received many compliments. Made of white silk faille and trimmed with pearl prasmentarie and white chiffon, it featured a simple V-neck and a wide scalloped overlay and cascading front. The long sleeves had double puffs to the elbow and fit closely to the wrist, allowing her to pull up her long white gloves easily, and the skirt was finished with a wide ruffled hem.

The Institute for the Deaf and Dumb ca. 1892.

The ball, like other large state affairs, was held in the mess hall of the Institute for the Deaf and Dumb because of it size, spacious grounds, and surrounding verandas. A torchlight parade led the Fosters to the ball and before the dance began, there were fireworks and many balloons and many people. An excerpt from a letter young Rose wrote to her cousin Sarah Towles soon after they returned to Dixie provides more details.

> . . . We had a nice time in Baton Rouge. We saw Papa take his othe [oath] of office and Mama, Bessie, Mary, Willia, and I were so proud of him. Just Bessie and I went to the ball with Mama and Papa. Mama had on a beautiful dress and she looked beautiful and she and Papa danced, and we stayed until half past one o'clock. Bessie and myself got sleepy and so Mama and Papa came home with us. There was over four thousand people there. . . .
>
> We are going to be very busy getting ready to go to Baton Rouge, in August. They are making the mansion pretty for us. Willia has had a very bad eye. . . . from your loving cousin Rose.

After Murphy saw his family safely home to Dixie, he returned to Baton Rouge, for he had much state business which required his attention. He and Rose decided that she and the children would stay at Dixie through most of that summer while he settled down in the executive offices and began the business of running the state. Another reason was that the Mansion was being renovated and a new wing added to accommodate the large family moving in. The proposed date for occupancy was July.

Warren Foster had offered to manage the Dixie fields while they were in Baton Rouge, but a reliable caretaker for the house and grounds, as well as the livestock and poultry, had to be found. There were hard decisions to be made, especially concerning the horses. In one of Murphy's letters to Rose, he wrote: "Tom Murphy wrote that he would take 'Dix' but Rose, I cannot separate her from her colt; besides if we let Tom take her, there will be no gentle horse for you to drive except 'May' and she is getting pretty old."

The children begged to take some of the barnyard residents with them, but their parents explained that it would be too hard on the animals and assured them that when they went to Baton Rouge their Papa would have some animals and chickens waiting for them there.

A letter from Murphy to his daughter, Rose, was carefully written for the benefit of all the children.

Baton Rouge, La.
June 3, 1892

My dear daughter,

 I was real glad to get your letter the other day and I am "stealing" time to write to you tonight. I get very lonesome, although I have my hands full. I want to get home so much, but every minute of my time is taken up from morning to night. I am so busy.

 You know I have moved from the Mansion and am boarding while the work is being done. The work on the house is getting along very well. I think I will have you all a nice home when it is finished I am going to fix you and Bessie a nice room.

 I am having a stable built, large enough for three horses and one cow. Papa wants you all to come over as soon as possible and I am going to have everything nice and ready.

 You must write and tell me all about the place. Tell Mary she must write to Papa too.

 Give your Mama a kiss, and love and kisses for all,

Your affectionate Papa,
Murphy J. Foster

Murphy returned for a brief visit to Dixie in July to see his family and to help with preparations for the move. Rose, a very organized and efficient person, had left little undone. He had always been able to depend on her to run Dixie, handle the fiances, and rear the children; therefore he was not surprised that she had given new meaning to the word *organization*. When he returned to Baton Rouge, he wrote her about his own schedule.

July 23, 1882

Dear Wife,

 Since my return here I have been crowded with business. My office is filled with gentlemen from morning till late at night. Everybody is crazy for an office and everybody gets mad if they do not get an office. However, I suppose the rush will be over in the next two months.

 I sent you the other day by registered letter forty dollars, and as yet I have heard nothing from the letter nor has the receipt been returned. I hope the letter did not miscarry.

The house and addition is nearly completed. I think you will be well pleased with the arrangement. The addition you will find comfortable with all modern improvements. I had a bath room for the children put in the back of the hall upstairs.

The main building looks well—in fact handsome. I will have the carpets put down next week. I think you will be delighted with my selection. Now, Rose, our home here you will find comfortable and pleasant, and all it needs now is your womanly traits.

I want you to come down to the city on the 31st of this month in order to select some furnishings. I will bring a list of what is on hand here and what is needed. Then I shall try to return home with you so that I can make final arrangements for you and the children to come here.

I shall have a fine bay horse for your surrey. I understand he is a magnificent animal and well adapted for family use. I was sorry he was not a dapple grey, but, since he is only loaned to me, I can't be too choosy.

Kiss the children and tell Miss Johnson I am having her room papered with bright and cheerful paper.

Your affectionate husband,
Murphy

In early August the Mansion was ready for the Foster family and the governor was excited. An excerpt from his last letter tells of the final touches.

. . . the rooms are finished and I think you will find everything harmonizes well. The mechanics will finish the pipes, water connections and everything wil be ready for you all by next Monday.

Tomorrow I am going to get us a few chickens so that you and the children will find everything homelike. The horse sent by Mr. Thompson is a very fine looking animal, but I do not know if he is perfectly safe. I drove him the other evening and he seemed to shy a good deal. This, however, I attribute to his first trip in the country. My little mare is well and looks quite pretty.

I shall leave here on the 19th, after my meeting with the school board. I am tired of this bachelor life, and how glad I will be to get you and the children over here. . . .

Rose spent her days sorting and packing trunks and deciding what to leave at Dixie. Her final effort was to make a complete list of linens which she was leaving at Dixie for use during holidays and summers. After packing the linens in moth balls, she made and tacked the following hand-written list on the right door of the closet under the garret steps. The list remains there today.

THINGS TO BE LEFT AT DIXIE
August, 1892

16 large, new sheets, made in 1891
6 large old sheets made in 1885
2 small old sheets made in 1885

White Spreads

5 perfectly good Marseilles spreads
3 ordinary white spreads

Colored Spreads

1 large blue and white spread
1 large brown and white spread
1 faded red and white

Bolster Cases
10 good Bolster cases

Pillow Cases
22 good, large pillowcases
7 torn, large pillowcases
5 good, small pillowcases

Towels
3 1/2 dozen in all, viz:
8 large, handsome towels, same quality, different borders
6 nice linen towels, alike in quality, but different
10 coarse linen towels, all alike in borders
2 coarse linen towels, solid red border
5 good linen towels, faded red and white, borders
7 very common towels, 5 of one border, 1 of another and 1 of another
5 washstand [illegible]
2 worked table scarves
2 white [illegible]
Signed: Rose K. Foster

On the left door of the old closet was another list:

List of Table Linens
2 large, new white tablecloths
2 small new white tablecloths
4 old white tablecloths
2 good, red

Napkins
12 large, new white napkins
11 smaller new white napkins
14 solid red napkins
10 red and gray napkins
1 worked tea tray cover

Blankets
2 prs Blue bordered blankets
2 prs Red bordered blankets
1 pr Red and Blue bordered blankets
2 old single blankets

Quilts
6 large quilts
2 small quilts
4 old quilts

Lace Curtains
3 sets of lace curtains, 4 pcs each set
2 sets of scrim curtains, 4 pcs each set
1 set silkoline curtains, 4 pcs each set
1 set brown and yellow cheese cloth, 3 pcs and one mantel

With the packing done and the lists complete, little was left to do except repeat household instructions and wait for Murphy to come for them. They were embarking upon a new life and they didn't know what to expect.

CHAPTER TWELVE

In mid-August 1892, Murphy arrived at Dixie to help the family make the final break. The children needed him to be with them when they said good-bye to their home and animals, especially their much-loved chickens, turkeys, and ducks. Since many of the animals had been farmed out to various relatives for Murphy's tenure of office, they would not be there to greet the children when they came home for holidays. Some, however, were to remain for the children's enjoyment and also for the family to have milk and food and transportation for holiday and vacation times. Rose needed his support, too, for it was especially difficult for her to say good-bye to Dixie since she had overseen its emergence from a rundown Reconstruction era casualty to a living, breathing home. Every inch of this tree-shaded structure was dear to her: it had comforted her in her loneliness and her sorrow and provided love and security for her family. She had bonded with it when as a bride, she planned and participated in its restoration. Although a caretaker and his wife would keep it up, the house wouldn't be the same without her and especially the children. She also knew that when she joined the accelerated political pace in Baton Rouge, there would be moments when her shy nature would cry out for Dixie. But she had to remind herself that this move was the culmination of their dream, what Murphy had always wanted, and what the state needed. The house in Baton Rouge would be fine and she would love it, too, because finally, the family would all be together.

They moved into the Mansion on August 16, 1892. Since it was partly furnished, Rose took from Dixie only the furniture she would need. The nursery at the Mansion had beds for Mary, five; Willia, three; and Prescott, two; while ten-year-old Rose and eight-year-old Bessie would have their own room. Their many trunks, boxes, portmanteaus, hat boxes, and children's toys filled several wagons; and three surreys were required to transport the Foster family; Francis, the children's nurse; Lizzie, Rose's housemaid; and Miss Georgie to the train station.

All their family and friends waited at the station to see them off. A band played while well-wishing and flowery speeches filled the air. Wide-eyed with excitement, the girls momentarily forgot their animals, and Prescott was concerned about the white handkerchief-waving. Anxiously the children gazed down the tracks, and soon a low mournful whistle sounded. Clutching their papa's pants legs, the little ones watched the heavy black smoke that hung in the air and the racing locomotive that appeared not to be stopping. Then came the sound of screeching brakes and bumping cars that seemed as if they would pile up on one another. The door opened and steps emerged, and good-byes were said again as the baggage was loaded.

After the Foster family entered their special car, the conductor called his final "all aboard" and their journey began amid hand-waving and kiss-throwing. After spending the night in New Orleans, they continued on to Baton Rouge where Murphy went immediately to his office, and Rose went to the Mansion to begin the laborious task of unpacking.

Rose later reminisced about the disorder and commotion in the house that day: "We were surrounded with confusion, the children were running around, some were hungry, some wanted to go outside, and I didn't even know what time it was. So I gave the Mansion's janitor Andrew, five dollars and I said, 'Please go out and get me a clock. I don't care what it looks like. I just need to have it run.' And sure enough he did, and he wound it, and I put it on the mantel. To this day I don't know why I felt that urgent need for a clock, but somehow or other it helped me get organized better than I ever could without it."

By dinner time, life was a bit calmer, and the four girls were allowed to sit at the table with their parents. Murphy beamed with pleasure and said to Rose, "Just another reason, dear wife, that I am so glad to have proclaimed this Thanksgiving an official holiday. Louisiana has shed its lottery, we are sending a united Democratic delegation up to the National Convention in Chicago, and now I have us back together as a family again." Then looking at his children, he said, "You know, your mother and I have had a rule when you are at the adult table, that children should be seen and not heard. But since this is our first night in our new house, you can talk as much as Mama and I do, just be sure you don't interrupt us or any of your sisters when one of us is speaking."

As the chatter erupted, the questions multiplied. "Mama, when do we go to school? Who gets to take the first bath? Do you think the chickens are lonely at Dixie? Papa, where is your office? Can we come see you?" On and on they prattled while Rose and Murphy looked at each other with gratitude in their eyes that this would not be a nightly affair.

Schools were the first priority. Rose, Bessie, and Mary were already registered in Miss Wills' school in Baton Rouge, and piano lessons were solved when Rose found a letter waiting for her at the Mansion:

Baton Rouge, La.
July 30, 1892

Mrs. M. J. Foster,
     Having organized a music class in this city and knowing that you intended to reside here, I write to you hoping to secure your little daughters as pupils. Can furnish you first-class recommendations, from teachers, in the Cincinnati Conservatory of Music, where I have spent

the past year and a half, fitting myself for the responsible position, as teacher. I received a fine certificate from that Institution, certifying my ability. Hoping to hear from you at an early date, I am very sincerely,

(Miss) Lucie Bates

Rose and Mary were naturals at the piano, but Bessie enjoyed neither the lessons nor the practice. Her father came home one day during her practice, and she was delighted to hear him remark to her mother, "Rose, I do feel we are spending money uselessly on Bessie's music lessons. Let her stop trying." Bessie's music career ended that day.

Since both Rose and Murphy were hospitable, the Mansion doors were always open. Callers came with their children; and whether walking, riding, or driving buggies or drays along North Boulevard, neighborhood residents were soon introduced to little girls playing hopscotch or waving at them. Their pony which lived in the side yard was an added attraction, and their rooster initiated wake-up calls to the neighborhood.

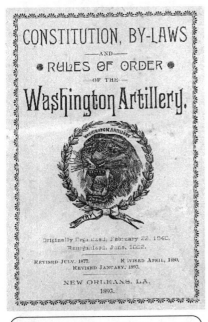

Constitution and by-laws of the Washington Artillery, 1893.

Not all was well in the state. Although Murphy was enjoying his family, the demands of his office were weighty and continuous. In the fall of 1892, a strike in New Orleans threatened the city. The first general strike in the nation to include both skilled and unskilled labor, it was called to establish collective bargaining and closed shops. When Murphy went down, he found a tense situation. Forty-two unions—including musicians, mercantile clerks, gas and water workers, electric light trimmers and streetcar drivers—were participating. Peaceful negotiations had proved futile, and violence seemed almost certain. To avoid rioting, Murphy called out the state's Washington Artillery and other militia units to maintain order, and he urged the people not to gather in crowds. His level-headed actions convinced the strikers of his serious intentions. He refused to recognize the unions as a body, but he negotiated with management to grant workers a higher pay scale and overtime pay.

As a result of his presence and his efforts, the strike lasted only three days and the grateful city gave Murphy a testimonial dinner to thank him for saving New Orleans from chaos. The papers in the city, which had never backed him in the lottery fight, became his staunch supporters. "Now," Rose told him, "it will be easier for me to read their editorials. They were not fair to you during the election." There was pride in the Capitol, too. The Daily Advocate of November 17, 1892, noted, "The New Orleans City Council, at its meeting Tuesday night, tendered a vote of thanks to Governor Foster for his action in settling the city's strike. Governor Foster ended peacefully what in many cities has ended violently."

In the spring of 1893, the Mississippi River flooded and thousands of people were left homeless. The governor arranged for refugee camps to be set up, and Rose, in an effort to alleviate suffering set up headquarters for the Ladies Aid Society in the Mansion to gather clothes and food for the victims.

Emergencies and special situations occurred almost daily. After the flood water subsided, Murphy was again called to New Orleans to participate in an important historical event. Varina Howell Davis, widow of Confederate States President Jefferson Davis, having decided to move her husband's remains from New Orleans to Richmond, Virginia, had been working for quite some time with the Jefferson Davis Monument Association and New Orleans officials to effect this transfer. The day selected for the interment in Richmond was May 31, Decoration Day [now Memorial Day], a day set aside by Southern women to honor their Confederate dead.

After President Davis's remains were disinterred from a vault in Metairie Cemetery, they were moved to Memorial Hall where a formal public ceremony was held with Murphy as the first speaker. He had prepared his speech carefully, sharing it with Rose and the girls after giving the children a brief history lesson on the Confederacy.

As he spoke, he recalled the first funeral of the President in 1889. Then he explained that Mrs. Davis had chosen Richmond as her husband's final resting place because it was the burial place for thousands of Confederate soldiers. Reminding those present that this gathering was not one to remember war, but to pay tribute to Davis's memory, he went on to say, " . . . when time has dissipated the sectionalism, as thank God it is rapidly doing, and mellowed the heart-burning of the great Civil War, then will Americans point with pride alike to Davis and Lee, Lincoln and Grant, and the great leaders on either side, as men of whom a people may be justly proud." He was careful to separate the South's reverence for its dead from any sectional implications, and his words served the notice of his hopes. With the ending of his remarks, the ceremony soon came to a close, and the coffin was put aboard a caisson and taken to a

Richmond-bound train which had scheduled many stops along the way to allow Southerners to pay their last respects.

The summer of 1893 brought another exciting trip. Chicago was having its World Columbian Exposition to celebrate the four hundredth anniversary of Christopher Columbus's voyages to the Americas. Each state was asked to participate and Louisiana enthusiastically accepted the invitation. Murphy and several of his staff members planned to go for the dedication of the Louisiana Building, but Rose received her own personal invitation.

The Louisiana Board of Managers
of the
World's Columbian Exposition
request the pleasure of your presence
at the

Dedicatory Ceremonies
of the
Louisiana State Building,
on Thursday afternoon, August tenth,
eighteen hundred and ninety three,
at three o'clock.
Jackson Park,
Chicago, Illinois.

Both Rose and the children, who were staying at Dixie for the summer, were delighted with the prospect of attending the World's Fair. She could leave the little ones with her mother-in-law and the Dixie staff and take Rose and Bessie with her. Her fanciful little essay on her trip (written several years later) indicates that the great Exposition interested her and that she enjoyed herself.

MY CABINET

Should these little reminiscences ever fall into strangers' hands I hope its title will not expect me to tell them of such august personages as cabinet ministers, for I have never been a ruler—if you will except my province of home and my seven little subjects—and I only wish to write a true history of my cabinet—a little oaken case that [illegible word] one corner of our dining room at the Mansion, the shelves of which are filled with little souvenirs, gathered here and there, the association connected with each constituting its value.

The upper shelves are filled with various little articles collected during my visit to the World's Fair that serve to bring to mind the scenes and recollections of that time more delightfully than all my past or future reading can do. I love my various little souvenirs, and so often it has occurred to me that I should jot down my many pleasant recollections, that I have at last yielded to my inclination, and if you will follow me I shall endeavor to make you understand why I value them so much.

To begin at the very beginning I feel that before describing some of the scenes of the "beautiful White City," I must first tell you of the delightful trip when, with the Washington Artillery Company of New Orleans, we left for Chicago the morning of August 5, 1893. Together with Mr. Foster, Rose and Bessie—our two eldest daughters— we left Baton Rouge on the fourth of August. On the need for accommodations, and after the train's usual daily trip, we reached New Orleans and the old Hotel Royale where we were joined by Mr. Foster's mother, his brothers Prescott and Don Foster, and Don's wife.

We reached Chicago on the evening of the 6th of August, 1893. We came on the "special" by the Illinois Central Railroad in company with the Washington Artillery and Mr. Foster's personal staff for the purpose of celebrating "Louisiana Day" and seeing as much as possible of the wonderful World's Fair.

I went with Rose and Bessie to the Fair the first morning. Also with us was Miss Kate Minor, a friend who is one of Louisiana's lady commissioners. She volunteered to act as my guide until I could get my "bearings" in the beautiful "White City."

After buying our tickets at the 57th Street entrance we went into the grounds, the children going through a separate pass gate from the one we took, owing to the difference in the price paid. The separate gates were only a few feet apart and we soon met, with smiling remarks made over the rapidity with which we had been ushered in.

Everyone is in a hurry in Chicago, and especially so in Jackson Park. We soon made our way with the crowd which, at this early hour in the morning, had their faces turned toward the ground.

We crossed the bridge just in front of the Eskimo's Village and went straight down the broad white walk with state buildings on either side until we came to our own state's building which stands modestly between the more impressive looking buildings of Minnesota and Missouri.

It is a building neither imposing nor beautiful, but to every Louisianian who is so fortunate as to visit the World's Fair, this simple structure holds out the promise of a warm welcome, and it is with state pride that they recognize the familiar outlines of an old time Southern home.

Among the souvenirs brought home and put in my cabinet:

> 18 little mother of pearl pitchers of all colors—green, navy blue, pale blue, lavender, yellow, one navy with a rosebud, and black and white.

> wooden slippers from Swedish building
> 3 cartridges (little cases)
> Pen Holders given at the Venetian glass works
> A Gypsy kettle of dogwood
> A Shamrock for Good Luck—The Grail may roam
> for many a mile
> But his heart is in his own green isle. (Quotation
> found on a Pine Box found in the Irish Exhibit).

Unfortunately, Rose's ponderous duties intervened, for she never finished her souvenir memoirs.

The weather in the area was so wonderful that Murphy persuaded her to stay and get a real change of climate. Reminding her that "I have been to the springs and spas many times for my health while you stayed home and took care of babies," he announced, "Now my dear wife, it is your turn. I'll go back and I'll stay at Dixie part of the time, and between Miss Wade and my mother we will take good care of the young ones. Rose and Bessie will have a good time and the experience [of a new place] will help their education."

Although Rose was hesitant, she knew he was right; the change would be beneficial, and the fact that her good friends, the Garigs and the Ballards, were also going to stay was an added inducement. They all stayed in the same boarding house—the Schofield Cottages in Kilbourn, Wisconsin. Rose and the girls stayed until mid-September. She was pleasantly surprised when she received her bill for the three of them—$28.00 for two-weeks' room and board.

Murphy did very well with all his responsibilities. Only in his last letter did Rose detect any plaintive notes: "I am in a world of trouble about public matters. One trouble is scarcely off before another is on. . . . Our people seem a little discontented and turbulent. But I presume this is the fate of all public men. I am getting along as well as can be expected under the circumstances. But I am so glad you are thriving in that cool weather. I want you to come home perfectly sound. Ma says the little ones are fine and Mary gave me a letter to send you . . ."

> Dear Mamma,
>   I want to see you so much. Hope you are having a nice time. The squirrels are fat as ever. Polly laughs and cries in the evenings. This evening, yours has a rising on his foot. We are all well and good.
>   Love to all
>   Your loving child
>   Mary.

After reading their letters, Rose knew that Murphy's martyrdom was wearing thin and that the children needed her. It was time to go home.

CHAPTER THIRTEEN

By the end of 1893, the family had adapted to its new life. Rose and Murphy made every effort to give the children a normal life despite their position. The children had neighborhood friends with whom they exchanged visits but only with permission. Mary forgot her mother's admonitions one day, and when Rose found where she had gone, she brought her home, put her in the corner, and made her recite a verse from Longfellow:

> Stay, stay at home, my heart, and rest
> Home keeping hearts are happiest
> For those who wander they know not where
> Are full of trouble and full of care
> To stay at home is best.

Mary never forgot the poem and taught it to both of her children.

Murphy enjoyed his home life and spent as much time as possible horseback riding with the children. With one or another of the children sitting in front of him and holding tightly to the pommel of the saddle, he savored his early evening rides. They became familiar figures around Baton Rouge. Prescott at age three had become so comfortable in the saddle that the governor began to allow him to sit alone while he led the horse.

Prescott Foster at age 3.

Murphy was not only a good father, but he was becoming a good governor. At the end of his first two years in office, this account appeared in a local publication:

> When Murphy J. Foster was inaugurated Governor of Louisiana he announced that he would, in all things, endeavor to do his duty to the people of the whole State. How well he has fulfilled his promise is well known to everybody. Taking his seat at a time when bad blood still existed among the factions, and matters generally were most unsettled, he has brought order out of chaos, cleared the atmosphere of clouds and has almost totally eradicated that feeling which marked his advent in office. This has not been accomplished without effort. A

wise head, true heart and Christian spirit were requisite to attain it and that it has been attained is to the eternal credit of our chief of state. . . . We cannot but feel safe while he remains our pilot. . . . " [from an un-dated news clipping found in a scrapbook]

On September 12, 1894, the citizens of the state were elated when word was received that Rose had given birth to a baby girl—Louisiana Navarro. The first girl to be born in the Mansion, her arrival brought many letters of congratula-tions, but Rose's favorite was from her old friend and classmate at St. Michaels—Caroline Tarlton Brady of Franklin:

> Your announcement of Miss Louisiana's birth arrived this morning. Oh, Rose I am so glad your trouble is over and the little one safe and sound. If she is like those who preceded her she is indeed worthy of the name given her. Whom does she resemble? And how are you feeling? But, Rose, you have those babies so easily I envy you. . . .
>
> Have you become wedded to society, Rose, or are you still the do-mestic Rose of old? I don't think you will ever change. Kiss the chil-dren for me and, dear Rose, God grant that you live long, have good health that you may enjoy the gifts of God bestowed on you in the form of your happy family. Believe me, always the same true friend.
>
> Caro

The name "Louisiana" was a bit difficult for the younger Fosters, so they called her "Nana." The public was so pleased with her being named after the state that they scarcely paid attention to "Navarro"—her middle name. Murphy had asked that she be given this name in honor of his great grandfather, Felix Martin Navarro, who had come over with the first Spanish governor after France ceded Louisiana to Spain. "I want her to have Navarro in her name; then she will remind us of both early and current Louisiana," Murphy told Rose.

Louisiana did seem to have a bit of flamenco in her nature. She started her flamboyant movements and noise-making very early in the form of colic. Her parents got very little sleep in that period. Upon returning from the Capitol after a very frustrating day, Murphy heard Louisiana's wails resounding off the walls. Cradling and bouncing the baby in his arms, he commented, "I declare, Rose, I don't know what gives us the most trouble—Louisiana, the state, or Lou-isiana, the infant." Once the colic subsided, however, she became a joy to all. As she grew, she was beautiful and fiery, and she danced a graceful tango.

Louisiana Navarro Foster

With six children, Rose tried to keep her social activities to a minimum, but she remained active in the Baton Rouge Women's Club which directed its efforts toward improving the appearance of the city. They encouraged tree planting along the boulevards and streets and held benefits to raise money for this purpose. Rose offered the Mansion for their bake sales and teas, and the children happily served as tea girls. The ladies also lobbied for grants from the legislature to bolster their cause, and in Baton Rouge today many of those one-hundred-year-old oaks, magnolias, and crepe myrtles stand as proof of their far-sighted efforts.

Christmas of 1894 was a special day in the Mansion. From the time the children were old enough to recite or sing, they had participated in the family pastime after supper—doing readings, song-fests, or reenacting scenes from children's stories or even famous Shakespearean scenes. The practice continued after they moved to Baton Rouge, and the young thespians were improving their skills rapidly. Knowing how much they enjoyed displaying their dramatic talents, Rose and Murphy decided to eliminate presents for all and give one special present to the group—a full stage. They hired a carpenter to construct one that could be left in the ballroom until an adult affair required its use. After the children went to bed on Christmas Eve, the carpenter and Rose and Murphy put up the stage. Then Rose and Murphy decorated it with a large "Merry Christmas" sign over the top and propped up one small present for each child around the stage. Mary reminisced to her children later: "When we woke up Christmas morning Mama and Papa took us downstairs, and they made us put our hands over our eyes, and then they led us into the ballroom, and then they said 'open your eyes' and there before us was this beautifully decorated stage with steps leading up and the 'Merry Christmas' sign staring at us and then they said 'Now everyone has to sing a song or say a poem or play a tune, and if you can, then you can join the Foster troupe of actors and actresses.' Oh my, I can still feel the chills and thrills we felt at that moment, and do you know we all remembered something we had learned and we took our turns and even Prescott sang 'Old MacDonald Had a Farm.' And did we have a good time with that stage all the rest of the years we lived in Baton Rouge! Later when L. S. U. boys used to come around to see Rose and Bessie, they helped us out on plays. We even gave Nana a part when she was about two years old. We dressed her up in one of Press's outfits and we let her be one of the orphans in *Oliver Twist*. We always celebrated birthdays with a reading or a song or scene from a play and the birthday girl or Prescott sat in a special chair and heard his or her praises sung."

In early 1895, Murphy went to Washington on business and from there he wrote Rose, "I am going to have lunch with President Cleveland tomorrow. . . . tell the girls I hope to get a glimpse of Ruth and Esther [the Cleveland's little daughters], for I know they are not as pretty and sweet and good as our own little daughters."

Rose and Murphy began the tradition of inviting the Baton Rouge Fire Department to their home after the parade which the firemen had every year to celebrate George Washington's birthday. There was only one complication; Murphy wanted to offer the guests a choice of drinks, but Rose objected, insisting that only fruit punch be served because of the children. She was afraid that the firemen would be thirsty after their strenuous efforts, and serving strong drinks would make them rowdy and noisy. Giving in but protesting that he was sure they would not enjoy themselves as much, Murphy predicted that the custom would soon die. But he was wrong; the temperate reception was held with plenty of cold punch and tasty food and with all the little Fosters joining in. There was community singing with young Rose and Mary taking turns at the piano, and the reception at the Mansion became an annual affair.

Louisiana had been enjoying a period of peace and prosperity under Foster. The state was sound financially, and a more harmonious relation existed among the political factions. This period, however, was only a lull between the storms. Congress under President Cleveland's Democratic administration passed the Wilson Tariff Bill, leaving sugar on the free list and causing a volley of protest from the Louisiana delegation and sugar interests. The planters, some of whom were personal and political friends, promised to bolt the Democratic party and

vote Republican. Thus, the harmony which the governor had so carefully nurtured was shattered. He refused to go along with the party break, saying "No one feels more deeply than I do. All that my family possess is wrapped up in sugar interests of St. Mary [Parish]. All of my associations are interwoven with that interest, yet my love for my state, its peace, happiness, and prosperity and my love for the Democratic party . . . cause me to cling closer to the party in the hour when many of its friends are leaving it. . . ." In spite of this plea for unity; he lost a great many supporters.

Another issue was that of free silver. Some wanted unlimited coinage; others insisted on keeping silver at a sixteen-to-one ratio to gold.

In the late summer of 1895, Rose, who with the children, was visiting Alice Wade at Ouida, received a letter from him explaining the necessity of his remaining in the capital. ". . . I am sorry I can't join you and Cousin Alice, but I am quite busy here. As the campaign approaches the number of visitors increase and each day since you left at least two or three, and sometimes eight or nine parties come to Baton Rouge to discuss the situation, etc. . . . I intended to go to the city tomorrow, but I am in receipt of telegrams and letters asking for appointments, and as they are important I shall have to abandon the city trip. Heard has returned, and his presence gives me a wise companion with whom to discuss our problems. . . ."

In October the factions who had been unhappy with Foster's stand on the tariff bill called a meeting in New Orleans to try to nominate someone to run against him, but were unsuccessful; and in December 1896 the State Nominating Committee renominated Foster by acclamation minus one vote. Other candidates on the ticket included R. S. Snyder, Jr., lieutenant governor; John T. Michel, secretary of state; A. V. Fournet, treasurer; W. W. Heard, auditor; M. J. Cunningham, attorney general; and J. V. Calhoun, superintendent of education.

Included in their platform was the prepared and endorsed suffrage amendment which was to be voted on in the state election. This amendment declared that, in addition to requiring the age and residence qualifications, the voter must be able to read the state constitution in his mother tongue or shall be a bona fide owner of property, real or personal, located in the state and assessed to him at a cash valuation of not less than $200.00. Because the Negroes at that time had little, if any education, and very few owned property, this requirement in effect deprived most of them of the voting privilege.

On Murphy's return from the Convention, he and Rose discussed this issue long into the night. Feelings against the extremes of Reconstruction and carpetbaggers, such as herding of long lines of Negroes who had been told how to vote, caused many hours of thoughtful analysis in those who were torn both ways. In speaking of his hard-arrived-at decision, Murphy defended it to Rose, "I know I shall be vilified for pushing this amendment. I wish extremes did not always get the attention. But we cannot allow this state to be governed by ignorance at the polls. One day we will see education take supremacy over basic emotions. And what we are championing today—the denial of the most basic premise of our democracy—will be repudiated. But right now something has to be done." Rose agreed, adding, "Extreme policies serve neither side. Reconstruction in Louisiana was worse than in any other Southern state. We had more carpetbaggers and scoundrels perpetrating fraud, and their lack of respect for the Negro was obvious in the way they herded them to the polls and told them how to vote. Now you and your administration, Mr. Foster, will be blamed forever for this."

Smiling, he answered, "Well you know this blame will come in later years. Our descendants will have to explain this to the critics. Right now my problem is the tariff bill and most of the sugar planters are going to want my scalp. We have a rough campaign ahead."

Rose chuckled. "It can't be any rougher than your first meeting with those reconstructionists in 1872 when you were elected on the McEnery ticket and you all were trying to meet, and President Grant sided with those awful Kellogg people, and you all were taken out of your meeting and marched to the drunkards' cell in the jail by General Longstreet and his soldiers."

"That's right. I had forgotten that, Rose. I remember I told you that story on our first buggy ride—I was so charmed by you, I just wanted to tell you everything, bad and good, then if you even spoke to me, I knew I'd have a chance with you."

"Well, you did impress me—so much that I removed General Longstreet's picture from my Confederate Generals book and replaced it with my father's picture. To think he would do that to his fellow Southerners."

"Just obeying orders, I guess. I must admit they didn't keep us there long. When Kellogg heard where they had put us he ordered us released immediately."

"I still say, dear husband, this upcoming campaign can't be any worse. You will have another four years; of this I am sure."

Rose was correct, but the campaign was a bitter one. The governor was accused of bossism, of deserting the sugar planters, and being a political schemer. Feelings were so high that it even affected the children. One day, Mary came home from school crying. "Papa, my friend, Jimmy S—— says he hates me because his papa hates you, and he's not going to play with me any more. What does it all mean?"

Murphy took Mary on his knee and patting her, said, "I don't know why Jimmy's papa doesn't like me. I never did anything for him. But when some people try to do too much for other people, those people get unhappy with themselves and they strike out at those who might be trying to help."

Rose reminded the children that since they were growing up, and with their father in politics, they must be prepared for more experiences like Mary had, and they were not to worry about it, because once campaigns are over the politicians usually make up. She added, "But each of you must take care of your dear papa any way that you can—write him, rub his head, walk with him and talk with him. You all will be the best tonic he can have."

Murphy, in New Orleans on Valentine's Day, received three valentines: one from Prescott, one from Willia, and one from Mary. Young Rose and Bessie wrote letters to him regularly, and when he came back from one trip, Rose delighted him with the news that another little Foster was on the way.

St. Valentine's Day greeting cards to Murphy J. Foster from Willia (left),
Prescott (center), and Mary (right).

When the April election was held, Murphy was re-elected, but the fusion party of Republicans and Populists wanted a recount, so it was three more weeks before Murphy was officially declared the winner. The suffrage amendment was defeated. Murphy lost his own and other sugar parishes, but one interesting feature of the election was that he carried more of the parishes with a majority of Negro voters than did his opponent, John N. Pharr. His comment to Rose was, "It is good that I have friends among both races."

CHAPTER FOURTEEN

In July the Fosters received an invitation from Mr. and Mrs. Henry Hester of New Orleans to join their party in their private railroad car for a two-weeks' trip to the Midwest. Their itinerary included Memphis; St Louis; Chicago; Madison, Wisconsin; Minnetonka Beach, Minnesota; and Dubuque, Iowa. Mr. Hester, secretary of the New Orleans Cotton Exchange and a strong supporter of the governor, felt that after the grueling campaign, he had well earned a nice vacation.

Rose, almost seven months pregnant, declined the invitation, so the Hesters suggested that she allow her twelve and fourteen-year-old daughters to go. Although a bit apprehensive, Rose agreed and she never regretted her decision; it was a trip neither girl ever forgot. Rose's sister Sarah, along with her four children, came to keep Rose and her four younger children company, and their visit was one for Rose to remember. The Mansion was a very busy place for those two weeks.

The traveling party left from New Orleans, and Memphis was their first stop. Two versions of their day in that city are preserved: a newspaper account from *The Memphis Scimitar* and young Rose's account of that day:

My dear Mama,

I am going to write to you and tell you how we spent the day in Memphis. I am writing at night on our way to St. Louis. I would have used a postal card, but as I have lots to tell you I am going to write a letter.

When we got on the train in New Orleans Tuesday they had a nice dinner for us which I enjoyed very much. We reached Memphis at 7 o'clock and, after eating breakfast, some very nice gentlemen came up in the car and Mr. Hester who knew them introduced them to us.

The Mayor was with them and they went off and got some carriages and brought their daughters and wives too, which made it very pleasant for us. We drove all around Memphis on Main Street and on the other principle roads.

As the Mayor was with us, we were allowed to drive on the large bridge over the Mississippi which is only for trains. It was just lovely, and I took some pictures of it.

We went to the Cotton Exchange where Papa and Mr. Hester were introduced to a lot of gentlemen. After dinner the men who had so kindly shown us around, got a street car and we went twelve miles out in the country to the summer resort where I took some more pictures.

We will arrive in St. Louis tomorrow morning. Mr. and Mrs. Hester are very nice and Mr. Hester Jr. is as nice as possible. Our car is just lovely. It is not the same one we went to Chicago on summer before last.

Although I am having such a nice time, I only wish, Mama, that I could let you take my place and for me to take all of your troubles, but never mind, if I can't help you now I can help you when I get older and I hope that, by you and Aunt Sarah being alone and quiet, you will feel better.

Give my love to all. You must excuse this writing and I don't think you can read it, but that's because I am writing on the train. Hoping that you will be much better, I am,

Your little daughter Rose

Post cards from Bess also kept their mother fully informed of their activities. The first one was from Chicago:

Dear Mama,

The air up here is so refreshing that I have been out taking in a little of it. We arrived here early this morning, and when I got up I found it necessary to put on my blazer. How are you all. You must keep well. Is Aunt Sarah with you? Papa told me to tell you he wrote you a long letter and I suppose he told you the news. Papa and Mr. Hester have gone to find Mr. Harrihan. All well. Love and kisses to all. Lovingly, Bess

July 19—We are about to leave Chicago. We received your telegram and were so glad to hear from you, and that you are all well, and Aunt Sarah is with you. Mama, I wish you would telegraph to us often. You can do so by sending them to Chicago, care of Mr. Harrihan and he will forward them. Mama, you must keep well and you and Aunt Sarah must have those nice times you always have together. PAPA HAS SHAVED OFF HIS BEARD! Love and kisses to you and Aunt Sarah. Lovingly, Bess

July 19—Dear Mama,

After driving around Madison we got on the train and we are now at Freeport, Illinois where we will stay an hour and then leave for Dubuque. My little watch keeps perfect time and I am delighted. Mama, I miss you all so much. Give my love and kisses to all. Lovingly, Bess

July 20, Dubuque—We are now in Dubuque and will go out in about an hour to see the city. My appetite is increasing all the time. I know you and Aunt Sarah are having a nice time but all the same I wish you were with us. Rose has taken 2 dozen pictures. Love and kisses, Bess

July 14—Minnetonka Beach—Dear Mama—We are already in sight of Minnetonka and if I make any mistakes, please excuse them. We are going out fishing in the lake this evening and how I hope I will catch lots of fish. We did not go to Minneapolis this evening, and we won't go until we come back. All well here. Lovingly, Bess

The Fosters enjoyed their trip immensely, but were happy to be home because they had all been concerned for Rose's health. On September 17, 1896, Martha Demaret Foster was welcomed into the Mansion by her happy parents and six siblings. Ten-year-old Mary managed to contain her happiness one day before writing to her friend Julie in Franklin.

725 North Boulevard
Baton Rouge, Louisiana
September 18, 1896

Dear Julie,
    I expect you heard about the other little baby that's come. It is the sweetest little baby! Her hair, what little she has, is just as black and it looks like it is going to curl . .
.
    You ought to see Nana [Louisiana] over the baby. Well, there is no more news. I must close. Love to all from your devoted friend.
                    Mary Lucy Foster

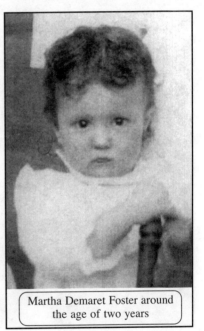

Martha Demaret Foster around the age of two years

In the spring, Rose, along with the five youngest children, made one of her regular visits to Ouida Plantation to see Alice Wade. Because of their studies, Rose and Bessie were left with their father. It was a happy but unexpectedly prolonged vacation. Instead of two weeks, the visit lasted almost two months because the Mississippi flooded, making both

Governor Foster without his customary beard

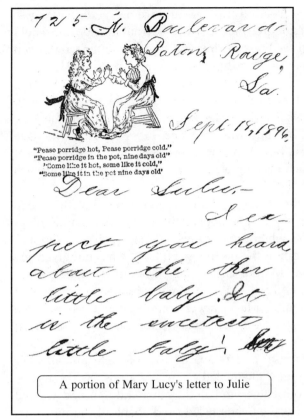

725. N. Baulevard
Baton Rouge,
La.

Sept 17, 1896

"Pease porridge hot, Pease porridge cold."
"Pease porridge in the pot, nine days old"
"Come like it hot, some like it cold,"
"Some like it in the pot nine days old'

Dear Sister,—
I ex-
pect you heard
about the other
little baby. It
is the sweetest
little baby! Mary

A portion of Mary Lucy's letter to Julie

roads and rails impassable. When the waters finally receded, the babies got sick; therefore Rose again had to postpone her return home until they were well enough to travel.

The older girls missed their mother and felt very neglected; however Rose's letters indicate that she was enjoying the peace and solitude of Ouida. The first card was from Bess:

> My dearest Mama, it has been almost a week since you left and this makes the sixth missive I have written to you and we have not had a line from you yet. I am going to write you two postals this evening. I have been feeling weak and faint and had short breath all day and now am feeling wretchedly. How are all of you. Won't they all soon be better so you can come back to your homesick Bess. Mama, please hurry and come back. I can enjoy nothing nor can look forward to anything for, as sure as I do, I see that space of time that has to be passed without you. Lovingly, Your daughter Bess

Rose responded to the plaintive note as soon as possible:

> Sunday morning
> Ouida, March 29, 1897
>
> My dear little girls,
>   I never look around for any of the children that I don't miss you two and I feel as though you ought to be right here with us. Yet I try to feel differently because I know this is for your good that I left you behind. You ought not to miss this time from your studies.

We have had a very pleasant trip here and we are getting along so nicely. Louisiana does not give me a particle of trouble and you would be amused if you could see Prescott dressing himself out and out, even to combing his own hair and washing his face and hands. He is the first one up in the morning, and, although I do not let him go beyond the front and back yard, he finds diversion in climbing trees and playing in the lot where the calves and pigs range. Now and then the little gang of pigs will get out into the yard and Press has the exquisite pleasure of moving them out. While it seems to me that there is a great deal of sameness in such past time he finds fresh pleasure in it each day.

Nana runs behind the others all the time and, while I always keep her in sight, she thinks she is as independent as the others and enjoys herself accordingly, and when night comes she sleeps like a top and wakes up bright and fresh in the morning. So far she has not given me any trouble whatsoever. Martha is the same dear little smiling baby that everybody praises and pets. Willia already romps and plays and looks so much better again. Mary never complains and seems to be enjoying herself too, so you see I have every reason to feel encouraged about the children.

Last night "Aunt Louisa" and I gave all five of them an "all over bath" and this morning they all smelled so fresh and sweet. Yesterday Aunt Sarah and I took our babies and all the other children and walked up to the woods known as the Evans woods and spent all the morning. We sat down and talked of old times when we were growing up here while our children romped and played under the trees within our sight. We had lunch and a jug of both water and milk and all together we had such a happy time.

I wish I could make you understand how much I feel refreshed by this sweet country which is so pure and fresh. As I sat in the woods, I wished for you all and Papa and the power to put into words a fitting description of the beauties of nature that surround us. I wish I could make you see it all as it appeared to me—the wild beauty of the woods where all the dark green of the magnolias, mingled with the pale green of the beech and elm, with here and there a glimpse of white and gold as the dogwood blossom and the yellow jasmine struggled to be seen. There came to me with the soft, fresh breeze a quiet satisfaction that has done me such good. I hope we have many lovely days like yesterday.

Monday morning—Although yesterday dawned bright and promising it soon began to grow cloudy and by night a perfect gale was blowing which ended with quite a storm. As a matter of course I thought of cyclones and tornadoes and everything that was fearful, and I did not close my eyes until the wind and rain had ceased. At the same time I kept up sufficient courage to hide my fears from the children and made them go to sleep with the assurance that there wasn't any danger.

This morning the day began quite as promising as it did yesterday, but is now so cloudy that I fear we are going to have a heavy rain once again. I do hope not, for the children love to be out of doors. The croquet set is a great source of pleasure to them and there is so much nice shade that even in the middle of the day they can still play outside and not get too much sun.

Aunt Sarah has such a sweet little baby and we all think it is improving. May God spare it to us is my silent prayer whenever I look at it, for Aunt Sarah and Grandma cling to it so that it is right pitiful to watch their anxiety about it.

I have thought of your Saturday night frolics and hope you have enjoyed it as much as usual. I want you to have all the pleasure that you can, only try to remember all that I wish my dear little girls to be. I hope that you will at all times remember never to be rough in your manners, and avoid all silly, ugly sounding slang that is so prevalent today, and above all be kind to each other.

Monday evening—Cousin Mary Ryland and Francina Brandon have just left after spending the evening, and as I want to get my letter off by tonight's messenger for mailing tomorrow I must hurry and close. I wish you would send me at once by mail some little half length stockings for Martha—2 pair black and 2 pair white. Also please send me all my shirt cuffs and a half dozen white collars like those you bought for yourselves. You can take my collars for yourselves as mine are too high in the throat for me. I send for these as Miss Walsh did not finish my waists with cuffs and collars as I requested her to do.

Remember me to Miss Anne and tell her I hope you girls are not giving her any trouble, and you must be considerate of her in every way. I hope it is needless to tell you to take good care of your father. With much love in which all join me.

Devotedly,
Your mother

This is another letter Rose wrote her daughters before returning home.

Ouida
April 20, 1897

My dear little girls,

The date of my letter brings to mind that just sixteen years ago to-day I was married, and being here at Ouida brings the day back to mind with even greater clarity. The sun shines just as brightly, the roses here on the gallery are blooming just as sweetly as they did that day, yet my heart is filled with sadness because your father is absent and your Aunt Annie and Aunt Sarah are gone, too—Aunt Sarah left last week to return home and your Aunt Annie has gone to her everlasting abode.

Instead of the happy stir and bustle that pervaded old Ouida that day, the house today is more quiet. "Grandma" goes about her domestic duties, I sit in my room writing quietly, and the stillness is broken only by the buzz of the bumble bees and the laughter of the children as they pursue them, for they, like Mr. Bakewell, seem bent on destroying the poor little bees.

Martha and your little cousin Annie, seated in their buggies at a safe distance in the shadow of the trees, look earnestly at the sport while Louisiana plays nearby with her tin cup and soap bubbles.

I am trying to draw you a picture of Ouida today. One day is very much like another—quiet, and yet never monotonous, for I am enjoying the perfect restfulness.

Children, you must not beg me to come home now. It is best for me and best for the children to stay here awhile, and you must not distress me by begging me to return. I miss you and your father dreadfully, and I feel each day like writing to tell you to come up here, but then I do not for I know it would make a break in your studies, and while these younger children can miss the time from school, you two cannot. Tell Miss Virginia not to expect the young ones to return for the closing exercises. I don't intend for them to go to school any more this season.

Martha is the same bright little baby and Nana is always getting off some remark that amuses everyone. Mary and Willia are very helpful, and even Prescott takes pride in being useful.

Now, my dear little daughters, you must be sweet and cheerful little girls, give us little trouble as possible and keep well. I have not received one newspaper since I came up from Baton Rouge and I miss the news so much. Rose, I would like you and Bess to send me a paper. Your father is kept so busy that I doubt he has the time and you can easily get them after he brings them home and has finished reading them. Also please send me The Baton Rouge Truth. I recently sub-scribed to it and my first issue came in March.

Did you send me the safety pins, toilet pins, hair pins and narrow tape or linen bobbin I asked you to send? I am making Martha sum-mer flannels and I need the bobbin as a drawstring around the neck.

The weather continues so cold that the children have all had to wear their shoes, and if it stays this cold another week or two they will need another pair apiece. I brought their old shoes but they have already finished them. Willia's rubbers have gone all to pieces and Prescott's have begun to do the same. Nana is the proudest mortal of her rubbers and she looks so cute in them.

Did you give those bills to your father as I told you to do? I hope so. I made a sort of memorandum of what bills are due outside of the statements I had, but the morning I left I settled some of them. I put the receipts in that same tin box. Your father gave me fifty dollars the morning I left, and as I had enough for my expenses up here I gave Bess ten of it for her guitar, paid Miss Bow and Miss Walsh 15 and then gave the rest to the servants for their salaries. Also paid the gardener.

Please go to Mr. Rosenfields and get the children tie shoes made out of cotton cloth. Mary wears 13, Willia 11, Prescott 10 and Louisiana 5. Also get 2 pairs of stockings apiece. After this I won't have any wants for a long time. Give your father my love and much love to you too.

Devotedly,
Mother

The girls sent postcards to their mother regularly, but by the time May came around, they were not just lonesome; they were concerned about their social obligations. Bessie's postcard was specific. Dated May 3, 1897, it read, "We received your last letter, Mama. Am so sorry about the baby being a little sick and we hope she will soon be well, but Mama, please, please, come home. You know we want to entertain the fraternity boys before May 17."

Reading this, Rose made a mental note to talk to Murphy about finding a nice and reasonably priced boarding school for Rose and Bess. They were too pretty and L. S. U. was too near.

Nature took its toll on Louisiana and her people throughout that year of 1897. As soon as the flood waters receded, a terrible hurricane hit the Louisiana coast causing more death and devastation. Then came the worst of all night-mares—the yellow fever epidemic. The first cases were reported late that summer between Baton Rouge and New Orleans.

The Foster family was vacationing at Dixie when word reached the gover-nor that the fever was spreading. Although the governor had to return to Baton

Rouge immediately, he and Rose decided that she and the children should stay at Dixie. The epidemic was not as deadly as the one in 1878, but the authorities took no chances and placed quarantine stations around the cities of Baton Rouge and New Orleans and even the little town of Franklin, which had some cases. Rose and Murphy were separated almost three months.

Quarantine enforcement camp, Baton Rouge

Not only was Baton Rouge quarantined, but vigilante camps were established to enforce the quarantine. A letter to Rose from her husband in September, 1897, described conditions in Baton Rouge:

> . . . I was so glad to get your letter and the three from the girls. I hope you are getting mine. I know nothing of the mail. Some days the mail comes and some days not. The Southern Pacific route is uncertain. This is why I wired you. It was more to show the perturbed condition of the public mind. Baton Rouge is practically deserted. The State House looks like an empty banquet hall. W. W. Heard, State Auditor, and Speaker Lee and all have left with their families, and it is estimated that at least one thousand of the people have left the city. All schools are closed, all public institutions shut down and all public meetings prohibited.

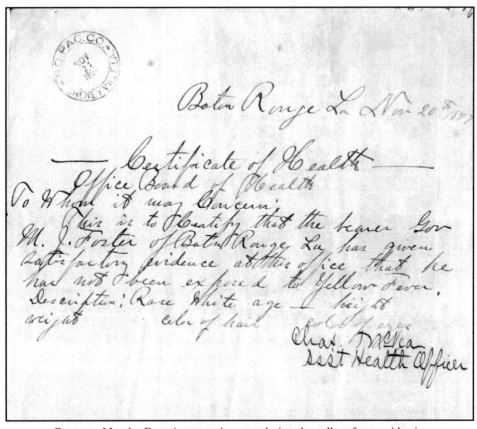

Governor Murphy Foster's quarantine pass during the yellow fever epidemic

I have a very lonely and lonesome life. The dreariness of the city is almost unbearable. I see no one but the few remaining officials and occasional citizens. I am keeping house with Aunt Lizzie duly installed. I tried the restaurant, but was taken with a little fever and concluded I could get along better and cheaper in milk, eggs and fifteen cent beefsteak than at a public hotel. I don't know whether the fever will get here or not. The situation is critical around us to say the least.

The outlook in New Orleans is rather gloomy, and the fever is daily increasing. Rose, it does seem as if our poor state is doomed—drought, pestilence and floods all in one year are enough to dishearten and discourage the bravest. . . .

By November the situation was still serious and Murphy was more depressed:

. . . The wind has suddenly whipped around to the north and its mournful mutterings on the outside make the library dreadfully lonesome. No one is here and I have a genuine and friendly feeling for a new dog which Robertson gave me today. He is lying here before the fire and seems to enjoy its afterglow. By the way, if I can't get you all back soon I will have as many dogs as children.

The good news is that there are no more new cases of fever and I think the worst is over and I hope, after tonight, all preventive regulations against us will be abolished. I made another attempt yesterday to get through Alexandria, but Mr. Bolton wired that the health authorities would permit no one to enter or pass through their city, so I will have to bide my time.

The convention meets here on the 9th and I am exceedingly anxious to get home [to Dixie] and return as it is important, in fact absolutely necessary that I should be in attendance.

The refugees are fast returning. Their tales of woe are interesting. Lt. Governor Snyder returned after a trip all over the continent and it is ludicrous to hear his experience. For instance, he and Heard, with their families and little children innocently stopped at Union City about six o'clock one evening. They had been up two nights with but little to eat. It was dusty and hot and they were literally fagged out, and poor Mrs. Snyder was so lame she could only walk with the aid of crutches. After they registered a policeman tapped them on the shoulder and told them they were wanted by the mayor.

When they arrived before his majesty they were charged with violating the quarantine regulations and rendered themselves liable to fine and imprisonment. Snyder says Heard made the "speech of his life," and after begging and pleading they were finally permitted to remain till the next morning when, with bag and baggage, they were escorted to the first train. Snyder says the people were almost mad enough to mob them.

They went to Nashville and there had trouble—thence to Arkansas and more trouble, and finally they reached their homes in north Louisiana.

I shall come home as soon as I can. I am sick of this life and when we meet it will be "for good" as our little ones say. Give them all my love and tell them their Papa wants to see them and their mama so much. . . .

The last weeks of the quarantine allowed Murphy to lay the groundwork for the 1898 Constitutional Convention, and in December, he wrote Rose ". . . I was so gratified to receive your words of praise in what my preparations have been with regards to our Convention next year. I wish I could describe how much I treasure such feelings on your part. While words of praise for my efforts are pouring in from every side, yet, Rose I would rather have one word of sincere praise from you than all these other flattering commendations. . . . I am trying to close the Convention work, the state's year end report, and then on to New Orleans to try to solve their very difficult Board Of Health problems as delicately as I can. I should be home in three or four days and we will have Christmas and New Years at Dixie."

The holidays were special that year. There had been so many separations that being together again as a family at Dixie nourished their spirits. On New Year's Eve Rose and Murphy enjoyed one of their late-night talks after all the children had gone to bed.

"Mr. Foster," Rose said, "I have a feeling this New Year will be a challenge for us. You have this Convention coming up, and I have to solve the problem of a school for Rose and Bess. I realized the importance of a school for them last spring when I was at Ouida and received cards from them urging me to come home by a certain day, for it was their turn to entertain those 'fraternity' boys from L. S. U."

Murphy chuckled. "Well, Rose, they are mighty pretty young ladies and Mary and Willia won't be far behind them. How old are they now? I lose track."

"Rose is fifteen; Bess, fourteen; Mary, eleven; and Willia, almost ten. Now Mary and Willia are fine in their day school in Baton Rouge, but Rose and Bessie need to be sent off to a boarding school where they can not only learn lessons, but social graces, and independence from their family while being carefully chaperoned."

Murphy added, "And a school that is not expensive. This is a foremost consideration too. I fear our work is going to be cut out for us. However I will do some careful inquiring when we go back to Baton Rouge."

"I plan to ask around, too," Rose offered. "I know my Aunt Mary Ker in Natchez will want them to come to Stanton Hall, but that is far too expensive, even though your salary has been raised to almost $5,000 now."

"Thank you for realizing this, Rose. Money is always such a problem, but we are blessed in so many other ways. Which reminds me—I hope to get more money for public education. Superintendent John McNeese of the Calcasieu Schools came to see me in December when we were laying the groundwork for the Convention. He wants us to include in our constitution an article which would authorize parishes to levy taxes on themselves for school purposes. I'm also going to try to get him some state money. We owe it to our citizens to get their children better public schools. There are so few of them now."

When Rose and the children returned to Baton Rouge after the holidays, she was almost as busy as her husband. She had to put the children back in school there and get the household to functioning again after the months of oc-cupation by her lonely husband and his dogs. She later said, "The first thing I had to do was to give the Mansion a good fumigating. It was very, very musty."

By the time the Constitutional Convention of 1898 was called to order on February 8, Rose was ready to welcome any of the one hundred thirty-four delegates as guests in her house, and although most of them stayed in hotels, some accepted the hospitality of the Fosters and enjoyed the atmosphere of home life and little children.

The delegates passed amendments on a variety of public-interest issues. The suffrage amendment restricted voting privileges to those who could read and write or had assets of at least $200. The Convention also passed an amend-ment which encouraged foreigners to take up residence in Louisiana. Public education got a big boost. Age limits for attendance were placed on students six to eighteen, and kindergartens were authorized from ages four to six. All state funds appropriated for schools were apportioned to different parishes on a per student basis.

Amendments relative to public offices and taxes were passed. The state superintendent's office was changed from appointive to elective with a four-year term. His salary was set at $2,000 per annum with the stipulation that the en-tire expense of his office would not exceed $4,000.00. A State Board of Education was established, as well as parish boards whose members were to be elected. A poll tax of $1.00, to be dedicated to public schools—but not to private ones—was levied on all adult males between twenty-one and sixty. Even the office of the governor had limits set. The new constitution stated that no person elected un-der this constitution was eligible to succeed himself, but that he could run again after being out of office for one or more terms. Thus Murphy J. Foster was the last governor to succeed himself until 1976. Days went into months as they negotiated, cut and added, compromised, pruned and sharpened, clarified and illuminated. The convention lasted over four months.

Meanwhile the country had other concerns. During the first week of the Convention, the battleship Maine was blown up in Havana harbor, and the Spanish-American War began. President McKinley called for volunteers, and Louisiana furnished two regiments of infantry and three batteries of artillery, but since the war lasted only four months, none of the volunteers saw any fight-ing. By the time the convention ended on May 15, 1898, the war was almost over.

CHAPTER FIFTEEN

After the convention the family returned to Dixie. Rose was pregnant again, and she appreciated the cooler country breezes. She and Murphy discussed selection of a school for the girls and decided before he returned to Baton Rouge on Southern Female College in West Point, Mississippi.

The girls and their parents had mixed feelings about their going away; therefore there had to be some discussion. It would be the first break in the family circle, but they all knew that was inevitable. The tuition was reasonable, their going together would ease their initial homesickness, and the school had a good reputation. It had been founded in 1854, first as Union College at Oxford, Mississippi, but later moved to West Point where they had better buildings and railroad advantages. Young ladies were taught "by precept and example to be thoughtful and prudent in preserving, developing and cultivating the body."

One hundred sixty-nine young ladies representing thirteen states, as well as fifty-nine local girls, were enrolled. The school's purpose was stated in the catalog: "to cultivate our students socially as well as to develop them mentally and physically. Our aim is to have them better prepared in both mind and heart to bear the responsibilities and enjoy the blessings of life. Teachers are instructed to meet the young ladies while promenading in the hall or on the campus and to show themselves friendly, kind and sympathetic on all occasions. . . ."

The school's regulations were also very clear. "Students will be charged board and tuition from the date of entrance until the close of school. There will be no refund except at the discretion of the committee. It shall be very discourteous for any parent to withdraw his daughter from the college before gaining the consent of the President. Pupils must not borrow nor lend money or any other valuables. All packages shall be prepaid. Young ladies should deposit their spending money with the President. They shall not be allowed to overdraw their deposit. Young ladies are advised to practice economy. A medical fee of $5.00 will be charged, and a competent physician will visit the college daily. The length of a school month is 28 days. No boxes or eatables allowed except by special permission of the Lady Principal."

Rose and Bessie read the catalog with their parents and agreed to abide by the rules. The Fosters appreciated the school's emphasis on language, literature, history, and music. They felt that these studies would be an intellectual continuation of what they had always shared with their children—awareness and appreciation of scholars and musicians, past and present.

Rose escaped a great deal of shopping in getting the girls' clothing ready because they were required to wear uniforms. The dress uniform, which could

C. M. Williams, Sec.,   Agatha Moseley, Lady Prin.,   A. N. Eshman, Pres.

West Point, Miss., *Dec. 7th,* 189*8*

M*iss* Bessie Foster

Gov.

In Account with **Southern Female College,**
La.

Extraordinary Advantages

In Music, Art and Elocution.

TERMS: 10¢ Interest after 10 days.

Dec 10   To 2nd Part of contract   148 | 10

According to announcement in the catalogue, Dec. 10" is our second collection day, therefore we send you this memorandum in advance, and beg leave to remain,

Very truly,

A. W. Hiran

Your daughters are doing good work. We wrote you at length about one month ago, concerning their progress, and we, beg leave to know whether or not you received said letter

A. W.

Receipt for tuition payment and report on Bessie Foster's academic progress,
Southern Female College

be made at the school after the students' arrival, was $9.33. The everyday uniform, shepherd plaid calico, could be made at home or at school. Always economical, Rose decided she could save money by getting their seamstress in Franklin to make them. They were registered for the 1898-99 term which began on September 1.

While Rose was busy at Dixie, her husband was in Baton Rouge with the legislators. A special session was held in August to give New Orleans and the parishes the right to issue bonds in order to pay for public improvements and to levy special taxes when they were petitioned to do so by at least a third of the property-owning taxpayers. The legislators also voted to appropriate $10,000 to make improvements on the State Capitol and surrounding grounds. Rose was instrumental in enlisting the support of the "Woman's Club," of which she was a member, to help with the project.

Included also was a small appropriation for the Mansion. Rose appreciated the funds, for in spite of the care she gave the Mansion, the natural wear and tear of six-and-a-half years caused by a large family was beginning to show. Since getting the girls off to school, having the baby, and getting her committee started on streets and capitol grounds improvements were her highest priorities for that year, she was pleased that the money would not be available until the following year.

The family missed the girls and everyone was delighted when the first letter arrived from the Southern Female Academy. It was from a homesick Bessie:

West Point, Mississippi
Tuesday, Sept. 11, 1898

Dear Mama and Papa,

We finally have a little time between classes and I shall write you all a few lines in answer to your sweet and much appreciated letters which we received last night.

You asked about the teachers, Mama. Well, some I like very well, others not so much. Most of them are graduates of this school, and I don't find them especially brilliant, but they can still teach us a great deal, I know.

We have now begun the regular routine of work, and it certainly keeps us busy going from one place to another. Rose and I have entered as Juniors and have some pretty hard studies, among these trigonometry.

They are very strict on you up here. Every time you turn around you are in danger of breaking some rule. If you spill anything on the table at meal times you have to pay a nickel.

Miss Jenkins, our music teacher wears her dresses to her ankles and talks in a mysterious manner. My guitar teacher is just lovely. Miss Campbell, the elocution teacher, recites very well and doesn't believe in anything like "ranting."

Rose's music teacher is a man with a high voice and I'm glad I don't have to take from him for I know I would giggle every time he sang. Miss Lease, the English teacher and Miss Mosley, the principal, frighten me to death—they are so particular. Last but not least is Mr. Eshman, always dignified with a pale smile now and then. He frightens me too.

But enough of school. I like it well enough and shall perk up in time, but how I miss you all. I am certainly sorry the fever is starting again in Franklin. I hope we have an early freeze and kill it out.

I wish I could come home with this letter. Thank the children for all their nice letters and with love for them and the servants I am

Your loving daughter,
Bess

Murphy James Foster, Jr., was born October 1. The news spread quickly that the Fosters finally had another son, and the governor received congratulatory messages on his namesake from all over the state. Rose was as delighted as he, and the new little boy's sisters and Prescott wrote a special play in his honor. Up in West Point, Mississippi, Rose and Bessie received a telegram announcing his arrival. Although welcoming a new member of the family was not new to them, they were very happy and more homesick than ever.

The yellow fever which had struck Franklin in September became an epidemic, and before it subsided, over six hundred cases had been confirmed. Eleven people died. Dr. Dixie Foster, Murphy's brother, sent his wife away from Franklin while he stayed to treat the sick. Then he, too, came down with the disease, but after several weeks he recovered. When his wife was allowed to come home, she wrote Rose: ". . .When I reached home I discovered a most decided yellow fever odor which still permeated the whole house. Though the hour was 2:00 A. M. I was very loathe to retire, fearful of fatal results. I have lost no time, Rose, in cleaning and moving and airing everything. I am just now beginning to feel comfortable here again. . . ."

By the spring of 1899, Rose and Murphy were ready to let out some contracts for improvements on the Mansion. As she later recounted, Mr. Foster said, "Rose, you are well suited to handle these contracts. Not only do you have the experience of overseeing Dixie, but you like to paint and fix and add on and you know this is not my strong point." Rose was in her element. Estimates came in, contractors were approved, and by the end of the summer, the Mansion was a much-improved place.

Baton Rouge April 25ᵗʰ 199

Mrs M. J. Foster.

City.

Madam.

I propose to do the following described work and to furnish the necessary material therefore for the sum of Four Hundred and Ninety Dollars #490 ⁰⁰⁄₀₀

To raise and level up wing building and to build 15 new pillars under same. To also rebuild the old ones where necessary

To put new ridge board on roof

To put in new Valley at intersection of main building and repair entire roof of wing

To put up new gutters on above building

To put up new gutters on Kitchen building

To repair Chimney top

To repair all blinds

To replace broken sash cord

To repair rear steps east end of gallery main building

To rebuild front steps

To ceil the front and rear gallery ceilings 2ⁿᵈ story main building

Contractor's estimate for repairs to the governor's mansion, Baton Rouge

With Murphy's gubernatorial years coming to an end, the Nominating Convention of 1899 was an important one, but one aspect of it was personally distressing to Rose and Murphy—a break between Murphy and his cousin Senator Donelson Caffery. The disagreement between them had begun during the 1896 Presidential election. Murphy had supported the Democratic nominee, William Jennings Bryan, who supported free silver. Caffery, considering this silver policy radicalism, supported the gold plank.

The 1899 convention began by nominating W. W. Heard for governor. The convention went on record in its platform approving Murphy's conservative and business-like administration. It complimented the governor for placing the state on a cash basis, and it pledged to continue his administrative policies. But Senator Caffery and his son, Donelson Caffery, Jr., bolted the convention and formed an opposition slate within the party. Suffrage and free coinage of silver took second place to the personal attacks on Murphy. They accused him of being a dictator and a boss. As the campaign progressed, the Heard ticket, supported by Murphy, increased its lead and on April 20, 1900, was elected by a 4-1 majority over the Caffery ticket.

Murphy's last day in office was May 21, 1900, and the next day, the Democratic legislature unanimously elected him to succeed Caffery at the expiration of his term on March 3, 1901. Credit is due to both the Caffery and Foster families that these bitter "turn of the century" political and philosophical differences did not affect their long ties of friendship between the families. Four generations later their friendship is as strong as ever.

Rose's last days in the Mansion were busy ones with farewell gatherings and packing and cleaning. There was letter writing to alert the members of the staff at Dixie to prepare for their imminent return. The Ladies' Club gave Rose a diamond watch; and Murphy's friends and associates surprised him with a party at the Grouchy Hotel, where they presented him with an initialized gold stop watch with repeater and split second, complete with chain. They also gave him a locket with a miniature of him and Rose on one side and a picture of their eight children on the other.

Rose and Bessie graduated from Southern Female Academy six days before their father's last day in office.

They, with Mary, who had completed her first year at Southern, returned to Baton Rouge in time to help with the final packing, and on the day of departure, dressing the younger ones and getting them to the station. With not a little sadness they left the big house that had been their home for eight years and the friends to whom they had grown so close. Those friends gave them a warm send off—candies and toys for the children and fond good-byes to their parents, and a promise from the Heards to check the Mansion for any left-behind juvenile treasures.

Rose and Bessie with their class at Southern Female Academy, ca. 1899

As they gathered the children and walked down the steps of the Mansion to the carriages that would start them on their journey to the train and back to their beloved Dixie, both Rose and her husband knew they had tried to serve their state well. A new chapter in their lives would begin.

Another group of friends and business associates greeted them in New Orleans where they were to change trains and continue their journey to Franklin on the Sunset Limited. Members of the Washington Artillery, local politicians, Rose's sister Sarah Towles and her family, Rose's close friend Miss Kate McCall met them at the station. With a few minutes to spare between trains, the nurses walked the three younger ones and friends took charge of the older ones while Murphy checked on the transfer of the many trunks and boxes. Rose enjoyed chatting with her friends.

By the time they reached Franklin, they were dusty and tired, but the days being long, they were able to reach Franklin before dark where they were met by the Fosters, the Tarltons, and Millings, and other friends who had sent their carriages to haul the luggage to Dixie. A brass band and enthusiastic cheers met them as they alighted from the train. Since there had been no rain, the road to Dixie was passable.

CHAPTER SIXTEEN

The Fosters welcomed Dixie, and Dixie welcomed them. It was good to be home, and better still to have the family all together again. Murphy would not take office as a senator until the following spring; and since his salary ended with his last day as governor, he planned to return to his law practice in Franklin.

Dixie Plantation House

The caretakers, John and Susan Williams, had readied the house, and Rose was thankful she had kept so many linens at Dixie. Susan had made the beds and filled the washstand pitchers with water. Rose designated two of the upstairs bedrooms for Rose, Bessie, Mary, and Willia, the four older children; and the third room for Prescott and Louisiana. The front room was left for guests. Rose and Murphy kept the two little children Martha and Murphy J. downstairs with them, while Louise Evans, the nurse; and Janie Crockett, the maid; stayed downstairs in a back bedroom.

There was much to be done to restore Dixie to its former state. Since he planned to replace them, Murphy had sold his horses, carriage, and other stock before they left Baton Rouge. Although several farm animals had been left on the place, he needed riding horses. Murphy and his daughters were equally excited about purchasing the horses, and eight-year-old Prescott was begging for a pony.

Rose Ker Foster with Sarah and Murphy J. Foster, Jr. (standing) (1903)

Rose immediately wrote to Cousin Alice Wade to visit her: "it is wonderful, dear cousin, to be back at Dixie, but I need you to help me get these myriad children and house organized. I have already told Mr. Foster the first thing we need is a bathroom. There are so many of us, and Franklin has real plumbers now and we can get the necessary fixtures. I plan to economize in other ways, but you must help me persuade Mr. Foster. He is more interested in horses, and he is still attached to taking his bath in front of the fireplace in his bedroom. For myself, with those little ones around us always, I prefer the quiet of a separate bathroom. And they certainly are getting popular. I have seen quite a few in Franklin. . . ."

The crop on Dixie that year was a fine one. Sugarcane was the major crop with cotton as a secondary one. The Dixie crops had been good during their absence; however, Rose, anticipating many expenses as their children grew, had saved some of that income.

In planning for the new bathroom Rose had begun to consider the layout of the house. It had two ells, named according to their location, the kitchen ell and the dairy ell. The latter was near the carriage house and barn, where the milk was brought and stored in crocks. Rose decided that when she had her bathroom built, she would put a little bedroom off the hall leading to the dairy ell for Martha when she grew older and did not want to share a room with her little brother. Rose knew that later the two boys would share a room, and Louisiana would graduate to the older girls' room when they left home.

Realizing that she could not move her large family to Washington on Murphy's $5,000-per-annum salary, and that if he lived alone, he could live more cheaply, she silently continued her plans to make Dixie accommodate her family and provide Murphy with as much family support as possible. She would visit him at least once or twice, and each of the older children would visit him once during each session. Then, between sessions, he would be home most of the time.

In another of their "after-the-children-are-in-bed" talks, they discussed their children's immediate future. He reflected, "Rose, the girls are growing fast. I don't think it will be too many years before we'll be having weddings at Dixie. Rose, Bess, and Mary—they're all mighty pretty."

"Yes, I've thought about that, too, Mr. Foster," Rose answered. But right now we have to get them educated and make Dixie a little more comfortable now that there are ten of us in the house instead of seven."

His eyes twinkled. "I know, Wife, like a bathroom, for instance?"

"Well, yes, that too. It's not just our large family, the girls are wanting to have house parties, and our living will be so much more comfortable. I hope Cousin Alice comes down from Ouida to give me moral support."

"Just remember, we have to replenish the stock and the poultry, and you know how the children love sheep and goats, and the fences need mending."

"I understand, and we will respect each other's selections. You let me improve Dixie when I have saved some income from the crops, and you feel free to buy your animals when you have a little extra from your earnings. And when the weddings come, I will have them as economically as possible."

"We can't neglect their education, either. Rose and Bessie can go to Natchez and attend Stanton Hall for a year. Doesn't your Aunt Mary Ker teach up there?"

"Yes, and she's a good teacher and she'll keep a motherly eye on them."

"Rose, we're really fortunate to have a good public school in Franklin. Mr. Ives, the principal, is a fine educator, and we are lucky to have him here. Mary and Willia can finish high school here, and before long Prescott, Louisiana, Martha and Murphy J. will be enrolled."

In the summer of 1900 an important member was added to the household— Angelle Verdun, a seamstress. With so many in the house, Rose could not keep up with all the sewing, and her friend Mrs. Milling, the wife of Murphy's new law partner, recommended Angelle, who came to Dixie to sew two days each week for the next forty years. Versatile and dexterous, she made clothes for col-lege-bound Rose and Bess to the youngest, as well as sheets, curtains, or any other sewing that the household needed. Etched in the minds of all who knew her was the small figure at Rose's sewing machine guiding the fabric under the presser foot while her feet rocked back and forth on the treadle. Angelle was of racial mixture, but she ate with neither the blacks nor the whites, preferring to take her meals at the machine. Always cheerful, and hiding what misgivings she might have had about her station in life, she became very dear to the chil-dren, always sharing in their delight of their new-found treasures with her "*Ahhh, mes enfants, très interessant.*" She had several children of her own but no apparent husband.

Murphy purchased three riding horses that summer, and Rose and Bess helped their father train them before they left for school.

About that time Rose and Murphy took a rare vacation. Murphy accepted an invitation to speak in California, and in addition to his wife, he took his two older daughters. His brother, Dr. Dixie Foster, also accompanied them. With the exception of Dixie, all had Southern Pacific passes; thus the family's trans-portation cost nothing and Murphy was given a stipend for speaking. It was essentially a sight-seeing trip, so they took in all the sights of nature that the area offered. They saw Yosemite National Park from horseback, or in the la-dies' case, muleback. Later when family and friends viewed the photographs taken there, they teased Rose about how utterly miserable she looked on top of her mule. She responded, "I don't know why they put Rose, Bess, and me atop mules and gave the horses to Mr. Foster, Dixie, and the guides; but I wouldn't have been any happier on a horse."

Rose with one of the family's riding horses, Dixie Plantation

Cousin Alice Wade arrived from Ouida shortly after their return home; and she not only helped Rose plan the first bathroom at Dixie, she also helped her plan the garden which would be planted. With ten family members, plus the household and yard staff to feed, it couldn't be small.

Her supplier was Joseph A. Schindler and Co. in New Orleans, with whom she had done business before going to Baton Rouge. With Franklin's temperate climate, she could plant all year long, depending upon which vegetables grew best during the different seasons.

After Rose and Bess left for Stanton Hall, the next four—Mary, Willia, Prescott, and Louisiana—were enrolled in the public school which included elementary grades one through seven and high school grades eight through graduation, at grade eleven. The enrollment of four new children gave the school a real boost. Murphy had long been a strong supporter of public education; both he and Rose felt that public education performed a special service in promoting understanding among children from diverse backgrounds.

The town of Franklin was growing. In their eight years in Baton Rouge and their involvement with Dixie when they were home, they had lost touch with the growth of the town and its civic improvements. Mr. Robicheaux's new city market had opened on Willow Street, complete with its own cold storage room. Most of the streets had been overlaid with shells, and some of the sidewalks concreted. To accommodate the increasing number of steamboats, a new dock had been built at the foot of Willow Street; and eight trains stopped at the depot or freight office each day. However, It would be a few years before the trains would cut down on the steamboat traffic.

A bill for seeds purchased by Rose

By the next spring, Rose and Murphy had gotten the domestic front on a firm footing. Horses, cows, a goat, a donkey named "Mutt," a pony for Prescott, and a surrey for Rose had been added to the pasture, chickens to the hen house, and ducks and turkey to their pens. With the farm and garden producing, the household should be self-sufficient.

Murphy reported to the Senate in early 1901. Mary later remembered how hard it was for them to tell their father goodbye. "Willia and I cried and Willia said, 'but Papa, who will you practice your speeches with?' You see, during his campaigns and other times he spoke, we took turns tagging along and listening when he was practicing his speeches. We all went to the station with him that day, and his last words to us were 'Remember to help your mother, and don't ever refuse to do what she asks you to do. I promise to do my best for you and our state, and I want each one of you to promise to write to me regularly.'"

CHAPTER SEVENTEEN

Rose found dealing with teenagers the next few years as busy and challenging as she had expected. She consented for Rose and Bess, young ladies now, to have their first house party in July, 1902. The party lasted from one to two weeks, depending on the distance the guests had to travel and the weather. At this first gathering, there were four girls and four boys. They were all quartered on the second floor—the boys on one side, the girls on the other. The success of their party will live on as long as the house at Dixie survives; it is etched into a pane of glass in one of the front upstairs hall windows.

Mary and Willia, fifteen and thirteen, respectively, had agreed to give up their room to the out-of-town guests. For their generosity, Rose granted special privileges to them: both to sit at the table with the older ones, Mary to play the piano, and Willia to join the chorus for the songfest. However they could not go on the hay rides and boat rides, nor could they join the card games. Rose assured them that their time would come; in another year or two they could have their own house party. Rose kept her promise, but to them the wait was interminable.

During this first house party, Rose took the whole group out to Cote Blanche Island on Vermilion Bay, a resort island with a long beach over which stood a bluff of about fifty feet.

The fresh air and the therapeutic salt water made it attractive to tourists, although there were some private homes there. Steps led from the top of the bluff down to the water; on top of the bluff was a covered platform where the less venturesome could sit on benches, enjoying the breezes while watching the frolic going on below. In the evening, the platform was used for very genteel "spooning." Since Rose had included in her group, Mary, Willia, Prescott, and Louisiana (as a part of their compensation), chaperoning was easy; the younger ones were eager to monitor the conduct of the older ones.

While Rose was managing children and house parties, her husband was having a busy initiation into the Senate. His reputation for honesty in government, as well as his innate tact and enjoyment of people, served him well in his relationships with fellow senators. His interests centered on preservation of the sugar tariff, control of railroads' rate legislation, and flood control in the Mississippi Valley, and he kept his constituents well informed with what was going on in these matters, which so vitally affected them. The old Cochran Hotel served as his Washington home; it gave special rates for members of Congress whose families were not with them.

Back at Dixie the times were exciting. Another daughter came into the family—Sarah Ker Foster. Born on August 12, 1903, she, like the others before her, was given a big welcome by the entire family, including the senator, who was

The Foster family during the Cote Blanche outing

home between sessions. While he was home a young banker came out to see him on business. Taking one look at Bess, he began a whirlwind courtship, and they became engaged in less than two months. In January, 1904, Bessie and Harry Penick were married.

In addition to these domestic de-velopments, the Louisiana political system was changing, and in 1903, a voter's primary system was devel-oped. Many newspapers and citizens had been calling for nomination of state officers by popular vote in a primary instead of in convention by delegates. Murphy agreed with the idea and said that if such a process became a reality, then he would run for his seat in a primary, even

A member of the Foster family out for a buggy ride, ca. 1903.

though his first term would not expire for three years. He also said he would not leave the Senate, which was in its Winter Session, to come home and cam-paign, based on his belief that if the people thought him worthy of the office, they would vote for him. At that time the Cuban Tariff Bill was being debated, and he wanted to remain in Washington to help protect the sugar industry.

Rose understood, but with a newborn and wedding preparations, she felt a bit overwhelmed. She also worried that his absence would affect the campaign. As in his other races, he had opposition; but he relied on his brief visits home, letters to the press, and campaign statements. These efforts did suffice, and the voters nominated him by a two-to-one vote. Then the legislature voted him in, not only for the remaining three years of his first term but for a second term beginning on March 4, 1907. Rose thought it was a wonderful tribute to her husband, and his successful election was announced only a few days before Bessie's wedding.

The wedding was held in the Dixie living room in front of the pier glass mirror. Rose and Mary, who had come home from Stanton Hall, and Willia were her attendants. Baby Sarah was brought in by her nurse for the exchanging of vows, thus giving all the guests a first look at her and of all the Fosters together. Rose smiled and Murphy beamed as they drank in all the compliments on their tenth child and congratulations on their first son-in-law.

In the fall of 1904, young Rose went to Washington to visit her father and then on to New York to visit a classmate. While in New York, she met Henry Miller, a young man from a wealthy family in Tarrytown, New York. His family was close to the Prince family with whom Rose was visiting in New York City. Since Henry worked on Wall Street and Rose was taking an advanced piano course, they saw each other often. Before Rose knew what was happening, her daughter had fallen in love. Concern on her part over the suddenness of this rebel-yankee courtship was probably matched by that of his parents, so the senator from Louisiana said he would go to New York City to accompany his daughter to Tarrytown to meet the Millers.

The visit was a huge success, and Murphy's letter to Rose reassured her. He wrote, "The Millers are an old and well-established family, and they have a handsome home on the Hudson. Our Rose's demeanor had won them over completely. Henry's devotion is total, and he has already asked me for her hand in marriage. I told him he would have to come to Louisiana and meet you and the children and he has already set the time when he can come. I think, dear wife, you will like him and his sisters, and their closeness reminds me of our own girls. . . ."

Rose and Henry Miller were married at Dixie in the early spring of 1905 and went back to New York to live.

Murphy was one of six senators selected that summer by President Teddy Roosevelt to accompany Secretary of War Taft on a good will trip to Japan, Hong Kong, and the Philippines. Rose assured him she had no doubt why he was chosen: "The President knows your ability to get along with people, Mr. Foster, as well as your knowledge of Philippine sugar interest. But you will need all the tact you can muster to ease their worries over your stand on sugar imports."

The last session of the Fifty-eighth Congress adjourned on March 3, thus giving Murphy almost four months with Rose and his children before he left to join the Taft group in San Francisco in early July. He had time to spend with each of the children, especially Baby Sarah. Mary and Willia, who were attending Potter College in Bowling Green, Kentucky, to complete their formal education, came home for the summer and had almost six weeks with their father before he left. He and the older girls rode horses and practiced the young ones in their equitation. The only cloud on the horizon appeared when Rose's letters arrived, telling of her anxiety over Henry's being unable to throw off a bad cold.

In between activities, Murphy was learning about the countries he was to visit. His study became a family affair with Rose and the children participating in regular study sessions on the history, geography, and climate of each country. They even anticipated the questions he might be asked while in those countries. He answered each question, and they rehearsed him just as they had in the years past for his political speeches. When the time came for him to board the Sunset Limited for California, they had all widened their knowledge of the Orient, the Philippines, and the Spanish-American War. They asked for presents, each with her own special requests. Kimonos were the favorite.

Besides his wife, Secretary Taft was taking the president's daughter, Alice Roosevelt. Since she was reputed to be the toast of Washington and a no-holds-barred conversationalist, the family teased Murphy about watching out for the unpredictable young lady, knowing he would charm her. He responded to them at the table on his last night, "Don't worry, daughters, she can't hold a candle to your mother."

The War Department kept Rose informed of Murphy's whereabouts. The first news came in a newspaper clipping from Honolulu, their first stop. In late July they were entertained in Japan before going to the Philippines. From Manila, they went to Hong Kong, and then back to Japan to return to America. His letters came frequently:

> Pacific Mail S. S. Company
> Aboard the S. S. Manchuria
> August 3, 1905

My dear Wife,

I wrote you a short letter mailed from Nagasaki giving a simple outline of our tour through Japan. Today I will try and give you a more

Alice Roosevelt and William Howard Taft aboard the S. S. *Manchuria*

CB

𝔚𝔞𝔯 𝔇𝔢𝔭𝔞𝔯𝔱𝔪𝔢𝔫𝔱,
𝔅𝔲𝔯𝔢𝔞𝔲 𝔬𝔣 𝔍𝔫𝔰𝔲𝔩𝔞𝔯 𝔄𝔣𝔣𝔞𝔦𝔯𝔰,
𝔚𝔞𝔰𝔥𝔦𝔫𝔤𝔱𝔬𝔫. 𝔇.𝔠̇.

August 28, 1905.

Madam:

In line with previous letters informing you of the movements of Secretary Taft's party, I beg to state that a cablegram has just been received stating that all are well and that they leave Manila for Hongkong August 31st and will return to the United States on the "Korea", due to sail from Hongkong September 6th and scheduled to arrive in San Francisco October 4th.

Very respectfully,

Captain, 19th U. S. Infantry,
Acting Chief of Bureau.

Mrs. Murphy J. Foster,
    Franklin, La.

War Department report regarding Murphy J. Foster

detailed description of this magnificent nation and the splendid and brilliant reception from the moment we put forth on their shores to the moment we left.

On the arrival of our ship early Tuesday morning in Japanese waters we were met by a number of launches decorated with the flags of Japan and the United States, carrying bands which were playing our national anthems. Sky rockets were fired off and the whole bay was alive with all kinds of water craft filled with American and Japanese officials and citizens, all cheering and welcoming us to their shores.

These craft formed an escort. As we approached Yokohama more and more joined us—the handsome yacht, the graceful sailing boat, old fashioned canoes, the famous sampan, a flat-bottomed boat curiously propelled by half-clad oarsmen, and all styles of new sailing boats peculiar to the people of the east.

The wharves were crowded with people. The American legation, the representative of the Japanese government, officers of the municipalities and ladies and gentlemen dressed in all manner and styles of dress and costumes—from the silk hat and Prince Albert coat to the sandalfooted and kimono-garbed native.

We were escorted to carriages which were in waiting, and we were conducted to one of the detached palaces of the Emperor where refreshments were served. From this moment on we became the guests of the emperor and his flowerland. It was truly a beautiful spot and one always remembered.

The next day was the Emperor's luncheon for our party. I am enclosing the menu and the seating arrangement and the card of my luncheon partner, a Miss Kasagawa. The palace is in the heart of Tokyo, so we took a short train ride from Yokohama, and at the depot were met by Imperial carriages. As we were driven down the streets toward the palace a steady line of people formed a curious and almost fantastic procession. It was almost like Mardi Gras in New Orleans. We were cheered from the beginning to the end of the ride.

At the luncheon were the members of the Royal household. Many ladies of rank were there and I thoroughly enjoyed meeting the Royal princesses, and their very senior officials. We removed our shoes and were given soft shoes and we sat on the floor, with a Japanese placed between the Americans. There was music in the background and it was a most unforgettable meal and experience. I will tell you the details when I get home.

The last night we were entertained at dinner by the merchants and bankers of Tokyo. In between these formal affairs, I called on our

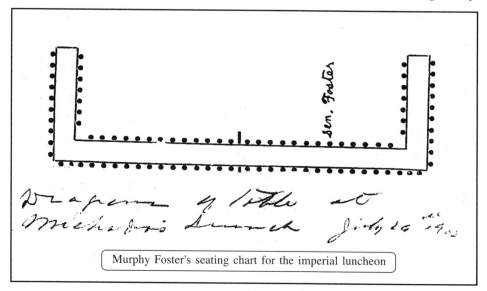

Murphy Foster's seating chart for the imperial luncheon

American minister, and the wives of General Okamura and Admiral Tojo (heroes of the war with Russia) called on Miss Roosevelt.

As I write this, I am hot. I am sitting here without a collar and my sleeves are rolled up. The nights in this immediate latitude are very warm.

We leave tomorrow for Manila and I must pack up. You can well imagine the process. The packing must be done in the hole of the boat and I dread it.

I have gotten some right pretty things for you and the children, but will do most of my purchasing on our return trip here after we visit Hong Kong, and before we leave for home. While I am having all this good time I think of you, dear Rose, more than you can know. How blessed I am, and how I want to be worthy of my beloved wife's love and confidence. I cannot tell you how happy I shall be to see you and the children again. I hope to write from Manila. I will be even busier there, for the sugar interests, I can assure you, are waiting for me!

With a heart full of love to you and children and my love to "Ma."

Affectionately your husband,
Murphy

U. S. Transport Logan,
August 14, 1905

My dear Wife,

We leave Manila in a few moments after a week of interrupted work and pleasure. The details of our stay I shall describe to you in a future letter. I have written you and other members of the family in every port we touched and I do hope the letters have come straight home, but I understand the delivery of the mail, or rather, the time of the mail reaching destinations is a little uncertain.

I cannot tell you, Rose dear, what my feelings were when I reached Manila and saw from the papers that yellow fever had made its dread appearance in New Orleans and in the state. Of course I do not know how much of the newspaper's report to believe, but I very much fear that the fever is now in an epidemic form and beyond all control.

The cablegrams report nearly three hundred deaths in New Orleans, and, if this is true, the disease is beyond all control and will more than likely spread, not only through the state, but more likely throughout the South. What this means I know too well. I cannot tell you, Wife, how perfectly desperate I felt, and still feel.

Your wire, of course, gave me great comfort, but I am still anxious and will continue to be all through this trip. What has become of Penick and Bess? My first thought was that they were in the hotbed and breeding place of the disease, and both being unacclimated, I actually dreaded, and still dread, the consequences for them.

Then you, my own dear wife, and all the little children, dearer than precious pearls to my life, are exposed, while here I am, helpless to comfort or to be of any assistance. I know that, in danger or trouble, the true spirit of the wife, the mother, and the fine, noble woman that you are, asserts itself even more. I have great confidence in you doing what is best and right. Yet, Rose, the situation must weigh so heavily upon you and I should be there to lighten and alleviate your load. I have never felt so miserable or helpless. When your answer to my cablegram came I was almost afraid to open it. When you said you were all right a great load was lifted from my mind.

My trip so far has been one of constant surprises and pleasure. I was surprised beyond expression at Manila. Its improvements, architecture, parks and places of public resort are all more or less modern and in contrast to Japan. Everything here is antipodal to us—the manners, customs, thoughts, everything is reserved. In Manila itself we find many Americans. They are officials, civil and military, with wives and families and they give an American appearance to this city, yet it belongs to another civilization.

With a heart full of love to you and each and every one of the children and my prayers that you remain well.

Affectionately your husband,
Murphy

The following is Rose's letter written to Murphy in San Francisco after his arrival from his trip to the Orient. The actual date of the letter was torn, but it was in late September since Murphy was due to arrive in the States around September 27, 1905.

September 1905

My dear Husband,

I am glad to welcome you back for it seems an age since you left. I wish I had only pleasant news for you, but this has been a very sad summer for all of us.

Henry died on the sixteenth of August up at Lake Placid. His case was that of galloping consumption, and although everything was done that was possible, nothing could save him, and yet he rallied so often that poor little Rose hoped until the very end. The end came peacefully. His heart was so weak that he turned on his side the night he died and said he wished to sleep, and in a very little while all was over without a struggle.

The saddest part of all is that not one of us could be with her. I could not go for yellow fever has been declared in the state since the 13th of July, and with it here in Pattersonville I did not dare leave the children, and Rose did not wish me to do so.

Harry and Bess have been all summer in New Orleans and they are still there. Bess, I think, wanted to leave, but Harry, like all those northern and western people, put business interest ahead of every other consideration, and as Bess could not leave him, she, too stayed. When the news of Henry's death came, I asked Bess to go to Rose, and Harry agreed to get a week's leave of absence but it was impossible for them to reach New York without going into a detention camp for twelve days, and so they had to give up going. I really believe everyone there would have been afraid of anyone from Louisiana, and perhaps it was for the best.

I would not tell you one word of all this until you reach home, but I feel that you must go to Rose at once from San Francisco. If you once get inside this state it will be almost impossible for you to get out of it. Rose writes that she is all right, but she weighs only 103 pounds and as I know, a physician goes to see her almost every day, I feel fearfully worried about her. I will not be satisfied until you see her, and I know this will also be your wish.

It is hard for us to have you so near us and then to wait still longer for your coming, but you will not have any trouble getting in from

New York, but would have a hard time getting into any other state from here.

Two nights ago I received your letter of August 14, written in Manilla, telling us of your having seen by the papers that we have yellow fever in Louisiana. Of course I knew it was more than probable that you would see it by the papers, and yet so long as there was a possibility of your not learning of it I deemed it best to not mention it in letters. We wished your trip to be of unalloyed pleasure, so Rose and I decided not to cable you of Henry's death. We knew you could do no good and we felt if you did know it would spoil your trip so we have purposely kept you in ignorance of our sorrow. This has been a hard summer and I am glad you have been spared the anxiety of it.

I have kept the children here at Dixie. Mrs. Milling kindly offered to make arrangements for us to go to Cote Blanche when her family and that of Prescott's [Foster] went out. I felt the fever could get there as well as here, and that here we would have every means at home of treating it, and at Cote Blanche we would be without everything needed.

I consider Prescott's trip out there a failure, for first, Emma was quite ill and had to return to New Iberia. Then Lelia's baby was quite sick and Martha and her baby became ill so they all had to return to town. Mrs. Milling has been having chills and fever ever since she went out, and I don't think she has returned yet.

Franklin, so far, has escaped, but how I do not know, for our quarantine was a farce at one time. My chief worry has been for Bess. I don't see how they can continue to escape the fever, although I must say that the nature of this fever is more like Dengue than Yellow Fever. Very few have died.

Dixie [Foster] and Tom Frere [both doctors] assured me that they would tell me of the first suspicious case and that, until then I need not be afraid of Franklin as things have gone on about the same. We have gone to town very seldom, but from time to time, we have had some from Franklin drop in here. But, I assure you, the first introduction of a "case" being in Franklin will find Dixie locked and barred to the outside world.

We have all kept well. Mary's friend, Perry Jones, was with us when the quarantine was declared and she has been a great source of pleasure and no trouble. She is cheerful, considerate and so sympathetic and helpful during our darkest hours.

We had some exciting times when the fever was first declared. Bess and Harry had been up the Sunday before and they insisted upon taking Murphy J. back with them. I consented for he had not been looking well and I hoped the trip would do him good. He had not been gone more than five days before Bess called me up by phone and said she was sending Murphy J. back that same day in the care of the conductor and she would explain by letter as she did not want to say any more on the phone. After we hung up I turned to Pres, who was standing by, and said I knew that Bess must have heard about Yellow Fever, and, sure enough, that was it.

I had sent Willia with them as far as New Orleans for she was going to see Effie Raymond in Baton Rouge. Willia, too, had looked frail. So as soon as Bess called about the fever in New Orleans, I called Willia and told her to take the next morning's train, and to come through New Orleans without stopping. I had checked with our Board of Health before I phoned her since I did not want her to get quarantined in New Orleans. She reached home without any incidents.

Sarah is now fine, but for a while she had been wretched owing to her cutting her jaw teeth and also having a number of boils. Now that the cool weather will soon be coming I feel sure she will soon be "ruling the house" once again. She is so sweet and attractive with it all that one doesn't rebel against her rule!

Mother has been with us ever since you left. We have all enjoyed your letters more than I can tell you. I shall assign them a place in my cabinet.

Mary and Prescott wrote several days ago and Willia wrote yesterday. I am sending this letter to the Palace Hotel and I feel sure you will ask them for mail. With ever so much love from all.

Your devoted wife
Rose

Mary later reminisced about the excitement when the Franklin station master told Warren Foster the approximate time the train would slow down in the Dixie fields and take the senator's trunks off the train. "Uncle Warren sent two wagons and a crew to pick up the trunks and take them to Dixie. Mama had gotten the trunk room off the downstairs back gallery cleared out just for Papa's trunks. He had the keys, so we couldn't get into them until he returned from seeing poor Rose, but how we speculated!! We all went down to the fields to see him wave to us, and we laughed and we cried to be so near to him and yet so far but we knew he had to go on up to Rose."

CHAPTER EIGHTEEN

In 1907 salaries of United States senators were raised from $5,000 to $7,500 per year [from inquiry to Senate Archives]. For the Fosters it could not have come at a better time. The cost of education, house repairs, and travel back and forth to Washington were all mounting up, and this extra income gave them both more peace of mind. It also allowed Rose to plan more improvements for Dixie.

She ordered and supervised the installation of gaslights into Dixie. In the 1890s it was discovered that calcium carbide mixed with water formed acetylene gas, which, when burned, gave out a bright light. By the 1900s, this system of lighting was popular in both homes and communities.

The system at Dixie was a great improvement, for until the gas lights were installed, approximately fifteen to twenty coal oil lamps had to be cleaned and their wicks trimmed every day. Although it was too expensive to install gas lights all over the house, they were placed in central areas, and even though they still had to be lighted, this task was far less time consuming than using coal oil lamps. Because of the danger of fire, a pump house, which contained the gas system, was placed at a safe distance from the house. Rose usually primed the pump herself, but Louisiana, the most mechanically inclined of the children, also learned the system and became Rose's chief assistant. The care and precautions Rose took in the installation enabled her to get, for an extra $30.00, a rider on their house insurance policy which included protection against any fire caused by their new lighting system.

Water for the kitchen and bathrooms came from the outside cisterns. These cisterns were elevated to allow gravity to force the water into the downstairs kitchen sink, tub, and lavatory.

With this project completed, she had a second bathroom built by enclosing a part of the upstairs back gallery, a pipe run from the cistern up the outside of the house, and a pump installed to carry the water up the pipe and into the bathtub. Living was getting easier all the time.

Cooking the food and heating the house required a great deal of wood and coal. The big stove in the kitchen had an oven and six burners. It was fired with wood, as were the fireplaces in the living and dining rooms, and two main bedrooms downstairs. The bedrooms upstairs had coal fireplaces, which were different from wood fire places in that they required an iron basket for the coal instead of andirons. Beside each fireplace sat a coal scuttle or a wood box, which the yardman kept filled. Every piece of newspaper was saved, especially in the winter, for lighting purposes.

Since Dixie had only six chimneys (four double and two single) to heat the entire house, small wood stoves with their own pipes were installed in the

DWELLING AND HOUSEHOLD FURNITURE FORM.

$ ...Nothing... On the.....two.....story..... frame.....Building, with....shingle.....Roof, and its additions, adjoining and communicating, occupied by...... .....assured...... ....as a Dwelling, including Foundations, Cisterns, Gas and Water Pipes and Connections, Gas Fixtures, and Electrical Equipments, Plumbing Work, Stationary Heating Apparatus, Door and Window Screens, Storm Doors and Windows, and all permanent fixtures belonging thereto and contained therein, situated..on his property known as "Dixie", about 1/2 mile South of Franklin, In St. Mary Parish, La...

$ ...1000......On Household and Kitchen Furniture, useful and ornamental, Beds, Bedding, Linen, Carpets, Curtains, Rugs, Pianoforte and other Musical Instruments, Piano or Organ Stool and Cover, Sewing Machine.

PERMIT TO USE ACETYLENE GAS.

In consideration of the following warranties on the part of the assured, permission is hereby granted to use Acetylene Gas on the premises described in this Policy, using a .... "Omega"..... Acetylene Gas Machine manufactured by The Sunlight Gas Machine Co., at New York.

The use of liquid Acetylene, or gas generated therefrom, or the location of an Acetylene Gas Machine on the premises described herein, is absolutely prohibited.

WARRANTED.

1. That the charging of the generator or the handling of calcium carbide shall be by daylight only.

2. That no artificial light shall be permitted within ten (10) feet, and that no fire shall be permitted within fifteen (15) feet of the generator.

3. That no calcium carbide shall be kept in the building where this Policy covers.

4. That no additions to or changes in the installation shall be made without notice to and the written consent of this company endorsed hereon.

CAUTIONS.

1. Calcium carbide should be kept in water tight metal cans, by itself, outside of any insured building, under lock and key, and where it is not exposed to the weather.

2. A regular time should be set for attending to and charging the apparatus during daylight hours only.

3. In charging generating chambers, clean all residuum carefully from the containers and remove it at once from the building. Separate the unexhausted carbide, if any, from the mass and return it to the container, adding new carbide as required. Be careful never to fill the container over the specified mark, as it is important to allow for the swelling of the carbide when it comes in contact with water. The proper action and economy of the machine is dependent upon the arrangement and amount of carbide placed in the generator. Carefully guard against the escape of gas.

4. Whenever recharging with carbide always replenish water supply.

5. Never deposit the residuum or exhausted material in the sewer pipes or near inflammable material.

6. Water tanks and water seals must always be kept filled with clean water.

7. Never install more than the equivalent of the number of half-foot burners for which the machine is rated.

8. Never test the generator or piping for leaks with a flame, and never apply flame to an outlet from which the burner has been removed.

9. Never use a lighted match, lamp, candle, lantern, or any open light near the machine.

10. See that the entire installation is in accordance with the rules of the National Board of Fire Underwriters, a copy of which may be obtained of your insurance agent, and obtain a written guarantee from the party installing same that these rules are complied with.

NOTE.—The failure to observe the above cautions is as liable to endanger LIFE as property.

This form attaches to, and is hereby made a part of Policy No..........29.23.............*of the* German American.......... *Insurance Company of*.........New York.

.... *Agents.*

.... *Agents.*

(left margin, vertical) JOHN C. LEWIS & CO., AGENTS, FRANKLIN, LA.

Insurance form permitting the Fosters to install a gas system at Dixie

smaller rooms. Their pipes were vented either to the outside or the ceiling. These stoves greatly improved the upstairs and downstairs halls; their pipes were three stories high to include the garret. Ever vigilant, Rose instilled fear and respect for fire in everyone, and no one went to bed without dousing every cinder in his stove or fireplace.

Fire did seriously threaten the house one time. Rose and Sarah were collecting eggs one afternoon when Sarah, then about six, called her mother's attention to the "big black smoke" at the top of the house. Rose called the yardman to run next door to the brick factory and ask the manager to send help. Then she sent Murphy J. racing to town on his pony to get help, while Mr. Bodin at the factory called on his workers to jump the fence into the Dixie yard and each bring a bucket. Forming a bucket brigade, they delivered water from the bayou, into the house and up the stairs to the attic, where the flames were just getting started. By the time help came from town, the heroes of the brick yard had saved the house. It had only one small hole in the roof. Apparently the hall stove pipes had overheated and charred the wood around the pipe until it burst into flames. When Murphy came home from Washington, he and Rose expressed their appreciation by having a picnic for all the workers at the brick factory.

Although prices were reasonable, there were always bills. To feed the household and the animals, to clothe and shoe them, to keep medicine in the house, and to pay for house repairs, Rose always had bills on her desk. She was regular in her payments, even if she could not always pay the full amount.

PHONE 222

FRANKLIN, LA. *Feb 29* 190*8*

MR. *M J Foster*

ST MARYS ——BOUGHT OF——

PACKING, ROPE, PAINTS, OILS, VARNISHES, BRUSHES, ETC. LIME, CEMENT AND SAND.

THE PLANTERS' HARDWARE COMPANY, LIMITED
——DEALERS IN——
HEAVY AND SHELF HARDWARE, PIPE AND FITTINGS,
SHIP CHANDLERY, ETC.
FARMING IMPLEMENTS, BUGGIES, PLOWS, TOOLS,
SADDLERY AND HARNESS, STOVES, ETC.

TERMS:—Strictly 30 Days, Interest After Maturity.—

Banner Print, Franklin

19 8 Pad Locks @ 85	2 80	
19 12 els Nails	48	
19 6 " " 10d	24	
19 8 " " 20d	12	
22 2 Reels Barb Wire 102/117) 219 els	9 32	
22 8 els Staples	40	
22 1 Hatchet	90	
25 Pr screen Door Hinges	15	14 41

Toward the beginning of his second term in the Senate, a Louisiana periodical published an article on Murphy and his family. Shown in the picture are Rose and Murphy and their five youngest children— Prescott, sixteen; Louisiana, twelve; Martha, ten; Murphy J., eight; and Sarah, three, along with some visiting cousins. Murphy J., anxious to get to school while the photographer and reporter were still there, was already astride his pony, Laura.

Murphy J. astride Laura

The oldest girls took their turns visiting their father in Washington. At one point during Mary's visit in 1906, Murphy wrote to Rose ". . . Mary is having a fine time, but she is keeping me busy. I have to help hook up her waist, comb her hair and see that her hat is on straight. I am becoming a first class maid. Next week she is going down to North Carolina with Senator Gregory's daughter for a visit. He will chaperone them down to Carolina and I have told Mary to come back in five days, for after that a visit becomes visitation . . ."

Prescott was fast growing up. At sixteen, he was sent by his parents to school in Ossining, New York. Since he had never been far away from home, Rose and Murphy selected the school because it was near his sister, Rose, who as a young widow, was still spending most of her time with her in-laws in Tarrytown. Mary chaperoned him on the trip up East before returning to Washington for her visit to their father. A letter from Mary to her mother tells a little about their trip:

August 1906

Dear Mama,

Pres and I had a really delightful trip, though the first day was quite warm. My cold, strange to relate, didn't bother me and I greased myself faithfully with Vaseline and Antiseptic....

Yesterday evening Rose met us at Jersey City and we came on out here to Braemaer [the Millers' house]. It is so beautiful here and Mrs. Miller and Janet have been so cordial and seem so glad to see us. Rose is sweeter than ever and looks so well. She seems perfectly delighted that Press has really gotten up here for school.

Pres, by the way, and please tell Willia, acted quite civilized about the mountains and the numbers of trains he saw after the first shock! Our trunks have not come as yet but I am sure they will. All of us miss all of you. I can hardly wait to see Papa. So much love, dear Mama, from your devoted daughter,

Mary

Pres did well in his northern school and from there, he went on to the University of Virginia.

During the early years of the twentieth century many showboats traveled the bayous, and Rose had her hands full when the children heard a calliope signaling that another showboat was on its way to Franklin to give a performance that night. After they dashed madly down to the bayou, their pleas would begin, "Mama, can we see the show tonight, please, please." Then along would come the showboat, with horn blowing, calliope belting out songs, and the carefully painted ladies waving and blowing kisses, while their tuxedoed gentlemen called out to the young Fosters to come. Rarely did Rose allow even the older girls to go to the shows and then they were chaperoned. The younger ones had to be content to see the glamorous boats and their actors from Dixie's back yard.

It would not be long before steamboats in general would cease to play the vital role they had once played in the commerce, travel, and entertainment in the South. Railroads were fast overtaking them. In 1909 a flotilla of the haunting paddle wheelers, with delegates led by President Taft, steamed down to a convention in New Orleans to show support for the continued use of steamboats as freight haulers. In spite of such efforts, the handwriting was on the wall, and as the years passed, they gradually disappeared.

Rose's beloved Cousin Alice Wade died in 1907. Rose and her sister Sarah Towles, buried her in the family cemetery at Ouida. Her tombstone reads "In Loving Memory of Alice."

Murphy 's mother died within a short time of Alice's death. With the passing of these two strong women, Rose and Murphy knew they were now the "older generation." Alice died at Ouida and Mrs. Foster in her home at Shady Retreat.

The children had known and loved them both, and their memories were kept alive by Rose and Murphy's recalling many of the stories about them.   Alice Wade's challenge of the Union soldier at Ellerslie, her hard work to raise her nieces and keep Ouida, and her devotion to them—these stories recounted by their parents, along with their visits to her through the years, created in the young Fosters a deep sense of commitment to all that she stood for.

Mary had her own special memory of Grandma Foster. One day when she was visiting at Dixie, Mary came tripping down the stairs in a new outfit. Her grandmother took one look and said, "Miss, that dress will never do. Your ankles are showing!" Mary answered, "Oh, but Grandma, it's the style," whereupon the lady from Shady Retreat answered, "Miss, if it were the style to kick your foot on a young man's shoulder, you would do it."

She told her daughter-in-law Rose that it was useless to try to get the gouges out of Dixie's hall floors. She had attended the wedding of General Pickett when he married "the Wilkins girl" at Dixie and remembered that many of Pickett's soldiers had come to the wedding in their uniforms, including their boots and spurs, which damaged Dixie's floors. To this day those spur marks are still on the floor. (Note: Mrs. Foster was referring to Sally Minge, the sister of Margaret Minge Wilkins, who lived at Dixie. Pickett and Sally Minge were married there in 1851).

In 1907 Paul Trowbridge, a local boy who had recently graduated from Vanderbilt Dental School, began visiting Dixie steadily. He had come home to Franklin to begin his practice. When the Fosters returned to Dixie from Baton Rouge, he was away at school and therefore did not know the Foster girls as well as did the other local boys. Rose and her daughters did, however, include him in house parties or dances when he was in town, and he was always the girls' favorite. Very handsome, lanky, and six feet tall, he was the youngest of four boys. His father had been mayor of Franklin but had died when Paul was only five. His mother reared him and his brothers at Shadyside Plantation, which was owned by her good friends the Barnetts, on Bayou Teche, about ten miles downstream from Dixie.

Rose and Murphy enjoyed him. They noticed his beautiful manners, his lovely sense of humor, his inclination toward practical jokes, his readiness to help others, and his sense of responsibility. They also noticed that he was paying more and more attention to Mary.

In the middle of June 1910, Mary and Paul were married in the Methodist Church with their reception at Dixie. After a honeymoon in Galveston, they established residence in Franklin.   The Fosters could not have been more pleased. Paul fit into the family almost naturally; he loved all Mary's siblings, and they loved him. His coming into the family was the beginning of a long and meaningful part of Rose's life, and Senator Foster and his new son-in-law were kindred spirits. Paul's interest in Dixie and the family gave Murphy more peace of mind than he had ever had during his months away from home

The children wrote their father regularly, and he kept in close touch with them.

In anticipation of her fiftieth birthday, Rose sent Murphy a new picture of herself. In his letter thanking her, he wrote ". . . Oh, Rose, looking at your lovely face makes me feel like a school boy again. I wish I could see you in person and give you a real kiss. Cousin Louis Murphy dropped by to see me and when he saw your picture he told me that your face showed him what a happy life we have had together. He made me feel even better and now all I think about is you and I need to think about the Senate's business. . . ."

January of the next year 1912 would bring national elections. Murphy planned to run again for his Senate seat, and Rose dreading another tiring campaign, hoped that he would have no opposition. However, in May 1911 Congressman Joseph Ransdell of Lake Providence announced his candidacy for Murphy's seat.

Congress being in Special Session all that summer, Murphy stayed in Washington most of the time. He fought long and hard to protect Louisiana's sugar interest which was being threatened by a bill before Congress to lower the tariff on sugar. When he succeeded in defeating the bill, he received for his efforts much credit in his home state. Congressman Ransdell, however, tried to discredit him by saying that he had done no more than any other senator from the sugar states and that he had been delinquent in helping the levee system and waterways in Louisiana.

The campaign began in earnest in the fall of 1911. Murphy opened his campaign at the Athenaeum in New Orleans on October 3rd. It was a hard-fought campaign with Murphy running on his past achievements as governor and Mr. Ransdell running more on local issues. He also used the facts that he was a North Louisianian and a Catholic. During the campaign many of Murphy's past supporters wrote or dropped by in person to say they felt they had to support Ransdell because they, too, were Catholics.

In December 1911, Murphy was defeated in his race for another term in the U. S. Senate by over 5,000 votes out of 110,000 cast. Sectionalism entered into the voting, for Murphy carried most of the southern parishes while Ransdell carried all of North Louisiana.

All of the Foster family was disappointed, but in trying to keep their spirits up Murphy reminded them of all the campaigns he had won and then told them to think about how the families of his defeated opponents had felt. He

Portrait of Rose Ker Foster, 1910

insisted that he had no regrets because the people had spoken and that life would go on. Since his term would not end until March 13, 1913, he promised them and the voters that he would continue to do his very best for them and for Louisiana.

Rose tried to be philosophical, but it was hard. She later said that she felt the hurt more than Murphy did. His mail was heavy, and the following two letters epitomize the contrast in emotional reactions involved in all political battles. The first is a letter from Prescott, then a student at the University of Virginia:

January 24, 1912

Dear Father,

Mother's telegram has just come and I hardly know how to write. To think that a people could be so ungrateful and treacherous to a man like you is beyond me. I know you want me to act like a man, and I am trying to, but it is SO HARD. Because I know you would have it, I am trying to keep myself from being too bitter.

Father, a man ought not to want to be senator for a people that will treat a man as Louisiana has treated you. You have given all of your time to raise the state and the people in it and this is your thanks.

I couldn't understand why people have been so bitter but now I can. When a young fellow sees a demonstration like this it makes him feel, "Why be good and upright, and why should you be anything but selfish? Right doesn't conquer, but the man who wins is the one who appeals to the baser natures of the mob."

I want to be with you, but I am glad I am not. I am too young to feel this way, but I want to kill the men who have wronged and betrayed you. I would really be afraid to meet one of those men for I would have a wild desire to hit anyone who was mixed up in this fight. If it had been an issue of merit and he had won, it could not hold a candle to you and the tenor of his entire campaign proved this.

I don't suppose that you have ever known how deep my affection is for you, and how this whole affair hurts me. I'll be through college in one more year, and, together we will start out. For me it will be greater than all the education in the books. I want to be with you and I want to leave right now. I know that there is nothing I can do but I want to be with you.

I am still hoping that there is some mistake in the returns, and I will wait every minute for another telegram. I know how hurt and disappointed you must be. But it is not a case of where you have done anything wrong. It is a case where mean and petty politicians tried to benefit themselves.

Father, the whole South is changing. The real, intellectual southern statesman is no longer the demand of the people, but it is the professional politician who will beg from them and lower himself any depth to get their support.

Write me as soon as you can and remember, Father, that if there was anything I could do, I would come to you right now. My duty to you, though, is to stay here and finish so I can be with you in a year.

Your devoted son,
Prescott

Life did go on. A March 12 letter from her husband contained a proposal: "I will come home in May, and if you will meet me in New Orleans and then we will go to Baton Rouge. I will select and send you your day gown material and you will get it made up in the most up-to-date fashion. . . ." She accepted his proposal and their reception in Baton Rouge was a very warm one.

CHAPTER NINETEEN

Later in 1912 Rose received word that her husband was ill in Washington. Since both of them had always had excellent health, the news was quite unexpected. The diagnosis was kidney dysfunction complicated by a heart condition. His doctor wrote Rose that he had secured a nurse for her husband and that he was a good patient except when he insisted on going to the Senate for important votes.

Rose asked Mary and Paul to stay at Dixie with the younger children so that she could go to Washington to see about Murphy. With daughter Willia accompanying her, they made the trip. They found him frail but in good spirits, and as soon as he could travel, they took him to Wytheville, Virginia, for rest and recuperation in the cooler air. While there, the senator received a letter from Paul bringing them all the news from Dixie and replying to a previous request from the Fosters that he and Mary move down to Dixie:

Franklin, La.
July 23, 1912

My dear Senator:

Was glad to know that you and the Madam are in Virginia. Hope you are feeling better, but don't overlook the fact that we are going to be just as glad to see you as the Madam and Willia were. All are well at Dixie and the children are as good as gold, and they have great respect for Mary and her management. We have great games of croquet every day, and, of course we get in the same arguments as usual over same.

The horses, cows, chickens, geese and ducks are all in good condition. The cats are especially in fine shape, and with the two new families that have arrived since the Madam left, and the new ones that are due to come within the near future, I expect to have enough by the time you arrive home to pull the carriage. I will have some at the depot to meet you. Of course, they might be so glad to see you that they will break out of harness when you leave the train. In that case you will have to walk home with the Madam, Willia and the serenading cats following. It is going to be a great day when you do get home and I know you, especially, will appreciate your reception.

It hasn't rained here since Sunday, but looks a little like it might at any time. The roads are not bad at all, and would be fine if they only had half a chance. When you get home I will be glad to discuss the

Dixie proposition that you mentioned in your letter to me. It's possible I think we could work things out.

Mary is feeling and looking fine now and I also feel extra good these days. Since I stopped smoking I weigh more than I did before my illness. From all accounts it looks like Tom Milling is going to win his race for District Attorney in St. Mary Parish and I sincerely hope he will.

Please tell the Madam that the feed is holding out alright, and the man is taking good care of the horses. The cook and house girl are also doing fine. We have breakfast at eight, dinner at one and supper at seven. Everyone seems pleased with the schedule. No matter who is late for meals, he or she has to suffer the consequences, but, so far, everyone is on time. On Sundays dinner is served promptly at noon and the servants get away early.

Murphy J. has gotten his jumper fixed and looks like a real jockey driving "Hobo" in it. We were all so glad to get the letter and postals from you Sunday, and to know that you are having a restful and beneficial visit. Will write again before you all leave. Our love to you and the Madam and Willia.

As ever, Paul

Murphy improved considerably in the two weeks in Virginia with Rose, and by August he was able to return to Washington for the last days of the session. Although they were still uneasy that he might have a relapse if his schedule became too strenuous, Rose and Willia returned to Dixie. Rose was eager for the session to conclude, knowing that the best medicine for him was to come home to her and the family and the animals.

When Murphy returned to Washington in December for his last months as a senator, he seemed fully recovered. One of his last letters to Rose from Washington arrived in late February:

Senate Chamber
Washington, D. C.
February 21, 1913

My dear Wife,

I am sending quite a number of boxes containing books and memorabilia of some years accumulation, and I suggest that you leave these things to be stored after I return. We shall have an interesting time finding space for them!

I am getting impatient about leaving here. While I shall sever strong ties of friendship with many of my friends, yet I know I am coming back home to far sweeter and tenderer companionship—that of my wife.

With much love,
Affectionately
Murphy

On March 3, 1913, his term of office expired. The Louisiana congressional delegation, in a gesture which proved the high regard which all political factions of the state felt for Murphy personally, unanimously recommended to President Wilson his appointment to the post of Collector of Customs in New Orleans. When President Wilson sent his nomination to the Senate, it was again unanimously approved.

Federal Customs House at New Orleans

During his last days in office, the Fosters and Trowbridges (Mary and her husband) made a decision that they would move down to Dixie, not only because of Murphy's health, but also because Mary and Paul were devoted to the place and such combinations of household were not unusual then. They all preferred that the move should be done after Murphy returned from Washington for the last time since this interim would give Mary and Paul time to transform what had been the milking ell at Dixie into their own private quarters. Knowing that they liked to socialize with other young people in town, Rose encouraged them to have their own entrance. Meals would be shared, as well as the rest of the house.

Murphy returned to Dixie in early March and stayed until he assumed his new position. Once again he was away from home, but this time it would be easier. The distance between Dixie and New Orleans was only one hundred miles, and the train service being excellent, he came home frequently. Not only was his traveling easier, his mind was easier knowing that the Trowbridges lived there with Rose.

Murphy assumed the post of thirty-eighth Collector of Customs in the port of New Orleans in August, 1914. Under the jurisdiction of the U. S. Treasury Department, his office was responsible for the collection of foreign goods brought into one of the nation's busiest ports. Because the revenues generated were substantial, there was a safe there which could hold 150,000,000 silver dollars. Revenue collection was not a small operation, for until 1913 when the income tax law was passed, tariffs brought in a large part of the federal government's revenue.

That same summer Europe was plunged into war with the assassination of

Rose on the running board of the Fosters' Chalmers touring car with her three eldest grandchildren (left to right): Rose Milling, Elizabeth Trowbridge, and Murphy Milling, 1916.

Archduke Ferdinand of Austria-Hungary, and although President Wilson proclaimed neutrality, America was put on alert, especially port cities such as New Orleans. Ships leaving the port of New Orleans were often intercepted, and Britain, because she ruled the seas at that time, would confiscate any goods which she suspected America might be sending to Germany's neutral neighbors. At the same time goods being sent to America from suspicious countries were intercepted. After awhile American anger cooled, and the country learned to live with British regulations and supported the British blockade. For a time the Foster family was affected but little by the war; later Prescott volunteered for the army.

Rose welcomed having her husband near again, and Dixie once again hummed along with everyone in place and satisfied. They rejoiced together in December, 1915, when Mary gave birth to a daughter, Mary Elizabeth Trowbridge, and again when several marriage plans were announced.

Rose's seamstress, Angelle Verdun, came to Dixie almost every day, along with another seamstress, Sally Runk, who was in charge of weddings, bridesmaid dresses, and trousseaus. Rose,

Murphy J. Foster
and Elizabeth Trowbridge, 1917

whose husband had died shortly after their marriage, married a young Franklin lawyer, Tom Milling; and Willia married John B. Hyde, a former classmate of Prescott's at Virginia. Shortly after their marriage, Prescott married his childhood sweetheart, Willie Palfrey, just before joining the army. The next year in April, Louisiana married a young surgeon, Lewis Crawford of New Orleans.

About the time the last of the weddings occurred, America declared war on Germany—April 7, 1917. Having two sons of fighting age, Rose experienced the usual motherly concerns about them. Murphy J was eighteen and finishing his sophomore year at the University of Virginia. Because of financial considerations—travel, out-of-state-tuition, and living expenses—he entered L. S. U., but he was far more interested in following his brother Pres, into the service. Since both Rose and Murphy urged him to wait a while, he joined the R. O. T. C. at L. S. U., but he still wanted to volunteer. Letters such as the following came often.

October 11

Dear Mother and Father,

Things have been pretty lonely over here in the barracks lately. These old cold rooms combined with Reveille at 6:30 AM on these cold mornings have a tendency to make a fellow rather blue. I am used to things, however, and nothing has any effect upon me. Even when I walked out from a quiz this morning in zoology and saw half the class answering the questions with books wide open, my blood didn't chill as it would have over such a sight at UVA.

Don't consider this a down and out letter, because I am in fine health and in very good spirits. I like it over here very much, and don't really mind the barracks so very much. I don't even miss being deprived of so many liberties and comforts nearly as much as I first thought I would. Of course I've met some awfully hard and tough fellows over here, but I have decided that the best thing to do is to meet these fellows fifty-fifty—talk out the corner of your mouth and be a real tough guy with them, and you'll find that these fellows will look up to you and do anything in the world for you.

I've found out that, even though I did enjoy two years of luxury at Virginia with the aristocrats, it does not pay to try to carry out the old aristocratic method over here. This is a democratic school from start to finish, and, after all, I believe that this type of school is better in the end. It is good for me, however, that I spent those two years in Virginia before coming here, rather than spending my first two years here and then going to Virginia.

Mother, not to bring up again an old subject over which many bloody battles were fought this summer, but whenever you and Father give me the word I am ready to go and take the aviation examination and try to go along with old Pres, and put the family on the map in this awful war. I don't know why, but I don't feel right at this time. When Pres has to really go into active service it is going to be almost impossible for me to keep out of some branch of the service. Remember, the age limit in the aviation service is nineteen.

Don't worry and think I might do anything rash on the spur of the moment, but I do want you all to be thinking along this line. Remember, I will go whenever you say the word.

To change the subject did Uncle Warren ever get his complication with Maggie straightened out? I know, Father, how you have worried about this and what grave importance this is to Uncle Warren. I am anxious to know if things were ever patched up?

Mother, will you please do me a favor by getting Mr. Gaston (Sigur) to send me a good sized bottle of that sulphur preparation. My skin is pretty good shape now, and I desire to keep it so. I think this preparation is as good as any I could use. Thanks.

I want like thunder to get a furlough at Thanksgiving and come back to Dixie for a day or so at least. The boys all tell me that it will be pretty hard to get. Maybe, Father, you could use the old pull but I know this is not likely!

If I can get home, I hope to get in a hunt or so and, with my military training of snapping empty guns, I shudder to think of what will happen to the poor little doves.

It is almost time for taps, and must run down and obey Article 25 in the Blue Book which commands every cadet to take a bath at least once a week. With a world of love to each and all.

Your devoted son,
Murphy J.

In the meantime, Prescott was training in San Antonio. Since officers had to buy their own uniforms, he had his troubles, too.

The St. Anthony
San Antonio, Texas
December 18, 1917

Dear Father,

Excuse the pencil, but I must write you hurriedly why I called upon you to get the money for Willie's trip. In the first place I just cannot be away from Willie on what may be my last Christmas, when it is possible for her to be with me.

When I was at home, I bought just about all the equipment that I thought I needed including the kind of suits I was ordered to get, and I had all of the money that was necessary to get me through.

This morning an order was read to us changing all of our equipment and ordering us to purchase at once a list of articles that will just about break a millionaire.

You know I came into this army with all kinds of ideas about the perfection of our country, and that a great many of the criticisms of it were unjust, but I have certainly received some terrible jolts.

I did not mind the training at all, but since we have been commissioned, we are now going to another school, drilling etc. just like we did. If some officer decides in his mind that I will not make a good officer, I will probably lose my commission. I joined the army to fight, but here I am, stuck off in some depot Brigade, and may stay here for the rest of the year. Kemper Williams and all of my other friends are here too.

To get back to this order though—our country is arguing over a whole lot of details and, as you know the men have not been issued rifles or uniforms. Yet we have to buy about seven hundred dollars worth of equipment, and buy it at once.

If you can arrange that money for Willie, and maybe fifty dollars more, then, if the government calls for me, I will give up my commission. I suppose I should have saved enough money in my work to pay for all of these things in cash, but I don't know anyone who has.

The only cheerful news that I can tell you is that (unless I lose my commission) it looks like I will be in the country another six months or more in this depot Brigade. Of course this is far from cheerful to me. I will try to write you soon when I am more optimistic.

With love to all,

Prescott

Rose and Foster's worries about sending their sons off to war were for nothing, for by the time Pres was ready to go overseas, the flu epidemic of 1918 devastated San Antonio and the army units training there. Prescott's case was one of the worst, and when he was finally better, Armistice was declared November 11, 1918. Murphy J. never got into the Air Corps. He volunteered for the Marines at the end of his junior year, and when the war ended he was still at Paris Island, South Carolina.

During this time, Martha was an undergraduate at Sophie Newcomb in New Orleans, but since that college did not offer a degree in education, she transferred to L. S. U. for teacher training. A quiet and serious student, she found the exuberance of the big university overwhelming. At her first football game, she was horrified when the revered captain of the football team, Arthur Herbert, was knocked unconscious. Later at a Kappa Alpha tea, she met Herbert. It was the attraction of opposites, and the beginning of a romance.

Back at Dixie, Rose kept busy with the farm and her diminishing family. Murphy came home frequently, but his last years at the Customs House were busy ones. In 1917, Congress passed the Eighteenth, better known as the Prohibition Amendment to the Constitution, which prohibited the manufacture, sale or transportation of intoxicating liquors." By early 1919 it had been ratified by the states and had become law.

The Louisiana coast, with its maze of inlets, bayous, and wetlands, became a happy haven for the bootleggers, just as they had been for Lafitte and his pirates a century earlier. It was not a long trip from Cuba, Mexico, and other Latin American countries to the Louisiana coast where the "rum runners" transferred the alcohol from boats into small fast launches piloted by men who knew the bayous. In that way, they eluded both Customs and the Coast Guard. Since there was never enough manpower to completely control the smuggling, as well as attend to the everyday export-import operations, Murphy's job became more and more burdensome, both mentally and physically, and soon he contracted a severe case of influenza.

Rose, seeing that he was not recovering as he should, urged him to retire, but he was reluctant to do so. In later years Rose spoke of their conversation:

"When I broached the subject of his retirement, his answer was   'Not only do we need the salary, Rose, but I can't desert my post when we are all being overwhelmed by this infernal smuggling.' Then I said to him, 'You did your best to keep this wretched prohibition from becoming law, and I am not going to allow it to break your health. Granted it's been an expensive five years, but we will weather that consideration. You are far more important.' 'I fear my working days are numbered, dear Wife, but not just now. I will give my group more responsibility. And I will tell all my political friends to get this law repealed just as soon as possible.'"

Rose's fears for her husband's health were well grounded. Heart and kidney complications followed his flu, and although neither problem seemed acute, their chronic effects dragged him down so much that all of the children were concerned. Mary kept all her siblings posted on his condition, and they wrote to him regularly. By mid-May his condition had deteriorated to the point that his doctors ordered complete bed rest. Martha, who was engaged to be married in late June to Arthur Herbert, stepped up her wedding date, and they were married in early June in the Senator's bedroom with Rose and other members of the family close by. The newlyweds sailed for Cuba afterwards where Arthur was working.

Murphy died on the morning of June 12, 1921. Although her children were scattered, Rose had all of them except Martha, who had just sailed for Cuba; and Murphy J., who was working in Honduras. Rose came from Shreveport; Bessie, from Ocean Springs, Mississippi; Willia, from Chatanooga; Louisiana, from Patterson; and Sarah, from Newcomb in New Orleans. Mary and Prescott lived in Franklin.

The family grieved in quiet comfort, remembering the gentle man who cared so much for his family and for his state. Their quiet did not last long, for word of the death of Senator Foster spread quickly, and by the time of his funeral, people had come from all over the state to pay their respects.

Rose, reading the editorials and the tributes paid to him and receiving the many callers who came by to express their sympathy, knew the challenges ahead for her. Remembering their forty years together, Rose, fifty-eight, had never felt more alone. Then she remembered something he had told her before he went to Washington. "Rose, you seem mighty shy and fragile to have me go so far away, but I know you can plan, you can raise children, you can build, you can nurse and you can handle money. These are mighty strong qualities for a lady to have." Before she retired that night, she went into his empty room and said, "Oh, Mr. Foster, I hope you're right."

SIX TUESDAY EVENING

THE NEW ORLEANS ITEM

Founded
in 1877

MEMBER OF THE ASSOCIATED PRESS. The Associated Press is exclusively entitled to the local use for publication of all news dispatches credited to it or not otherwise credited to this paper, and also the news published herein. All right of republication of special dispatches herein are also reserved.

724 Uni
Stree

OUTSIDE MAIL RATES		Daily	Sun.	Da.-Sun.			Daily	Sun.	Da.-Sun.	SEC
	1 Month	$ .85	$ .50	$ 1.00	6 Months		$4.50	$1.75	$ 6.00	CI
	3 Months	2.50	.90	3.00	1 Year		9.00	3.50	12.00	MA

Murphy J. Foster

A public career of more than 40 years, ended with the life of Murphy J. Foster, under whose governorship the Lottery was banished from Louisiana. It began with twelve years service in the State Senate, representing the district which included his native parish of St. Mary, during which his qualities of leadership and organizing ability attracted the attention of the enemies of the Louisiana Lottery, and caused his selection as their candidate for governor in 1892.

The task of ousting the Lottery from the state was no job for a weakling. Entrenched in power, with a host of specious defenders of standing and respectability, it ruled the state ruthlessly with one hand while it collected enormous tribute with the other. But its hour of doom struck when Foster, who could neither be bribed nor intimidated, became governor of Louisiana.

As governor, Mr. Foster served the state for eight years. At the close of his second term, he was elected United States Senator, and succeeded himself six years later. While his one accomplishment in the banishment of the Lottery from Louisiana made his fame secure in his native state, it was enhanced by his discharge of the duties of both high offices. During his second term as governor, a new constitution of the state was written and adopted the suffrage provisions of which put an end to a period of political corruption scarcely less dangerous than the Lottery itself. As United States Senator, he was a staunch and effective worker for the interests of Louisiana and the South and attained the regard and respect of his colleagues of all parties. Upon his retirement as senator, he became collector of the Port of New Orleans, serving in that capacity until his death.

Like all strong men, Murphy Foster made staunch friends and bitter enemies, but with the lapse of time the asperities aroused by his successful campaigns became obliterated, while the friendships endured. He had an acquaintance in Louisiana rarely attained by public men, a memory that never failed him and an ever loyal personal following. While long-continued ill health kept him out of active touch with the affairs of the state in his latter years, few men have been more generally missed or more widely mourned than this veteran leader in one of the state's most critical struggles.

News article from the June 14, 1921, issue

Soon after the funeral, Rose took stock of her financial situation. Since there were no pensions in those days and no more salary from her husband, she knew keeping up Dixie would be very difficult. However, the plantation was paid for, and income from the crops ought to see her through. Some of the children wanted her to live with them, but she would not hear of it. With Mary and Paul living in the house and sharing some of the costs, she would not be alone; and with Warren Foster, her brother-in-law, continuing to run the plantation, she knew she could handle Dixie. Upkeep of the house and yard would be one more challenge, but Paul and Johnny Brown, the yardman, were familiar with the place and well able to handle any chore. Rose purchased most of the staples at the Alice C store at a reasonable price, and Prescott, who had been taken into business at Alice C with his Uncle Warren, gave Rose a grocery allowance which she drew upon. Ham, pork, chickens, milk, butter, and eggs were home produced, and Paul, an ardent fisherman, brought in plenty of seafood. Sarah's older sisters and their husbands helped with payment of her tuition at Newcomb. Rose knew that the financial situation was hard on her daughter and that she was cutting corners in every way possible, so her light burned every night trying to plan ahead. She never doubted that she would save Dixie at all costs even though the entire family wondered how.

Making ends meet at Dixie Plantation during the 1920s

In April 1922, another granddaughter was welcomed into the Foster-Trowbridge family. Her birth was not a surprise, but her gender was. Eager for a boy, they had named her Paul, Jr., before her birth, but her name was quickly changed to Routh for her grandmother Rose Routh Ker Foster. *Routh* (pronounced *Ruth*) as a first name was always harder to explain than as a surname, but Routh never regretted that she had been given a family name even though she always had to explain the spelling. When she went to Natchez, she was pleased that she did not have to clarify her name since it was there Job Routh began his progeny.

Rose Ker Foster and her "shadow," Routh Trowbridge

The four Trowbridges lived together in the ell of the big house, but Routh was hard to contain, and as soon as she could walk became her grandmother's

shadow. They were always a great joy to each other, even in the days of colic
when Rose rocked and sang to her. Although Mary and Paul had hired a live-
in nurse, Rose still insisted on the baby spending a great deal of time with her.
It was soon evident that the pre-natal name Paul had, after all, been an appropriate choice for the child was a real tomboy who became her grandmother's
helper with household maintenance. She even had her own little tool box, and
she tagged behind Rose or her father or the yardman "fixing things."

Rose had hoped to see her daughter Sarah locate somewhere near her after
her graduation from Newcomb; however, she and her friend and classmate Olive Roberts from Shreveport obtained teaching jobs in Minden. Even though
she was sad to see her youngest child go so far away, Rose knew that Sarah
needed to work, and since her daughter Rose and her family lived in Shreveport, she knew Sarah would have a nearby support system. It was a hard
break and Rose often said, "Thank goodness I have the Trowbridges."

Workers filling sand bags during the 1927 flood

The flood of 1927 covered most of the Mississippi Delta from Cairo, Illinois,
to the Gulf of Mexico. It flooded the town of Franklin and the surrounding area,
severely hampering commerce. Dixie, sitting on the banks of Bayou Teche,
was threatened; but because the house was three to five feet off the ground, it
escaped damage. However the water did reach the back steps, where Paul's
boat was tied. Every available man went out to build local levees and fill
sandbags. Rose and Mary packed food and jugs of water for Paul and workers

from Dixie who joined the levee builders. One evening Paul came home and called out, "Mary, you and the Madam should have been with me today. Johnny Brown and Remus and I were working on the bayou side of the levee taking the filled sandbags from the fellows on top of the levee and placing them along the bottom to keep the water from swirling under the new levee. The water was pretty deep. All of a sudden Remus looked over and said, 'Dr. Paul, don't move. You got a helper coming outa your shirt.' I looked down and the biggest moccasin I've ever seen was getting out of my shirt. Thank goodness he was as anxious to get away from me as I was to see him go."

Mary almost fainted and Rose said, "Paul, I'm going to send you out with garlic tomorrow. That's supposed to keep them away."

Above left: Floodwaters lap against the back steps of Dixie.
Above right: The Trowbridges aboard a boat in Dixie's yard.

Everyone in the area was affected in some way by the flood. Many people were out of their homes for weeks, so extra food was cooked daily in the Dixie kitchen. Paul in his Model-T, accompanied by Elizabeth and Routh, distributed it to the flooded-out families. Then the chickens and livestock had to be checked daily to make sure their perches and stalls were free of water and snakes. Paul, between working on the levee, distributing food, and taking care of emergency patients, also performed this chore, making it an exciting boat excursion for Elizabeth and Routh. The front yard and front pasture remained dry, and often new cows, mules, and horses appeared: less fortunate neighbors had brought their livestock to Dixie's dry ground.

Later that year a letter from her son Murphy J. Jr., who worked as an engineer for the Andean Corporation in Cartagena, Columbia, asked Rose if his sister Sarah could visit him. He would send her a ticket and take good care of his "little sister." He also told his mother that he had requested that his sister bring a friend; he was lonely for "comely companionship." Sarah, who saved enough money to make the trip, was eager to go, and so was her roommate, Olive Roberts. They told their mothers they could each chaperone the other. Rose reluctantly gave her permission, but she almost rescinded it when she learned that the girls were going on a freighter instead of a passenger liner. Sarah immediately responded to her mother's objection, "Mama, how can you act up like this? You went on a steamboat all by yourself, and you were only eighteen. I am twenty four!" For once, Rose had no answer. When the Roberts family gave their permission, the girls set sail on their "banana boat" and reached Cartagena safely. Murphy J. met them with a friend and co-worker Monty Hayne from New Orleans.

It turned out to be blind dating at its most successful, for the girls later married these first two men they met as they stepped off the gangplank. While in Cartagena, they stayed at Murphy, J.'s house where he had a competent housekeeper and also a house pet, a mountain lion named Bozo.

The cat paid little attention to Sarah, for Murphy's attention had settled on Olive, and it was soon evident that Olive was his rival for Murphy's affections. Because of Bozo's jealousy, Murphy locked him up when he was not there with his guests, but the day before the visit was over, Bozo slipped out and immediately found Olive. Although he never growled, he quietly stalked her. She immediately called Murphy to return and told him she would not marry him until he got rid of his pet. Murphy agreed, but since they were leaving the next day and he refused to leave him in Cartagena, arrangements had to be made quickly. Having heard that a zoo in Shreveport wanted a mountain lion, he called and inquired about a home for him.   Delighted, zoo officials promised to build a special compound for him; however he arrived in Louisiana before the zoo was ready for him.

Murphy cabled Rose to ask if she and Paul could give him a temporary home. Dixie wasn't ready for the lion either, but Paul persuaded the Franklin Parish sheriff to give him a cell for a few nights. In the meantime, Rose emptied a storage shed and Paul made a strong clothes-line-type wire lead for him, so when Bozo arrived, everything was ready for him. All went well until Bozo

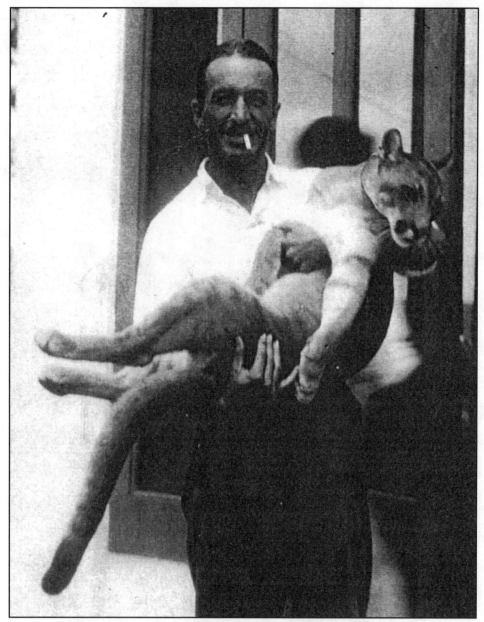

Murphy J. Foster, Jr., with "Bozo"

became ill with chills and fever. Rose called the zoo veterinarian and he prescribed medicine three times a day. Paul comforted and held Bozo while Rose
administered the medicine, and soon he was well again. When the zoo was
ready for him, they sent a special truck, and after a few fond farewell pats, Paul

said to Rose, "Madam, as a team you and I are unbeatable" to which she replied, "I'm glad you think so Paul, but let's rest on our laurels for awhile. No
more mountain lions." Murphy was very grateful and in appreciation he sent
Paul and Rose a pair of beautiful South American macaws, one bright blue and
the other bright red. They proved to be easier guests, and they lived in the
Dixie trees for over twenty years.

Paul Trowbridge
Murphy came up from Cartagena in 1928, and he and Olive were married

in Shreveport with all of the family attending. Among the pictures taken was one of Rose with her seven daughters. Olive, who had no sisters, said, "I want it to show off all my newly acquired sisters. I much prefer them to Bozo." Another wedding occurred in May of 1929 when Sarah and Monte Hayne were married at Dixie. Rain prevented the garden wedding they had planned, so it had to be shifted to the living room. Again the entire family was together, and excitement filled the air, especially for Routh, since it was the first Dixie wedding she could remember.

The crash of the stock market in October of 1929 upset Rose deeply. As more and more Wall Street investors jumped out of windows, she correctly forecast that the whole country would feel the repercussions. She could hardly imagine money being lost in the amounts which the news accounts described. Although she owned no stocks, it brought forth some of her deeply held feelings. She believed that the crash was brought on by the lifestyle of the roaring twenties—the decline in morals and manners, the emphasis on materialism and carefree prosperity, the failure of prohibition to control consumption of alcohol, and the rising popularity of speakeasies. The newspaper accounts of socialites in paddy wagons prompted her to remember her husband's prediction that prohibition would fail and gangsters would control the big cities. She heartily disapproved of women's Jazz Age behavior—wearing short skirts, short hair, lipstick and rouge, and smoking cigarettes. The novels of the popular Scott Fitzgerald, who not only wrote of the decadent but followed their lifestyle, were immoral and to be avoided. She cautioned every one of her daughters to observe conventionality and customs. The only innovation of the twenties that escaped her condemnation was the Charleston, a trendy dance. She saw no harm in it; in fact she enjoyed watching her granddaughter Elizabeth and her friends dance in the living room while Mary played the piano and seven-year-old Routh patted her feet to the music.

CHAPTER TWENTY-ONE

Rose was given a big challenge that year when Bess's husband asked to put an addition onto Dixie. He and Bess had had a troubled marriage for many years. She wanted a divorce, but he was unwilling. Wanting to keep up the semblance of marriage, he said she could travel anywhere she wanted—including Dixie—and he would come there for about two months twice a year. Harry, very wealthy, proposed to build sleeping porches and extra baths off their rooms upstairs and downstairs. In addition he wanted to extend the trunk room off the back gallery downstairs to make a kitchen for himself and quarters for Juan, his Filipino houseboy-chauffeur over the trunk room. They would both take their regular meals with the family, but being obese he wanted his own kitchen in order to cook and eat between meals.

Although she knew that the additions would ruin the symmetry of Dixie, Rose agreed to the proposal for several reasons. It would help make Bess's marriage more bearable for her, it would give the family more room, and it seemed best not to stir up his violent temper for fear he would burn Dixie. (He had lost both a house and an office by fire under mysterious circumstances.)

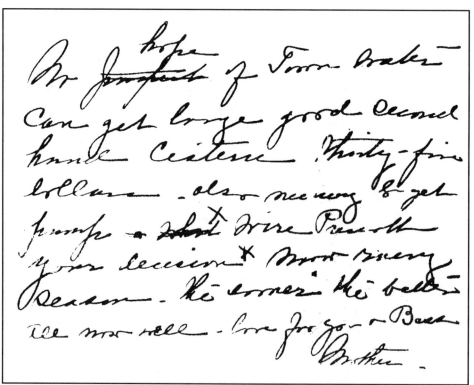

Telegram to Harry Penick from Rose pertaining to the addition of rooms at Dixie, 1930.

Putting on the addition was a big construction job, and Rose, along with son Pres and son-in-law Paul, supervised every step of the building process.

When the construction was completed and Harry came down for his first visit to his new quarters, Rose gave Routh a new job. In addition to having her rub her feet at night, Rose sent Routh creeping up the back gallery steps at night to smell for smoke. Rose then was doomed to worry about fire either way.

The household at Dixie was ever changing and was always stimulating. In late 1931 Sarah's husband lost his job in Cartagena, and since Sarah was expecting a baby, they returned to Dixie to live, at least temporarily. With them in the house, Bess there between trips, Martha and her family there from New Orleans most weekends, and Mary and her family in residence, the house stayed full. In addition to Rose's children and their families, other members of the Foster family dropped in often for visits or middle-of-the-day dinner. Warren Foster, Murphy's bachelor brother who lived at nearby Alice C. Plantation, and Pres and his family, who lived at Shady Retreat, came often. The group loved to play bridge, and although Rose did not share their enthusiasm for the game, she enjoyed their pleasure in the game. She never allowed card playing for money, however.

Rose's many grandchildren were a source of great pleasure but she was especially close to Routh and Elizabeth, both of whom had been born and reared there. Routh's tomboyish ways caused her some anxiety. Fairfax, who lived at Shady Retreat, was very dainty but Routh was a bit rough and loved physical activity. Rose, who had watched every step of her growing up, feared she would never become a lady. One day after Routh climbed very high in a tree, her grandmother scolded her, telling her she was far too venturesome. "To be a lady, you must learn more quiet ways." Then she pointed out that Fairfax was learning all the graces. After assuring her that she was trying, Routh answered that she loved the yard and animals and bayou more than the graces. "That you do, Routh, and I know someday you will be a lady, but I can see it is certainly not going to be for awhile." Bess, who had overheard the conversation, commented "I can just see what Routh will bring home for a husband—a logger or a baseball player, a real red beans and rice eater."

Elizabeth was also a great source of pleasure. She graduated from Franklin High and entered Sophie Newcomb College at fifteen. Mary and Paul, who were enthusiastic tennis players, had put in a court shortly after they moved to Dixie, and when they saw how well Elizabeth played, they improved the court. A nice tennis court drew crowds of young people to Dixie, and Rose loved to watch them play. Elizabeth went on to become state tennis champion.

Through the summer of 1932, talk of the Depression and politics was heated. Everyone blamed President Hoover, and although he was renominated by the Republicans, Franklin D. Roosevelt won the election in a landslide vote.

Everyone was singing "Happy Days Are Here Again," but they were still a good distance away. At Dixie tramps came through the gate in increasing numbers. Rose had given a standing order to the cook that she should not refuse any person a meal. The word spread and one day Paul found a scrawled notice on the gate, "Good Eats Inside." Scrawny cats also joined the homeless legions by the families— mother and kittens dropped over the fence in sacks. Rose decided that she would have to limit her cats to fifteen, and when the numbers increased, Paul brought chloroform down from his office and euthanized them. This caused Harry Penick to remark to Rose, "Madam, if I say I don't feel well, I don't want Paul putting me out of my misery."

With all the problems in the state and country, conversations were always lively at the dinner table. Huey Long was a favorite subject. He had been elected governor in 1928 and was now running for U. S. Senate. In Rose's opinion he was one of the most unprincipled and dangerous men in America. His meteoric rise to power was frightening to her, and she predicted nothing but trouble for the state. She had refused all invitations to political events in Baton Rouge since his election, and when he was elected to the Senate, she predicted he would run the state from Washington. "He is worse than Mr. Morris and his lottery people. Our state is in bondage again."

Rose's brother-in-law Warren Foster died in 1934, and Rose felt the loss very keenly since he and Dixie were her favorites of Murphy's brothers. He left the Alice C Plantation and sugar mill to Prescott, who worked for him. He also left each of his great nieces and nephews $5,000.

Hurt at being left out, Dr. Dixie Foster challenged the will. Ill feelings as well as litigation, in addition to her grief at the loss of Warren, distressed Rose, for she loved both of them. She felt that since Warren had made his own money and was in sound mind, it was his right to handle it in his own way. A handwriting expert was brought down from Washington; he testified that the will was legal. Although Prescott won his case, Dixie's relationship with Rose's family was never quite the same.

In the summer of 1936, Dixie was once again the scene of a wedding. Elizabeth Trowbridge married Harry Henslee, a Texan, in the Dixie garden. Since the economy was stabilizing and times were easing, the family went down when the wedding was over to Prescott's camp at Grand Isle for rest and relaxation. Rose delighted and surprised everyone by going "bathing" every day. "The warm salt waters of the Gulf are good for anything that ails you," she assured them.

Rose was seventy-four that year, and when she returned to Dixie another challenge awaited her. Before Bess's husband returned to Seattle, he gave Rose a pair of beautiful white turkeys. Naming them Paul and Mary in honor of his in-laws who resided there, he assured them that they would adorn the yard at

Bathers at Grand Isle (left to right): Marien Crawford, Bessie Penick,
Rose, Willia Hyde, Rose Hyde, and Louisiana Crawford.

Dixie. Everyone was delighted. Paul had a majestic air as he strolled posses-
sively around the yard with Mary clucking happily behind him. Unlike the
chickens, he preferred the front yard. When a car drove through the gate, it
was his signal to start preening. His plumes were magnificent, and he would
stiffen them into a fan-like background of white while he held his head high
and let his gullet emit a throaty gobble. Rose admired his looks; it was his atti-
tude that became the problem. After a month or two, Paul not only looked like
he owned the yard, he began to act like it. Whenever anyone walked outside,
he charged, ruffled his feathers, hissed, and then retreated.

At first, Rose was inclined to be tolerant. "Paul," she said one morning at
the breakfast table, "I think that gobbler is nursing a feeling of insecurity. He
is so devoted to his Mary that I think he fears for her."

"Insecurity!" Paul exclaimed. "Madam, that self-satisfied devil is a law
unto himself."

"I know," Rose answered, "but let's try facing him with gentle firmness.
After all, they are your and Mary's namesakes."

"I will try and you can try," Paul answered. "Routh can outrun him, but we both know my Mary is going to be no help. All she has to do is go out, see Paul around, and she's afraid to move."

"Yes," Rose agreed, "you and I have to administer the discipline. Paul, we should have been suspicious of Harry's gift from the beginning. Trust him to give something with Mephisthophelean ways under a beautiful body."

"Even though he's my namesake, he'd taste mighty good with dressing and gravy," Paul said hopefully.

"Then Mary would be lonesome," Rose said. "Have you noticed that he never hisses at her. No, we must simply show him we are his masters without resorting to murder."

No conclusions were reached after the period of training. Paul, by his mere presence, was able to effect an armed truce between himself and the gobbler. He did not bother Routh and her friends. Colo (the yardman), he liked, because he fed him, and whether by design or accident, he and Rose had few encounters.

Two incidents brought matters to a head. The first occurred when Rose and Mary had the Daughters of the American Revolution to lunch. When the luncheon was over, one of the guests asked if she could see the gardens. Mary quaked an "of course" and ran out to ask Paul to "do something about Paul."

Paul and Routh put the turkeys in the chicken yard, and before going back to his office, Paul reported that they were shut up. Rose and Mary relaxed and the tour was proceeding happily until one of the ladies turned toward a slow-moving, widely ruffled white figure. "Why look at that handsome turkey," she exclaimed. "I've never seen one any bigger, and isn't he tame, coming right at us."

"Ohhh," moaned Mary, "he must have flown the fence."

With a tempered note of explanation to the guests, Rose turned to Mary and said firmly, "Mary, take our friends in the house. I will see that he comes no further."

Rose found a stick and with it tried to stand her ground, hoping that the door steps weren't too far away. "Don't you come another step, you old reprobate," she warned, waving her weapon. "You think you own this place. Well, you don't, and Paul (this time with a note of pleading in her voice as she backed toward the gallery steps), stop that hissing! I don't want to hit you. That's it. I told you I'd stop you—I've been here a lot longer than you have."

She relaxed as the turkey stopped his pursuit. Then the zero hour came again as he resumed his stalking. "Paul, don't you shake your head at me, you white feathered czar. I'll chastise you severely."

By that time she had reached the steps, and her words were getting braver with each ascending step. Paul was not listening. She was off his territory, so he headed for the chicken yard to encourage his Mary to fly the fence.

Just at this point, Routh came around the corner. "You were a fine help, Routh! Stop smirking! I know you saw the whole performance! The nerve of that incorrigible wretch! I agree with your father. He will surely end his days in a pot. But," she continued, "I cannot help admiring such unadulterated gall. No matter, I must do something about him."

She meant to, but the right solution was hard to find. A few weeks passed and then Paul chased Olive, Murphy J.'s wife, up a step ladder to the top of the garage. Mary was not at home. Rose, hearing the shrieks, ran out and found Olive in a precarious position with Paul strutting back and forth in front of the ladder. Routh and Colo chased him away while Rose tried to calm her daughter-in-law.

"Olive, honey, come down now and you must stop crying. Your face is getting all blotched."

"I don't care," Olive wailed. "You let a killer run loose, and I won't come off this ladder until you promise me you will kill this creature."

Rose promised; that was the only way she could get Olive off the ladder.
In the meantime Routh had called her father and Murphy J., who came immediately with the smelling salts. Paul promised to come as soon as he had finished his last patient. When Olive was finally removed from the ladder, she reminded Rose, "You promised."

"I will, I will, honey," and turning to the yardman, she said, "Colo, go get your hatchet. The quicker the better."

Paul arrived just as Colo went into the hen house for the execution. But it was not to be easy. When he appeared with the hatchet, Paul sensed danger. He made his Mary go into a corner while be blocked the doorway, and waited for Colo to catch him. His gobbles grew louder, and every time Colo drew near, he jumped at him and threw him off balance. After several of these unsuccessful tries, Rose could stand it no longer. "Stop, Colo, stop!" she cried. "If he is that devoted to his Mary that he will sacrifice himself like this, I can't have it." Then she turned to her son-in-law. "What can I do, Paul? I promised Olive!"

He took her arm and said, "Madam, a thought just came to me. I recently heard about a new turkey farm that's opened down the road. They might like Paul and Mary for breeding purposes."

"That's it. That's the answer," she cried. "I'll call right now. Colo, shut the hen house door tight."

Information gave her the number and she came away from the phone with new life in her voice. "The owner said he would be delighted to have a good pair of breeders, and their truck will pick them up tomorrow morning.   The chickens will just have to roost in the trees tonight."

The turkey man was true to his word.   He had a few uneasy moments getting the turkeys into their pen for the ride, but it was successful, and as the truck pulled through the gate, there was a loud triumphant gobble.

Rose, sitting on the gallery, was heard to say.   "The old sinner.   Good riddance.   He was too tough to eat anyway."

Rose with her youngest grandchildren (left to right):
Mike Foster, Martha Herbert, and Warrene Hayne, ca. 1935

CHAPTER TWENTY-TWO

In 1936 a threat came to Dixie from the U. S. Corps of Engineers, who was attempting to alleviate flooding along the lower Mississippi. The plan required channeling excess water that came down the Mississippi into the man-made canals and on into the Gulf of Mexico. The project would relieve pressure on Bayou Teche and prevent a repetition of the 1927 flood. The end result would be beneficial, but in order to accomplish it, they had to make two canals in St. Mary Parish. After studies were made and possible locations considered, the final selection process came down to three sites, two of which would be chosen. One of the three sites was Dixie Plantation, and as the crow flies, it was the straightest and shortest route to the gulf. The plantation fields were long and narrow, and they didn't meander.

Rose and her family were very upset when they saw a copy of the early engineer studies which mapped out Dixie's possible fate. Because they understood the power of the government, they knew that even if they put up a good fight, they could lose in the end. The threat of Dixie's demolition became very real when six surveyors came into the yard. Using all kinds of instruments, they did their necessary work, leaving Dixie with a black cloud hovering over it. Months dragged into months while anxiety increased, and then finally the two chosen sites were announced. Dixie was not one of them. It would not be split by canals.

It seemed to Rose as if one problem could not be solved before another raised its head. By 1937 the country was in an even deeper depression. Banks foreclosed on mortgages, and planters in the Franklin area lost their farms daily. Prescott's Alice C was threatened; he had to raise a large amount of cash to save his plantations. Rose came to the rescue, and with the family's consent mortgaged Dixie. Since Pres had contributed to her support since Murphy's death, she felt that she should and could help him out. Telling him that the family policy was "united we stand, divided we fall," she signed the papers, risking her only possession. The story had a happy ending, however, for Pres saved his farms and Dixie was restored to Rose.

It was 1937, and the house came alive during the holidays. The daughters and sons tried to coordinate their visits so that they could see each other. Willia and John came from Washington, Rose and Tom and from New Orleans; Sarah and Monty and Warrene from Houston. Rose revelled in all of the activities. For her children, coming home to their mother and Dixie was like some kind of magic balm that lessened their burdens. Souls and problems were bared on the gallery and in the spacious hall where sat the grand piano whose top was a catch all for arriving guests. Tom Milling swore that he lost a pair of pants on the piano and his brothers-in-law teased that if he was silly enough to add his pants to the collection of things on top, then they had no further comment. They knew that when callers came, either Rose or Mary swooped things off the top and stashed them elsewhere.

The bridge table seldom went down. Players changed constantly, for no one could ever play for long at a time. The hardest-fought foursome pitted the city boys against the country boys. This game was played in Paul's room so they could shut the door. Paul and Pres always challenged Monty and Arthur to a game, and they played until the last minute when Arthur had to return to New Orleans or Monty had to get his family back to Houston. The only persons permitted to enter the room were Elizabeth and Fairfax because they brought juicy morsels of food.

One of the happy, bridge-playing weekends had a pall cast over it by Routh, then a senior in high school, who woke on Sunday morning with a terrible backache. By afternoon her kidneys shut down and her fever went up. While the family, including many cousins, rallied around her, her mother called Dr. Homer Gates, their physician, who prescribed lots of water. When the water didn't help, he catheterized her. With her physical pain abated, she slept, but when later in the night she woke with no pain and tried to get out of bed, her legs collapsed. Paul and Mary whispered the dreaded words "infantile paralysis" over her head while Rose stood by almost paralyzed herself. Routh had been at her heels all of her life, and she loved her as she did her own children. It was to be a bad time for all the Fosters since trouble for one was trouble for all. Louisiana's husband, Lewis Crawford, was a physician in Patterson, and both he and Dr. Gates came immediately and confirmed their fears. Lewis called in a New Orleans specialist, and Routh was sent by ambulance to New Orleans where she was treated at Touro Infirmary.

After months of therapy in New Orleans administered by Miss Sue Price, Routh recovered partial use of her legs. Miss Price worked tirelessly with one goal in mind—to prepare Routh to enter Sophie Newcomb. During her period of convalescence at Dixie, Rose shared most of her time with Routh.   Since Routh had missed her high school graduation ceremony, classmates sent a great many books, which Rose discussed with her. One day she brought a book of John J. Audubon bird prints. "Now, Daughter," she said, "I want you to see all those birds you shared the trees with." Another day she brought her an oscillating fan. With scorching days and a heavy cast, the new fan became Routh's best friend, that is, besides Rose. Fifteen months later, Routh entered Sophie Newcomb.

By the time Rose could draw an easy breath about Routh, she learned that Harry was divorcing Bess, cutting her off without a penny. This came as a blow to her. Seventy-six years old now, she could offer little help except the assurance that Bess would always have a home at Dixie. Bess, however, declined, saying she wanted to get a job and make her own way. "I can get a job in my friend Em's dress shop." Rose protested that Bess knew only how to wear clothes, not how to sell them, to which she answered, "Don't worry, Mama. You and Papa disciplined us, and now I'm going to discipline myself." And she did.

Rose invited a young engineer Lt. L. B. Wilby to dinner at the request of Bess, who through his grandmother, had learned that he was working in the Dixie area. At dinner he told Rose that he was a graduate of West Point, and had been ordered to the New Orleans Engineering District from the University of California where he had recently received a Master's degree in Civil Engineering. The conversation soon turned to Routh, with Rose telling him about her granddaughter and her recent bout with polio. Ironically, he too had had a light case of polio, and he thought he'd like to meet the granddaughter. Rose said that would be nice and gave him her address.

Rose visited her family in New Orleans frequently. One day, when Pres had driven her to the city, she told Routh about their usual non-stop political talk during the trip. Rose, as distrustful of Long's successsors as she had been of the Kingfish himself, reiterated that the state was in deep trouble. Although Huey had been dead three years, he had left a machine so entrenched with graft and corruption that evil permeated the entire state. She again expressed regret that Long had played upon the class warfare between the so-called "have's and have not's," adding, "You know he had a lot of good ideas, but he became power mad, and the people of this state have suffered. And now we have the same kind of people in office today. They are without principle. Let us pray the reform party goes in. I'm pleased that Pres is working so hard toward a viable slate to run against Governor Leche and his group, and I do enjoy talking politics with him. You know, your grandfather always kept me informed and shared his ideas with me."

During the fall of 1940 when Europe was engaged in a life-death struggle against Nazism and all of America speculated about whether America would enter the war, a political scandal was erupting in Louisiana, sending Governor Richard Leche and other high officials to prison. Thus the reform government that Prescott had been backing was ushered in with Sam Jones, a Lake Charles attorney, as governor. Rose was proud of her son's role in helping to clean up the state. Rose liked the new governor, whom she had met on more than one occasion, the first being during his campaign. While campaigning in St. Mary Parish, he had asked to meet her and she had enthusiastically agreed. Sitting on the front gallery, they entered into a lively discussion of his platform. His determination to execute sweeping reforms won her respect and support. After that visit, he returned to talk to her each time he was in the area.

Mr. Jones asked Rose to come to Baton Rouge as his special guest for the inaugural festivities, but she declined. She later told her family, "Governor

Jones has almost as big a challenge ahead of him as Mr. Foster did forty-eight years ago, but this time I will hear about his progress on the radio and read it in the newspapers."

Prescott was offered the job of highway commissioner, but he felt at first he could not accept it. Rose told him, "You have to do this, son. Mr. Jones will need those of you who worked so hard to elect him to help carry out his reforms. I know how your father depended on his true friends to help him weed out the corruptive influences of the lottery which had been ruling the state. You will just have to come home every weekend and check on your business." Prescott took his mother's advice and accepted the position on a temporary basis, handling his farm business just as she had suggested.

Oil exploration came to St. Mary's Parish in the late 1930s; and by 1940 Rose, for the first time in her life, began to have a little extra income from oil leases. Though nothing came of the prospect then, it gave hope for the future of oil in the area. Prescott, who was managing Dixie's land, laughed of the irony in an oil company scout's words to him, "You know, Mr. Foster, we usually strike oil when land owners don't need the money that much, like in your case." Prescott replied, "You don't know my mother and seven sisters!" It was several years before oil was struck on Dixie land and the little lease checks were much needed.

Hitler's invasion of Russia caused Rose to remember discussions she had had with Murphy. She told her family that she and Mr. Foster had never been supporters of the czars in Russia, and when the Russian Revolution began in 1917, they had high hopes for its first leader, Alexander Karensky. They felt he would have been a fair leader to replace Czar Nicholas II. "But," she said, "Mr. Karensky was too moderate for the rebels, and when that awful man Mr. Lenin and his Bolsheviks threw Mr. Karensky out, I knew Russia was lost. Now we can only hope those two evil empires will eat each other up."   But the Roosevelt administration saw otherwise and gave America's full support to Russia.

During this time, Routh became engaged to Lt. Langfitt B. Wilby, a third-generation West Pointer, thus giving Rose much concern about her going away. In September of 1941, Dixie hosted Routh's wedding reception with all of Rose's children and grandchildren present. Twenty-one relatives sat at the Dixie breakfast table the morning of the wedding. Other relatives and friends came and went all day, and happy chaos reigned. Always a gracious hostess, Rose sat on the front gallery and welcomed everyone. Then before retiring for her afternoon nap, she called Routh to come into her bedroom. "Daughter," she said, handing her a small package, "you will soon be one of those army nomads and we won't be seeing each other like we always have. This is not a wedding gift. This is from me to you and you can keep it with you. It doesn't weigh

Rose and her nine children, September 27, 1941
(left to right, bottom row): Sarah Foster Hayne, Mary Foster Trowbridge, Willia Foster Hyde
(middle row): Louisiana Foster Crawford, Bessie Foster Penick, Rose Ker Foster,
Rose Foster Milling, Martha, Foster Herbert
(back row): William Prescott Foster, Murphy J. Foster, Jr.

much." After Routh had opened it and exclaimed over the small silver vase, Rose gave her an emotional hug, saying "Go along with you now. Enjoy it and don't forget to let it remind you to be a lady."

Despite Paul and Mary's presence, Rose missed the fiery young girl who had become an army camp follower. When Routh wrote that she was a staff assistant for the Red Cross in Phoenix, Rose was pleased; she herself did volunteer Red Cross work. But when she learned that her granddaughter was working from midnight to 4:00 A. M. and being escorted home by policemen, she was horrified: "You must stop these night hours at once. What has happened to your sense of decorum? To be picked up by the police, just like any other common criminal, in the middle of the night, I simply can't imagine what you can be thinking of, and for your husband to allow you to do this, you tell him I am certainly going to give him a piece of my mind. . . ." From that point on, Routh's letters made no mention of her late working hours but rather focused on incidents she thought would entertain her grandmother.

Rose's past experiences in cutting financial corners helped in managing the plantation during the war years when food was rationed. Many army convoys passed Dixie, and somehow the practice got started of stopping at the Dixie gate and waiting to be served coffee and biscuits. Since both sugar and coffee were rationed, Rose was always on the lookout for extra food coupons for the soldiers.

Routh's husband went overseas in 1944, and pregnant, she returned to Dixie to add another generation born there. Rose, much attached to little Bill, could not bear to hear him cry. On this subject, she and Routh disagreed— amicably—and Rose eventually came to accept that grandchildren do not have to be picked up every time they cry.

It was during these war years that an Austrian refugee came to South Louisiana to paint portraits. Prescott hired him to paint a portrait of Rose, and she was one of his first subjects. The only problem was that he had to live in the house with his subjects to study their moods. Everyone was delighted when he said he loved bridge, and almost every night after baby Bill was put to bed, he and Routh would take on Mary and Paul at bridge. He was a good player, but not a good loser, and many times he irritated Paul who had suspected from the beginning that he was a sponger. When he asked Mary to do his laundry, Paul had a serious talk with him, telling him where the local laundry was located and that he would have to go to Peck's Hotel (at his own expense) if he could not be a more considerate guest. Fearing the loss of good food and a comfortable bed, Mr. D'Porto did mend his ways, and the portrait of Rose was beautiful. Prescott had a matching one of his father done from a photograph.

Portraits of Rose Ker Foster and Murphy J. Foster

Soon after the war was over, Routh, along with the baby, left Dixie to join her husband in Japan, arriving there in 1946. Rose was happy to welcome them back to Dixie in 1947, but tragedy had struck while they were en route home—Prescott had died suddenly of a heart attack. Mary, Routh's mother, later related the sequence of events leading to his death, as well as Rose's reaction: "Part of the trouble was the suddenness of your Uncle Press's death. We were completely unprepared. He and I were playing canasta in the living room when he said he had indigestion and he had to go home. Paul followed him up to his house and helped Aunt Willie get him in bed. Fifteen minutes later he was gone. Paul called me, and I had to tell Mama while he stayed with Willie. After I told her, she put her head in her hands and said, 'Oh, Daughter, I have lived too long.'"

Rose going for a jeep ride on her eighty-sixth birthday, November 17, 1947

Rose welcomed Routh and her family back from Japan in 1947. In spite of her joy at seeing them again, especially the baby, she was not the same vigorous person they had left. "It seemed as if a light had gone out of her," Routh later remembered. She missed Prescott and their visits on the gallery where he told her all the news and they exchanged comments on the farm and the politics. Knowing that she had not been out of the house since Prescott's death, Routh coaxed her into taking a ride in the army surplus jeep that she and her husband had bought in Japan for transportation home from California. On climbing into it (it had been enclosed with plywood), Rose asked with a chuckle, "How in the world did you all bring that baby across America in this awkward looking vehicle?" Grabbing her camera Routh snapped her picture before she could protest. After a long drive around the countryside, she thanked Routh and said, "I feel better now."

Rose made her last visit away from Dixie in the spring of 1952 when she went to Baton Rouge to see the L. S. U. rose garden and visit her daughter Sarah and her family. The press got word of her visit and sent a reporter for an interview.

Baton Rouge, La., Saturday Afternoon, April 26, 1952

Widow of Former Governor Foster Is Visiting Here

She may be 90, but you'd never know it talking to her or watching her quick, warm smile come and go.

The years since she was the first governor's lady to occupy a state-owned Executive Mansion have been kind to Mrs. Murphy Foster, who was here yesterday to see the LSU rose gardens.

The former governor's widow doesn't go out much any more, preferring to stay at home on Dixie Plantation near Franklin.

Two daughters, Mrs. John Hyde of Washington, D. C., and Mrs. Paul Trowbridge, a grandson, Murphy J. Foster III, and a great-grandson, Lorie Henslee, accompanied her here.

Her relatives here include her son-in-law and daughter, Mr. and Mrs. H. M. Hayne and their daughter, Warrene, and her grand-daughter and her husband Mr. and Mrs. James Bailey. Their children are James Jr., Prescott Foster and Virginia.

Had Nine Children

All in all, Mrs. Foster had nine children, seven girls and two boys. When she and her husband arrived in Baton Rouge for the inauguration in 1892, they were accompanied by five of their children, which may have had something to do with the state's decision to provide a residence for the "overnor."

COME TO SEE ROSES—Only the LSU rose gardens were able to lure Mrs. Murphy J. Foster, widow of the former governor, away from her residence at Dixie Plantation near Franklin. Though she liked Baton Rouge while she lived here, now, at 90, she says people must now come to see her. Shown with her is her great-grandson, Lorie Henslee.

In the summer of 1954 Dixie hosted the last wedding in Rose's lifetime when her granddaughter Warrene Hayne was married to Walter Suthon at Dixie. Rose basked in the warmth of yet another wedding there and her picture with the newly weds was the last she had taken.

The next year brought excitement of a new kind to Dixie—an oil well! Rose was very pleased but told the oil company representative that under no circumstances would there ever be a well in the Dixie yard. The well was short lived, however, and produced for only ten months, but it was a thrilling interval for the Foster family.

Rose Ker Foster with Warrene and Walter Suthon after their wedding at Dixie, 1954

In August of 1956 Rose was felled by a stroke, and she lived in her own twilight zone for the next two and a half years She spoke only once during that period. When Routh returned after three years overseas, she suddenly looked up and smiled, saying, "Why Routh. . . ." As quickly as the moment came, it was gone. She died on Valentine's Day 1959 at the age of ninety-seven.

She lay in state in the Dixie living room on a lovely February day while her many friends and relatives gathered there to show their love and pay their last respects to this extraordinary woman. Just before the service started, as people milled in and out of the house and yard, a pink Cadillac with Texas license came through the gate and inquired of Bill, Rose's fifteen-year-old grandson if the house was on tour. "I just said 'no,'" he later related. "I didn't think she would want me to tell them it was her funeral."

Rose Ker Foster's life had spanned four wars and two that were not called wars. She was buried next to her beloved husband in the Franklin cemetery, and on her headstone is this inscription:

A GENTLE WOMAN, NOBLY PLANNED
TO WARN, TO COMFORT AND COMMAND.

Rose Ker Foster on her ninetieth birthday, November 17, 1951

APPENDIX

ROSE KER FOSTER'S KER LINEAGE

David Ker married   Mary Beggs

Born in Ireland, 1758   Born in Ireland, March 30, 1757
Died in Natchez, January 21, 1805   Died in Natchez, November 11, 1847

Their son

Dr. John Ker married   Mary Baker of Kentucky
Born, North Carolina, June 27, 1789 Born Kentucky, January 13, 1803
Died Good Hope, Louisiana,   Died, Natchez, Mississippi,
   January 4, 1850   October 14, 1862

Their son

John Ker, Jr. married   Rosealtha Routh
Born Natchez, October 6, 1826   Born Natchez, March 9, 1829
Died Natchez circa late 1860s   Died Ker's Point, June 28, 1865

Their sixth child and fifth daughter

Rose Routh married   Murphy James Foster
Born Lake Catahoula,   Born Franklin, Louisiana,
   November 17, 1861   January 12, 1849
Died Franklin, La., February 14, 1959 Died Franklin, June 12, 1921

They had ten children (eight daughters and two sons)

Rose Routh Foster Milling
Born Franklin, August 4, 1882
Died Franklin, June 8, 1972

Elizabeth Ratliff Foster Penick
Born Franklin, December 26, 1883
Died New Orleans, October 3, 1974

Lucy Price Foster
Born Franklin, La., August 9, 1885
Died Franklin, June 21, 1886

Mary Lucy Foster Trowbridge
Born Franklin, La., December 10, 1886
Died Franklin, December 22, 1984

Willia Ker Foster Hyde
Born Franklin, La., January 12, 1888
Died Washington, D. C., March 31, 1993

William Prescott Foster
Born Franklin, July 19, 1890
Died Franklin, October 9, 1947

Louisiana Navarro Foster
Born Governor's Mansion, Baton Rouge, La., September 2, 1894
Died New Iberia, October 25, 1984

Martha Demaret Foster Herbert
Born Governor's Mansion, Baton Rouge, September 17. 1896
Died New Orleans, Ober 8, 1992

Murphy James Foster, Jr.
Born Governor's Mansion, Baton Rouge, October 1, 1898
Died Franklin, November 1, 1981

Sarah Ker Foster Hayne
Born Franklin, August 12, 1903
Died Franklin, May 25, 1992

ROSE KER FOSTER'S ROUTH LINEAGE

Jeremiah Routh went to Virginia from Wales in 1760. After his death in 1789 his children Job, Jeremiah, and Mary left Virginia and went to the Mississippi territory and settled in Natchez.

Job Routh married   Anne Miller

Of their eight children

Frencis Stebbins Routh married   Mary Haynes Lane
Born Natchez, June 9, 1804   Born Bayou Sara, June 8, 1808
Died Jena, Louisiana, May 28, 1878 Died Natchez, 1868

Their daughter

Rosaltha Routh married   John Ker, Jr.
Born Natchez, March 9, 1829   Born, October 6, 1826
Died, Lake Catahoula, May 26, 1865 Date of death uncertain

Their sixth child (fifth daughter)

Rose Routh Ker married   Murphy James Foster

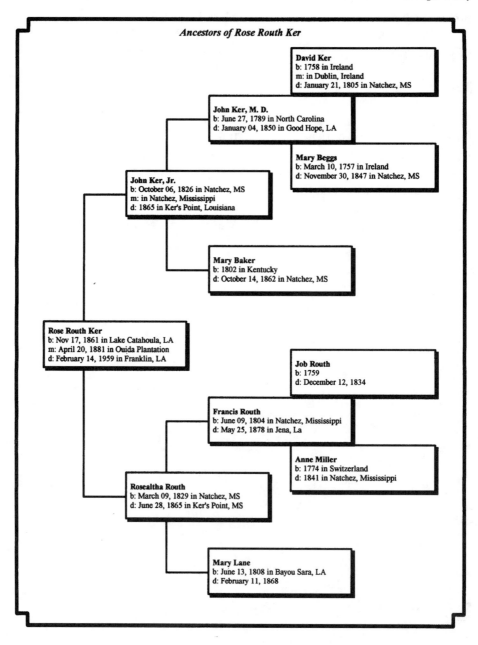

Ancestors of Rose Routh Ker

David Ker
b: 1758 in Ireland
m: in Dublin, Ireland
d: January 21, 1805 in Natchez, MS

John Ker, M. D.
b: June 27, 1789 in North Carolina
d: January 04, 1850 in Good Hope, LA

Mary Beggs
b: March 10, 1757 in Ireland
d: November 30, 1847 in Natchez, MS

John Ker, Jr.
b: October 06, 1826 in Natchez, MS
m: in Natchez, Mississippi
d: 1865 in Ker's Point, Louisiana

Mary Baker
b: 1802 in Kentucky
d: October 14, 1862 in Natchez, MS

Rose Routh Ker
b: Nov 17, 1861 in Lake Catahoula, LA
m: April 20, 1881 in Ouida Plantation
d: February 14, 1959 in Franklin, LA

Job Routh
b: 1759
d: December 12, 1834

Francis Routh
b: June 09, 1804 in Natchez, Mississippi
d: May 25, 1878 in Jena, La

Anne Miller
b: 1774 in Switzerland
d: 1841 in Natchez, Mississippi

Rosealtha Routh
b: March 09, 1829 in Natchez, MS
d: June 28, 1865 in Ker's Point, MS

Mary Lane
b: June 13, 1808 in Bayou Sara, LA
d: February 11, 1868

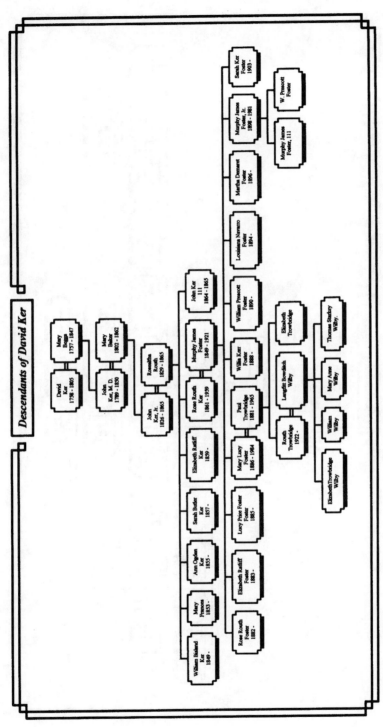

Descendants of David Ker

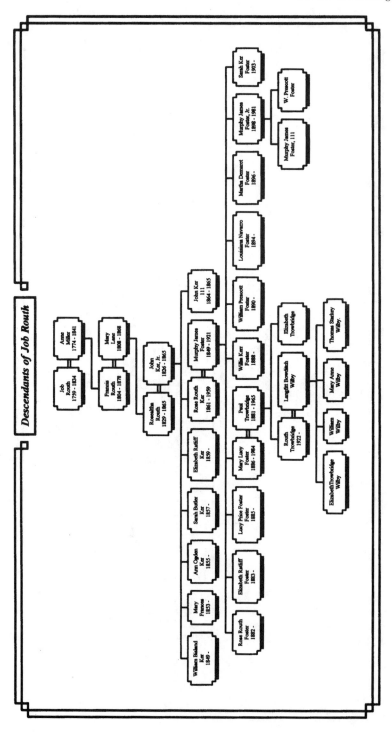

Descendants of Job Routh

- Job Routh, 1759 - 1834
- Anne Miller, 1774 - 1841
  - Francis Routh, 1804 - 1878
  - Mary Lane, 1806 - 1866
    - Rosaltha Routh, 1829 - 1865
    - John Ker, Jr., 1826 - 1865
      - William Richard Ker, 1849 -
      - Mary Frances, 1853 -
      - Ann Ogden Ker, 1855 -
      - Sarah Butler Ker, 1857 -
      - Elizabeth Ratliff Ker, 1859 -
      - Rose Routh Ker, 1861 - 1959
      - Murphy James Foster, 1849 - 1921
        - John Ker III, 1864 - 1865
        - Rose Routh Foster, 1882 -
        - Elizabeth Ratliff Foster, 1883 -
        - Lucy Price Foster, 1885 -
        - Mary Lucy Foster, 1886 - 1984
        - Paul Trowbridge, 1881 - 1965
          - William Kerr Foster, 1888 -
          - William Prescott, 1890 -
          - Louisiana Navarro Foster, 1894 -
          - Martha Dermott Foster, 1896 -
          - Murphy James Foster, Jr., 1898 - 1981
          - Sarah Ker Foster, 1903 -
            - Murphy James Foster, III
            - W. Prescott Foster
          - Routh Trowbridge, 1922 -
            - Langfitt Bownkksh Wilby
            - Elizabeth Trowbridge
              - Elizabeth Trowbridge Wilby
              - William Wilby
              - Mary Anne Wilby
              - Thomas Starkey Wilby.

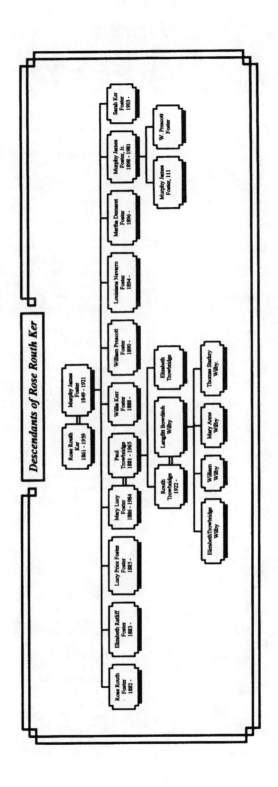

Descendants of Rose Routh Ker

Index